SCHLⵁⵁⵁ
IN THURINGIA

THE FASCINATING ROYAL
HISTORY OF GERMAN CASTLES

SUSAN SYMONS

Published by Roseland Books
The Old Rectory, St Just-in-Roseland, Truro, Cornwall, TR2 5JD
www.susansymons.com

ISBN: 978-1-8383845-0-0

For David (1932-2021) whose gift on my eighth birthday began my life-long love of books.

CONTENTS

1

INTRODUCTION

The federal state of Thuringia is unknown Germany to most English-speaking tourists; I had scarcely heard of Thuringia before starting to write about royal history. Thuringia is one of the smaller and least populated of Germany's federal states and yet until World War I (when Germany was a monarchy) it was made up of eight even smaller royal duchies and principalities. This multitude of royal families means there are more castles and palaces located more closely together in Thuringia than anywhere else in Germany. The competitive urge of the sovereigns of these small courts to display their rank and splendour has left a glorious legacy of dazzling castles and palaces. Thuringia is a treasure house of art, architecture, and royal history.

Schloss is the German word for castle or palace and the plural is *schlösser*. This book visits twenty-five castles and palaces in the federal state of Thuringia and tells colourful stories of the royal families connected with them. It includes schlösser from all eight former royal duchies and principalities that make up the present-day state. The book begins in what was the duchy of Saxe-Altenburg in the east of Thuringia, at an enchanting schloss named for the happy homecoming of a duke imprisoned for championing Martin Luther and the Reformation.

It ends in the breath-taking scenery of the Thuringian Forest with the principality of Schwarzburg-Rudolstadt and the schloss home of the last princess of the German monarchy before she was evicted by Hitler. The book uses the words *schloss* and *schlösser* in a wide definition to denote any type of royal residence – from a fortified castle, to a grand state palace, to a summer villa. As well as the twenty-five main schlösser, several more are explored more briefly. The twenty-five schlösser range in time from an eleventh-century hill-top castle where the royal story of Thuringia began (the Wartburg in chapter 5) to the last schloss built in Thuringia before the monarchy was abolished in 1918 (Neues Schloss Hummelshain in chapter 2). Appendix A at the back of this book has a hand-drawn map of Thuringia showing the approximate location of the twenty-five schlösser.

The eight Thuringian royal states at World War I

Saxe-Altenburg
Saxe-Coburg and Gotha
Saxe-Meiningen
Saxe-Weimar-Eisenach
Reuss Elder Line (Reuss-Greiz)
Reuss Younger Line (Reuss-Gera)
Schwarzburg-Sondershausen
Schwarzburg-Rudolstadt

See appendix B for more information on each state.

Schloss in Thuringia is the sixth book in my series on *The Fascinating Royal History of German Castles*. I cross-refer to the other books where appropriate, and for further information on the series see page 273 or visit my website (www.susansymons.com). I started to write about schlösser when my husband and I began to spend time in Germany. I am often asked the question 'What is your favourite part of Germany?'.

My answer, without hesitation, is always 'Thuringia'. Our first sight of this state was driving along the E40 motorway on a journey from Dresden to Frankfurt. Even from the motorway the scenery was so stunning we were determined to come back as soon as possible. Much of the picturesque countryside is covered by the Thuringian Forest, which sweeps in a great arc down from Eisenach in the west and past Saalfeld to the Bavarian border in the south-east (see the map in appendix A). With its scenic landscape of pine-covered hills and picture-postcard villages, the Thuringian Forest is a setting for fairy tales. The glorious countryside together with the state's location in the centre of the country is why Thuringia is often called *the Green Heart of Germany*. We have returned to Thuringia several times and there is a chapter on this state in each of two previous books (*Schloss II* and *Schloss III*). For the (ten) schlösser included again in this book, the content has been refreshed and extended with more historical information and new illustrations. The capital of Thuringia today is Erfurt, but until World War I there were different capital cities for each of the royal states and these are shown on the map in appendix A.

This book is organised with chapters by royal state and within each chapter a separate section for each schloss. The eight duchies and principalities were ruled by different branches of three ancient royal houses – Reuss, Schwarzburg, and the Ernestine Line of the Wettin. Chapters 2 to 5 cover the four duchies of the Ernestine Line (Saxe-Altenburg, Saxe-Coburg and Gotha, Saxe-Meiningen, and Saxe-Weimar-Eisenach); chapter 6 the two Reuss principalities (Reuss Elder Line and Reuss Younger Line); and chapter 7 those of the house of Schwarzburg (Schwarzburg-Sondershausen and Schwarzburg-Rudolstadt). For more information on the royal states see appendix B. The political map of Thuringia in the time of the monarchy was a kaleidoscope. None of the eight states was a continuous territory within a single boundary, but comprised lands in different pieces across the area. There were also stranded enclaves belonging to the kingdoms of Prussia and Saxony within Thuringia.

Titles, names, and epithets.

The hereditary titles of the rulers of the Thuringian royal states varied according to their size and importance. In descending order, a grand duke (grossherzog) was the ruler of a grand duchy; a duke (herzog) of a duchy; a prince (fürst) of a principality; and a count (graf) of a county. Landgrave (landgraf) and margrave (margraf) were ancient titles broadly equivalent to a duke. From the beginning of the eighteenth century there were a small number of kingdoms in Germany (such as Bavaria – see 'Schloss in Bavaria') but none of these was in Thuringia.

A complication is that rulers of the royal states often had the same first name, with some names being popular in particular families. The last four dukes of Saxe-Meiningen for example were Georg I, Bernhard II, Georg II, and Bernhard III. An extreme example of the re-use of the same name is the royal house of Reuss (see chapter 6) where for hundreds of years every single male child was given the same first name of Heinrich!

In the middle ages, epithets or descriptive words were used (rather than numbers) based on an individual's character or achievements. The first Wettin landgrave of Thuringia in the thirteenth century (he inherited it through his mother) is known as Heinrich the Illustrious. The epithets were not always so complimentary. Heinrich the Illustrious was followed by his son Albrecht the Unnatural (he tried to disinherit his own sons) and Friedrich the Bitten (with a bite scar on his cheek from a childhood mishap – see Tenneberg in chapter 3). I have often thought it would be fun to give epithets to modern politicians. I am sure readers can come up with many of their own but here are a few obvious ones to start with – Boris the Brexit (Johnson), Tony the Spin (Blair), Margaret the Iron (Thatcher).

After the fall of the German monarchy in 1918, former nobility was no longer recognised under the constitution of the new Weimar Republic. Since that time, royal titles have only been permitted as part of a surname. So, taking the head of house Saxe-Coburg and Gotha as an example, it is correct to say Andreas Prince of Saxe-Coburg and Gotha (and not Prince Andreas of Saxe-Coburg and Gotha).

Appendix C has numerous charts and family trees to supplement the text and help readers navigate the *Who's who* of royal genealogy. A thread that runs strongly through many of the royal stories in the book is the problem of inheritance. In the late seventeenth and eighteenth centuries the Thuringian royal families struggled to introduce the rule of primogeniture (inheritance by a single male heir), often not without a battle. Before this all sons had rights to inherit and were required to govern in collaboration. This frequently led to bitter family disagreements and sometimes even fraternal war. Duke Anton Ulrich (1687-1763) squabbled with his two brothers for forty years until their deaths eventually left him as sole ruler of Saxe-Meiningen (see Altenstein in chapter 4).

To settle the disputes, family lands were repeatedly divided to create new territories for younger sons and then reorganised again as these sub-branches died out. The constantly shifting picture makes unravelling the royal history of Thuringia rather tricky. At the height of fragmentation towards the end of the seventeenth century there were twenty-two different royal states in Thuringia – ten Ernestine Line, nine Reuss, and three Schwarzburg[1]. It was a must for the duke, count, or prince of each new state to build a splendid residence schloss to house his court. Ironically, the inheritance problem would later 'reverse' as the Thuringian royal families began to run out of male heirs. Anton Ulrich was sixty-seven years old when his son and successor was eventually born. Five of the eight ruling families in this book became extinct in the male line during the twentieth century (see appendix B).

A real joy in writing this book lay in exploring the stories of Thuringian royal women. Princesses are so often the unsung heroines of royal history and their lives are generally less well documented. Who knows the sad story of the banishment of Prince Consort Albert's mother? Who has heard of *the false queen of England* walled up alive in Tenneberg (chapter 3) for claiming to be Anne of Cleves (the fourth wife of Henry VIII)? No royal woman ruled any of the eight Thuringian royal states in her own right, but several ruled as regent for their young sons.

In her years in charge, Anton Ulrich's widow repaired the ravages of four decades of family infighting.

Princesses were important to cement diplomatic alliances or establish new lines of inheritance through marriage. Their lands in Thuringia came into the ownership of the house of Wettin through the marriage of a thirteenth-century princess called Jutta (Judith) of Thuringia (see chart 1 in appendix C). Thuringian princesses married into Europe's other royal families, including that of Great Britain. Who can name the Thuringian princess who became queen of Great Britain and the other who was expected to but never did? Through her great-great-grandfather (Prince Albert) Queen Elisabeth II is a direct descendant in the male line of the Thuringian dukes of Saxe-Coburg and Gotha. The ancestral schloss of the British royal family is at Saalfeld in Thuringia (chapter 3)!

One reason why Thuringia is less popular with British tourists than (say) neighbouring Bavaria may be because after World War II Thuringia was part of the German Democratic Republic (GDR or East Germany); and travel from Western Europe was restricted. The victorious Allies divided Germany into four military occupation zones – American, British, French, and Soviet. The Americans reached Thuringia first on 1 April 1945 and occupied the state. But they withdrew in early July, in accordance with the Yalta agreement reached between Churchill, Roosevelt, and Stalin. Thuringia became part of the Soviet occupation zone and later the GDR whilst Bavaria remained in the American zone and was part of West Germany (the Federal Republic of Germany).

On my first visit to Bavaria in the 1980s, I well remember driving into the countryside to see the border with Thuringia (between West and East Germany). It was a startling sight – like something from a film, with high fences, watch towers, border guards, and a 'no go' death zone. I was relieved to drive away. I did not visit Thuringia for the first time until thirty years later.

The contents of this book are a blend of historical information and my own observations and impressions from visiting the schlösser.

My comments are from the perspective of an overseas visitor who does not speak German and come from my personal experience. Another visitor at another time could have an entirely different experience. The sources consulted for the historical information are shown in the Notes section and the Bibliography at the back of the book. The book is illustrated throughout with a mixture of present-day photographs, old postcards, and royal portraits. There are one hundred illustrations in total. *Schloss in Thuringia* is not a detailed travel guide and readers should consult the schlösser websites or other information for opening hours, entry fees, and directions.

Appendix D provides an index of all the schlösser included in the *Schloss* series of books. Visiting these schlösser has given me a better understanding of the history of Germany and a more vivid picture of the historical royal characters and their personal stories than from just reading about them. I have found it fascinating to see the places where history happened.

A further joy of researching the *Schloss* books has been to discover new sources I have not read before. For this book they included a travelogue of his trip to Thuringia published by an English doctor in 1884. In the preface he writes that, after reading about the early Wettin ancestors of the prince of Wales (he meant of course Bertie, eldest son of Queen Victoria and later King Edward VII)

... an uncontrollable impulse possessed me to visit the more important localities [in Thuringia] connected with these romantic events; ...[2]

I know exactly how he felt! One romantic event is the happy homecoming of Duke Johann Friedrich I of Saxony (1503-1554) after he had lost his lands and title and spent five years in prison for his Protestant faith. He was reunited with his wife outside the new schloss at Wolfersdorf that she built during his absence. Their sixteenth-century love story is where my book begins.

The history of Germany.

It may be helpful for readers to have a broad outline of the political history of Germany as background for the stories in this book. The key point to bear in mind is that Germany was not a single nation-state but a federation of numerous independent territories, each with its own ruler and royal family. This was the case right up to the end of World War I, when the monarchy came to an end and Germany became a republic.

*For nearly a thousand years, the independent German states were held together as part of the **Holy Roman Empire**, under an elected emperor. The start of the empire is usually dated as 962, when Otto I was crowned; the end came in 1806 when Francis II disbanded the empire after it became unstable during the Napoleonic Wars. Over the next century there were then several successive groupings of the royal states – first the **Confederation of the Rhine** sponsored by Napoleon; then, from 1815, the **German Confederation** under Austrian presidency; and finally, from 1871, the **German Empire** with a Prussian kaiser (emperor).*

*At the end of World War I revolution swept across Germany and Kaiser Wilhelm II abdicated, followed swiftly by all the other royal rulers. A republic was declared and an armistice to end the war signed on 11 November 1918. The new **Weimar Republic** was a parliamentary democracy but was politically unstable from the start – tainted by the punitive peace terms and plagued by economic problems. In 1933 it was supplanted by a **Nazi dictatorship** under Hitler, who led Germany into World War II.*

*After the war Germany was divided into zones of occupation. This division hardened in 1949 when Germany became two separate countries – the Federal Republic of Germany (known as **West Germany**) and the German Democratic Republic (known as **East Germany or the GDR**). West Germany comprised the American, British, and French zones and was a parliamentary democracy with a capitalist economy. The GDR, previously the Soviet zone and including Thuringia, was communist and part of the Soviet bloc. The two countries were separated by an Iron Curtain until the fall of communism and the **Reunification of Germany** in 1990.*

2.

SAXE-ALTENBURG

The duchy of Saxe-Altenburg in north-east Thuringia was first created in 1603 as part of the Ernestine Line of the house of Wettin. When its branch of dukes died out in 1672, Altenburg passed through female inheritance to the dukes of Saxe-Gotha-Altenburg (their history is covered in chapter 3). When the dukes of Saxe-Gotha-Altenburg died out in turn, a stand-alone duchy of Saxe-Altenburg was recreated in 1826 and survived until the monarchy came to an end.

Saxe-Altenburg schlösser feature in some of the most evocative stories in German royal history – the kidnapping of the princes Ernst and Albrecht as children from Schloss Altenburg in 1455; the imprisonment of Johann Friedrich I and his longing to see the new schloss at Wolfersdorf before he died (he got there in 1552); the daughters and granddaughters of Duke Joseph of Saxe-Altenburg (reigned from 1834) who made important marriages and became queens ...

The last duke of Saxe-Altenburg was Ernst II (reigned from 1908). After the monarchy fell in 1918, the ex-duke retired to Schloss Fröhliche Wiederkunft (we visit this first) where he lived through a period of extraordinary upheaval – the Weimar Republic, Hitler's Third Reich, the Soviet Occupation, and on into the GDR (German

9

Democratic Republic or East Germany). The Saxe-Altenburg branch of the Ernestine line died out on the death of Ernst II's son, in 1991.

Fröhliche Wiederkunft

Fröhliche Wiederkunft at Wolfersdorf is a fairy-tale confection of neo-gothic towers, steep roofs, and stepped gables. The schloss is on an island in a lake and as we walked across the bridge the glorious colours of the buildings and the greenery were reflected in the water. There were tomatoes growing in the lakeside garden and mature trees shading the peaceful courtyard. Fröhliche Wiederkunft has a fascinating history, and an unusual name reflecting the romantic story of its beginnings. This is my favourite schloss in Thuringia.

1. Fröhliche Wiederkunft is a fairy-tale confection of towers, steep roofs, and stepped gables.

In 1552, Duke Johann Friedrich I of Saxony was released after five years of captivity. He travelled home across Thuringia to be reunited with his wife, Sybille of Kleve. Although arranged for dynastic reasons, their marriage was based on true affection and they were a devoted couple. On the evening of 15 September 1552 husband and wife met on the bridge at Wolfersdorf outside the new schloss that Sybille had built during his absence. Legend has it that Johann Friedrich took Sybille in his arms and said the schloss should be called Fröhliche Wiederkunft or Happy Return. This name is not modern or made-up; it was first documented only a few weeks after their reunion[1].

Johann Friedrich I (1503-1554), known as *the Noble* or *the Magnanimous*, is an important figure in the history of the Reformation. He was affectionately known to his subjects as Hanfried (an abbreviation of his name, Johann Friedrich). His life story is told in a remarkable way at Fröhliche Wiederkunft. Four large pictures, each divided into several scenes, depict key events of his life in chronological order. The provenance of these paintings is uncertain; they were discovered in storage and moved to Fröhliche Wiederkunft when Duke Joseph of Saxe-Altenburg rebuilt the schloss in the mid-nineteenth century. The artist of the paintings is not known, and experts think they probably date from between 1620 and 1650[2]. The originals are in the German Historical Museum in Berlin, but copies hang at Fröhliche Wiederkunft. The schloss is now a family home, events venue, and museum. There are many good reasons to visit Fröhliche Wiederkunft, not least the friendly welcome, picturesque buildings, and excellent café. The four intriguing pictures are a good reason in themselves.

The first picture in the cycle covers the youth of Johann Friedrich I and his marriage in 1527 to Sybille of Kleve (1512-1554). It emphasises his piety and strong adherence to the Protestant faith. Johann Friedrich was the sponsor of Martin Luther and in one scene he is shown collecting the offerings in church while Luther preaches a sermon[3]. In the wedding scene, Johann Friedrich and Sybille are married by Luther in a grand hall in front of witnesses. The couple had three sons and, through their second son Johann Wilhelm (1530-1573), were progenitors of the Ernestine Line branches covered in this book (see chart 3). Judging from her portrait by Lucas Cranach the Elder in 1526 (when she was fourteen), Sybille was a striking-looking girl with long, wavy, red-gold hair, pale skin, and a pointed face. Readers who enjoy Tudor history may like to know she was the elder sister of Anne of Cleves (English spelling) who was the fourth wife of Henry VIII for a few months in 1540. I have always thought Anne the smartest of Henry's six wives: when it became clear that the king did not fancy her, she agreed to a quick annulment. In return Henry granted her a generous pension and they remained on friendly terms.

2. Four remarkable pictures at Fröhliche Wiederkunft tell the life story of Johann Friedrich I.

Johann Friedrich I succeeded his father as prince-elector of Saxony in 1532. The next picture in the sequence gives the build-up to his rebellion against the Holy Roman emperor. As Emperor Karl V seeks to reimpose Catholicism as the true religion across the Holy Roman Empire, Johann Friedrich is forced to raise an army to defend his Protestant territories. Together with Landgrave Philipp of Hesse he became leader of a military alliance of the Protestant princes called the

Schmalkaldic League[4]. One scene in the second picture shows Johann Friedrich I conspiring with mercenaries while a spy (dressed in red) eaves-drops behind a curtain[5]. The spy is probably his cousin Margrave Moritz of Meissen[6]. Moritz was also a Protestant but chose to betray his cousin and his faith and side with the emperor from motives of political opportunism. He is often called *the Judas of Meissen*[7]. When Johann Friedrich I was defeated in battle and taken prisoner, Moritz was rewarded with his cousin's land and his title of prince-elector.

The third picture is set during the Schmalkaldic Wars (1546-1547) and charts the decisive battle of Mühlberg on 24 April 1547. The Protestant forces suffered a devastating defeat, and Johann Friedrich I kneels in surrender. The central scene of this picture illustrates another famous story about him. Johann Friedrich is shown playing chess with a fellow prisoner when the news arrives that the emperor has sentenced him to death. He displays great courage and appears unmoved, remarking only that his appalled opponent should pay attention to the game or he will lose the match[8]. To save his life and protect his family, Johann Friedrich I agreed to *the capitulation of Wittenberg* and signed over his prince-elector's rank and much of his lands to cousin Moritz. He staunchly refused to deny his faith or to cooperate in the emperor's attempts to find a religious compromise. His passive resistance made him a hero and a martyr to fellow Protestants. Our guide called him the Gandhi of the middle ages.

For five and a half years Johann Friedrich I remained a prisoner of the emperor. He was not incarcerated in a dungeon but forced to follow in the emperor's train as he travelled around the empire. The ex-elector could communicate with his wife and sons and in this way was able to oversee the building of his new schloss. Johann Friedrich's captivity was shared by a small suite of courtiers, including from 1550 his court painter, Lucas Cranach the Elder. Although an old man (born in 1472) the artist volunteered to join his patron in confinement. Many of his paintings from these years went to the new schloss at Wolfersdorf. Eventually Emperor Karl V tired of his recalcitrant and

The Ernestine Line of the house of Wettin

The royal house of Wettin can trace its ancestry back to the tenth century and takes its name from the ancestral schloss at Wettin (now in the German state of Saxony-Anhalt). Their lands in Thuringia were acquired through female inheritance in the mid-thirteenth century following the death of the last Ludowinger landgrave of Thuringia (see chart 1 in appendix C). The Wettin were margraves of Meissen from early in the twelfth century; in 1423 they became prince-electors of Saxony when the emperor endowed Margrave Friedrich I the Warlike (1370-1428) with this higher rank (chart 2). The title of prince-elector (or elector) was the most prestigious in the Holy Roman Empire. The small number of electors (seven at that time) were second only to the emperor and responsible for electing him.

In 1485 there was a lasting split when the brothers Ernst and Albrecht divided the house of Wettin to form two lines called the Ernestine and the Albertine. As the elder brother, Ernst retained the senior title of elector of Saxony, while his younger brother Albrecht became margrave of Meissen.

The Ernestine Line held the electorate of Saxony for only two generations. Ernst's grandson, Elector Johann Friedrich I the Noble (1503-1554), led a rebellion of the Protestant princes against the Catholic Holy Roman emperor. In 1547 he was defeated in battle and captured by the emperor; signing over the electorate to the Albertine Line was the price of saving his life. Thereafter the Albertine Line (who are featured in 'Schloss') were electors and later (from 1806) kings of Saxony; for a time, they were also kings of Poland. The Ernestine Line diminished in importance and retained only the lands in Thuringia.

The Ernestine Line have a fascinating history. After this fall from power in the sixteenth century they would rise again in the nineteenth and occupy numerous thrones. Following repeated reorganisations over centuries there were four surviving Ernestine Line duchies in Thuringia on the eve of World War I – Saxe-Altenburg (this chapter), Saxe-Coburg and Gotha (chapter 3), Saxe-Meiningen (chapter 4), and Saxe-Weimar-Eisenach (chapter 5). The prefix 'Saxe' is an abbreviated form of 'Saxony'.

awkward captive and at the end of August 1552 Johann Friedrich I was set free at Augsburg in Bavaria.

The last picture in the cycle covers Johann Friedrich I's release and the remaining years of his life. His health was poor, and he wrote to Sybille that he hoped God would not let him die before he found happiness at Wolfersdorf[9]. His journey home across Thuringia turned into a triumphal procession. The longed-for reunion with Sybille is depicted in the foreground of this fourth picture. The romantic story of their mutual attachment

3. Statue of Johann Friedrich I in the marketplace at Jena.

continues to the end. Sybille died on 21 February 1554, less than two years after her husband's return, aged forty-two. Johann Friedrich I followed her to the grave only ten days later, on 3 March. The couple were buried side by side in Weimar City Church.

Fröhliche Wiederkunft was built between 1547 and 1550 during Johann Friedrich's imprisonment. His old hunting lodge had been destroyed by Catholic troops in the Schmalkaldic Wars and he asked Sybille and their sons to build a new one at Wolfersdorf. In a letter to his wife Johann Friedrich suggests Sybille decorate her bedroom in plain white so it be adorned only by her beauty[10]. Imagine the excitement when workers peeled back several layers during restoration to find what might be that original white colour! The site for the new schloss was wet and marshy so the architect, Nikolaus (or Nickel) Gromann, created an artificial island by driving oak stakes eight metres into the ground. The schloss still rests on these today. Gromann was a master architect of the renaissance and his other great legacy at Fröhliche Wiederkunft is a cantilevered, self-supporting, wooden, spiral staircase. It forms a perfect helix (corkscrew shape) and has no central pillar.

After he resigned the electorship, Johann Friedrich I was left with his lands in Thuringia. His descendants divided this inheritance and Fröhliche Wiederkunft passed to the dukes of Saxe-Altenburg. In remained in their ownership until the Soviet Occupation Forces arrived at the end of World War II. The schloss was damaged in the Thirty Years War (1618-1648) and fell into dilapidation after the elder branch of Saxe-Altenburg dukes died out in 1672. Schloss Hummelshain (see below) became the preferred location for hunting. Fröhliche Wiederkunft was in a shocking condition and uninhabitable when it was rediscovered by Duke Joseph of Saxe-Altenburg (1781-1868) after his abdication.

Joseph was the second duke of the younger branch of Saxe-Altenburg dukes (see chart 10). He was forced to give up the throne during the revolutionary year of 1848. It was a time of turmoil for him. Joseph abdicated on 30 November 1848 – only two days after his wife of more than thirty years had died. The ex-duke had a strong interest in his family history and great admiration for Johann Friedrich I as the defender of the Reformation. He was also annoyed that the citizens of the nearby town of Jena had tried to claim ownership of Johann Friedrich I's memory by erecting a statue of him in the marketplace in 1858 (illustration 3), on the three-hundred-year anniversary of Jena University. (During his imprisonment Johann Friedrich had founded a school that later became the university.) Duke Joseph considered that the restoration of Johann Friedrich I's schloss would be a more fitting memorial to his illustrious ancestor.

From 1858 to 1863 Joseph reconstructed Fröhliche Wiederkunft in the neo-gothic style. This was a favoured architectural style with the nobility in the mid-nineteenth century. Stolzenfels on the Rhine was rebuilt by King Friedrich Wilhelm IV of Prussia in this romantic and imagined version of the past (see *Schloss III*); and Lichtenstein in the Swabian mountains by Count Wilhelm of Württemberg, a cousin of the king of Württemberg (*Schloss in Baden-Württemberg*). Joseph was determined not to do anything by halves[11]. He redesigned the exterior of Fröhliche Wiederkunft, extended the accommodation by adding extra wings, built a new stone bridge and crenelated entrance arch, and created some beautiful interiors. The project was expensive, and Joseph's four daughters made significant donations towards the costs. In the Reception Hall at Fröhliche Wiederkunft (where the tour begins) marble plaques commemorate the original construction of the schloss by Sybille and her sons and the financial contribution to the reconstruction by Joseph's daughters.

4. The Duke Joseph Hall.

The Duke Joseph Hall has beautiful carved woodwork and is painted in the colour ultramarine or royal blue. Before the development of synthetic dyes this intense blue was derived from the semi-precious stone lapis lazuli, making it the most expensive of pigments. The hall is a paean of praise to Joseph's famous ancestor. The apex of the gothic arches of the room divider are inscribed with the mottos of Johann Friedrich I – 'God helps us in need' on the left and 'My hope is in God' on the right. The middle arch has the motto of his wife Sybille –

'Always be honest'[12]. In his will Joseph directed that every year on his birthday (27 August) a ceremony should take place at Fröhliche Wiederkunft to remember him and to honour Johann Friedrich I. This tradition was upheld for fifty years, the last being held on 27 August 1918 just weeks before the monarchy fell.

As the German monarchy crumbled the last duke of Saxe-Altenburg, Ernst II (1871-1955), abdicated the throne on 13 November 1918. The ex-duke retained ownership of Fröhliche Wiederkunft and made it his home from March 1922. Ernst II carried out significant repairs and improvements, installing mains water, central heating, a new kitchen, bathrooms, and a lift. He had seen active service on the Western Front in World War I and suffered disabling wounds so that he found it hard to walk. Ernst II had a keen interest in science and astronomy and set up an observatory at the schloss. He was passionate about hunting and the head of his huge hunting dog called Roland (stuffed and mounted) still guards his master's rooms. Ernst II was also an inveterate womaniser. His wife of twenty-one years left him soon after the abdication and they divorced in 1920. He moved into Fröhliche Wiederkunft with his companion, the opera singer Marie Triebel. Marie was officially his housekeeper but in reality she was also his lover; the couple married in 1934.

Ernst II lived at Fröhliche Wiederkunft through thirty difficult years in German history. He proved a survivor who managed to reach an accommodation with harsh regimes. During the Hitler years he joined the Nazi party. The local Nazi group met at Fröhliche Wiederkunft and the building called the Fischerhaus (Fisherman's House), built by Duke Joseph as a chapel, was used by the SS[13]. When the Soviet Forces arrived, Fröhliche Wiederkunft was looted by soldiers but still Ernst II stayed on. He did not flee to the Western zone of occupation. Ernst II's sister Elisabeth was the widow of a Russian grand duke (see Altenburg). Ernst II spoke fluent Russian and one suggestion is that he was an old friend of the Soviet commanding officer from their youthful time together at the St Petersburg Cadet School[14].

Ernst II was granted the right to live in Fröhliche Wiederkunft for life by the Soviet administration and issued with an identity card in the name of Freiherr (Baron) Ernst von Reiseneck. This was a subsidiary title he used after the abdication. The last years of his life were spent in straightened circumstances in a few rooms of the south wing. Ernst II had to sell off or barter his remaining possessions to survive; at times he was dependant on the charity of his former subjects. Ernst II of Saxe-Altenburg died at Fröhliche Wiederkunft on 22 March 1955. His second wife, Marie Triebel, had no right of residence and was forced to leave the schloss.

After his death the schloss was turned into a juvenile correction facility for youths with behavioural

5. Ernst II of Saxe-Altenburg.

issues. What remained of the contents (and had not already been expropriated, sold, or stolen) was cleared to different museums. The four remarkable pictures telling the life story of Johann Friedrich I went to the German Historical Museum in Berlin. Rooms were divided and interiors altered to make bedrooms, classrooms, and workshops. The Duke Joseph Hall was converted to a cafeteria and the smaller room next door filled with concrete to become the toilets. After Germany was reunited in 1990, Fröhliche Wiederkunft was one of many Thuringia schlösser in poor condition and hoping for a new 'Duke Joseph' who would be passionate about its rescue. By a stroke of good fortune it found him. In 2007 Fröhliche Wiederkunft was privatised and is being sympathetically restored in close cooperation with the Thuringia State Office for Monument Preservation and Archaeology.

Altenburg

The history of Altenburg goes back to the beginning of the Holy Roman Empire. There was a watchtower there as long ago as the tenth century. In the sixteenth century the Ernestine electors of Saxony built a renaissance schloss and the dukes of Saxe-Altenburg Elder Branch took this for their residence when the duchy of Saxe-Altenburg was first created in 1603. In the eighteenth century the renaissance schloss was rebuilt and extended in the baroque style. This was during the period that Altenburg was part of a combined duchy of Saxe-Gotha-Altenburg. When the stand-alone duchy was recreated in 1826, Altenburg was restored, refurbished, and extended by the new dukes of Saxe-Altenburg Younger Branch.

When he visited in September 1884, Dr Shephard Thomas Taylor described Altenburg as

... a large and imposing edifice, standing at a considerable elevation on an escarped rock. It is one of the few ancient castles that are still inhabited by their princely owners; and ... consists of an older part, and a newer portion more adapted to modern civilisation[15].

The first sight of Altenburg is a cobbled entrance drive, built as part of the baroque remodelling. Flanked at the bottom by obelisks with statues of the gods, the drive sweeps up the hill and into the courtyard through a triumphal arch topped by a ducal crown (illustration 7). On the left is the schlosskirche (castle church) consecrated in 1413; on the right (out of sight in illustration 7) the Prinzenpalais (prince's palace) dating from 1868. The large courtyard is ringed by buildings of all ages and it is well worth taking time to look around. Each building has a label, translated into English, with a brief outline of its history. The symbol of Altenburg is an ancient tower called the Flasche (Flask) dating from the eleventh century.

6. Altenburg (left to right) corps de logis, schloss church, and prince's palace.

Somewhat surprisingly, there is no immediate sight of the main schloss building from the courtyard. The corps de logis (main building) is tucked away off to one side in a smaller courtyard, with the view of its grand front elevation obscured by the adjacent wings. The museum with the duke's apartments occupies the first and second floors (second and third floors in American English). The lower floor focuses on the Younger Branch of dukes and the higher floor on the Elder Branch. The town of Altenburg was an important centre for the manufacture of playing cards and the ground floor is a Spielkartenmuseum (museum of playing cards). Most other visitors headed for this. The original collection was removed and taken to the Soviet Union as part of reparations after World War II but has been gradually built up again.

On 17 November 1826, Duke Friedrich of Saxe-Hildburghausen (1763-1834) left his old duchy to take up a new role as duke of Saxe-Altenburg[16]. It must have been quite a wrench for him; Friedrich was sixty-three years old and had reigned as duke of Saxe-Hildburghausen for forty-six years. In the reorganisation of Ernestine Line duchies that followed the death of the last duke of Saxe-Gotha-Altenburg in 1825, Friedrich ceded Hildburghausen to the duke of Saxe-Meiningen and in

The dukes of Saxe-Altenburg Elder Branch

The duchy of Saxe-Altenburg was created in 1603 following the death of Duke Friedrich Wilhelm I of Saxony (1562-1602). Friedrich Wilhelm I was the grandson of the ex-Elector Johann Friedrich I and ruled Ernestine lands in Thuringia jointly with his younger brother Johann of Weimar (1570-1605). On his death Friedrich Wilhelm I left three small sons born in 1597, 1599 and 1600. A fourth son was born posthumously in 1603. Their guardian negotiated a division of lands with their uncle and a new duchy of Saxe-Altenburg became their inheritance[17].

When he grew up, the new duchy was ruled by the eldest son, Johann Philipp (1597-1639) on behalf of his brothers. Chart 4 is the family tree of the dukes of Saxe-Altenburg Elder Branch. The second and third brothers died unmarried during the Thirty Years' War (1618-1648). Friedrich II (1599-1625) died in battle and Johann Wilhelm II (1600-1632) from fever.

Johann Philipp's only child was a daughter called Elisabeth Sophia. When he died in 1639, his youngest brother, Friedrich Wilhelm II Posthumous (1603-1669), became the sole duke of Saxe-Altenburg.

Friedrich Wilhelm II reigned for thirty years. He married twice but had only one surviving son, born in 1657. When his father died, eleven-year-old Friedrich Wilhelm III (1657-1672) became the third duke. But he reigned for only three years; on his death in 1672 the Saxe-Altenburg Elder Branch became extinct in the male line.

The marriage of the only child of Duke Johann Philipp would now prove crucial to the future of the duchy. In 1636 Elisabeth Sophia (1619-1680) married Duke Ernst the Pious of Saxe-Gotha (1601-1675). In the reorganisation that followed the death of Friedrich Wilhelm III, the bulk of Saxe-Altenburg went to Saxe-Gotha by virtue of the inheritance rights of Elisabeth Sophia. Her husband became Duke Ernst I of the amalgamated duchy of Saxe-Gotha-Altenburg (see Friedenstein in chapter 3).

return received Altenburg. The independent duchy of Saxe-Altenburg was recreated after a hundred and fifty years and Friedrich became first duke of the Saxe-Altenburg Younger Branch. Four further dukes would follow him before the monarchy came to an end (chart 10). See also Hildburghausen in chapter 4 for the earlier dukes of Saxe-Hildburghausen.

In 1834 Friedrich was succeeded as duke of Saxe-Altenburg by his son Joseph (1789-1868). A wonderful portrait of Joseph with his family hangs in the duke's apartments on the first floor of the corps de logis at Altenburg. This is a copy of the original in St Petersburg painted by Joseph Stieler (court painter to the Bavarian kings) in 1847[18]. The best portraits not only show a true likeness but also tell a story. The message of this portrait is the important marriages of Duke Joseph's daughters. Joseph was married to Amalie of Württemberg (1799-1848) and they had six daughters in succession, but no son. Chart 11 is a list of the daughters of Duke Joseph. The four who survived childhood are all depicted in the Stieler portrait in one way or another.

Joseph takes centre stage in the picture seated on a throne-like chair with his wife Amalie sitting next to him. Standing next to Joseph are their second and third grown-up daughters – Therese (born in 1823) and Elisabeth (born 1826). Therese was the only daughter never to marry; Elisabeth would marry Peter II of Oldenburg in 1852. He was heir to the grand duchy of Oldenburg and succeeded his father as reigning grand duke the following year.

The eldest daughter, Marie (born in 1818) is included in the Stieler picture by way of her separate portrait in an ornate gilt frame propped up next to Duchess Amalie. In 1843 Marie married Prince Georg of Hannover, heir to the Hanoverian throne. They would become king and queen of Hannover in 1851. Georg was blind from childhood due to illness in one eye and an unfortunate accident to the other. In a portrait within a portrait within a portrait, Georg is also included in the Stieler picture. His portrait is shown on a vase standing next to his wife in her portrait.

7. Entrance to Altenburg through the triumphal arch.

The youngest surviving daughter, Alexandra born in 1830, made the best match of the sisters and married Grand Duke Konstantin Nikolaievich of Russia, the second son of Tsar Nikolaus I. Through her marriage Altenburg had a strong connection to the Romanov royal family. The Stieler picture was painted as a wedding gift to the young couple from Saxe-Altenburg[19]. Alexandra is included in the family portrait in a most intriguing way. Duchess Amalie points to yet another picture on an easel off to one side and Joseph and their two daughters look towards it. This picture is apparently a portrait of Alexandra. But we can see only the outside edge of the frame and not the sitter. Konstantin and Alexandra were married in the Winter Palace, St Petersburg on 11 September 1848[20]. Alexandra converted to Russian orthodoxy on her marriage and took the name Alexandra Iosifovna. Known as Aunt Sanny she would become a 'grande dame' (great lady) of the Romanov family.

A huge full-length portrait of Alexandra Iosifovna, painted in 1857, dominates the room named after her at Altenburg. The Alexandra

Room throbs in crimson and gold with silk drapes, glittering mirrors, and a highly polished inlaid wooden floor. Alexandra Iosifovna has been described as '... a striking young woman, tall and thin, with a luxuriant cascade of dark hair that fell in soft ringlets ...'[21]. When Konstantin Nikolaievich first met her at Altenburg he was immediately smitten. He wrote,

> I don't know what is happening to me. It's as if I am a completely new person. Just one thought moves me, just one image fills my eyes: forever and only she, my angel, my universe. I really do think I am in love. But what can it mean? I've only known her just a few hours and already I'm up to my eyes in passion![22]

Konstantin Nikolaievich (1827-1892) and Alexandra Iosifovna (1830-1911) founded the Konstantinovichi branch of the Romanov royal family. Their story has more twists and turns than a television soap opera and is permeated by tragedy. The Konstantinovichi lived a life of almost unimaginable wealth and luxury in some of Russia's most beautiful palaces – the Marble Palace in St Petersburg built by Catherine the Great for her favourite, Grigory Orlov; the summer retreat of Strelna on the Gulf of Finland near Peterhof, now the residence of Russia's President Putin; the perfect palace of Pavlovsk near Tsarskoye Selo created by Konstantin Nikolaievich's grandmother, Empress Marie Feodorovna; and the paradise of Oreanda on the Black Sea coast in the Crimea. Their marriage got off to a good start and six children were born between 1850 and 1862 – four boys and two girls. But over time the relationship of Konstantin Nikolaievich and Alexandra Iosifovna fell apart and their family life was dysfunctional.

The elder daughter was Olga, born in 1851. When she was just sixteen her parents encouraged Olga into a marriage with King George I of Greece (elected to the Greek throne in 1863). Olga was still a child and left home unwillingly with a suitcase full of her favourite dolls and toys[23]. The younger daughter was Vera, born in 1854. Vera had behavioural problems as a child, possibly caused or exacerbated by a medical condition. Her parents found this hard to deal with and doctors suggested sending Vera to an institution[24]. Instead, when she was nine Vera was given away to her father's sister, Queen Olga of Württemberg, who had no children of her own[25]. The arrangement was formalised by adoption in 1871. By that time Konstantin Nikolaievich was cruelly referring to Alexandra Iosifovna as his 'government-issue wife'[26] and openly carrying on an affair with a ballerina. But perhaps the family nadir was reached in 1874 with a scandal over the eldest son. Nikolai (born 1850) was a feckless and dissipated youth. He was found guilty of stealing Alexandra Iosifovna's diamonds in cahoots with his American mistress; declared insane; and sent into exile in the Asian part of the Russian Empire!

The second son, Konstantin Konstantinovich (1858-1915), became head of the Konstantinovichi when his father died in 1892. After the antics of his elder brother, there was enormous pressure on him to conform. He met his second cousin, Elisabeth of Saxe-Altenburg (1865-1927), when he went to Altenburg for a family funeral[27] and was pushed towards marriage with her by his mother[28]. Konstantin Konstantinovich and Elisabeth Mavrikievna (as she became on their marriage in 1884) had nine children – six boys and three girls. Konstantin Konstantinovich was talented, intelligent, and artistic; he wrote poetry and plays under the pseudonym of KR (Konstantin Romanov). He was devoted to his family but there were hidden secrets. The private diaries published long after his death, reveal him as a practising homosexual who was in turmoil over his feelings[29].

World War I brought suffering and tragedy to the Konstantinovichi. The favourite son of Konstantin Konstantinovich was killed in action in October 1914. The grand duke never got over this blow and died of a heart attack the following year. Three more of his sons were butchered by the Bolsheviks in July 1918 during the Russian Revolution. When the news reached their widowed mother, Elisabeth Mavrikievna fled Russia in October 1918 with her youngest son and daughter. She made her way back to her childhood home and spent her last years in the Prinzenpalais at Altenburg.

Grand Duchess Elisabeth Mavrikievna was a sister of Duke Ernst II, the last reigning duke of Saxe-Altenburg. Another must-see room at Altenburg is the library of Ernst II, refurbished when he came to the throne in 1908. This is at the other end of the first-floor enfilade to the Alexandra Room. Panelled in dark wood and lined with bookcases, the library features a six-metre-long central library table on which were displayed reproductions of old photographs and newspapers for visitors to look at. Fascinating material! Above the fireplace is an arresting bronze relief showing an action scene from the kidnapping of the Saxon princes. This famous royal event took place at Altenburg in 1455. During his guided tour of the schloss in 1884, Dr Shephard Thomas Taylor was so thrilled to

8. Artist's impression of the kidnapping of the Saxon princes in 1455.

be shown the actual room from which the two sleeping boy princes were abducted that he tipped the guide an extra shilling[30]. But his excitement later turned to disgust when he discovered it was not possible to pinpoint a particular room as the building had been so much altered in the centuries since[31]! The sculpture in the library portrays the moment when two kidnappers are about to make their getaway on horseback, each with a boy prince on the pummel of his saddle. The picture is full of movement – the horses rear, the boys struggle, and the cloak of a kidnapper billows above his head.

The kidnapping of the Saxon princes

The kidnapping of the Saxon princes is a famous royal story from history. On the night of 7 July 1455, a knight called Kunz von Kauffungen scaled the walls of Schloss Altenburg and abducted the two young sons of Elector Friedrich II the Mild of Saxony. The elector was away from Altenburg and Prince Ernst (fourteen) and his brother Albrecht (twelve) were alone with their mother and her ladies. Kauffungen and his small band of followers had an accomplice inside the schloss. The kitchen boy Hans Schwalbe opened a window and threw down a rope ladder for the intruders. They overpowered the attendants and successfully made off with the boys.

Kunz von Kauffungen was a nobleman with a grievance. He supported Friedrich II in the elector's war against his brother but felt he was not adequately recompensed for his loyalty. The kidnapping did not redress his grievance. He was apprehended with Prince Albrecht on the same night as the kidnapping; his followers released Prince Ernst a few days later, on the promise of a pardon. Kunz von Kauffungen was executed. Legend has it that the kitchen boy was walled up alive at Altenburg.

The story of the Altenburg Prinzenraub (stealing of the princes) has captured the imagination over centuries. There is an annual re-enactment at Altenburg. The kidnapping is also celebrated in many works of literature and art. In an 1823 portrait of the young princes Ernst and Albrecht of Saxe-Coburg-Saalfeld with their mother, the boys are dressed in period costume as the kidnapped Saxon princes. Albrecht (five-years-old in the picture) would grow up to become Prince Consort Albert, the husband of Queen Victoria. Albert was an Ernestine Line prince: his family story is told in chapter 3.

Altenburg has a complicated ticketing arrangement which is not easy to fathom if you do not speak German. Visitors need one ticket for a self-guided tour of the duke's apartments and another ticket for a guided tour of the schloss church and the ballroom. We did not find out about the guided tour until it was too late in the day to take one. Like some other schlösser in what used to be East Germany, Altenburg also had an outmoded requirement to buy a photo permit in addition to the entrance tickets. We bought a permit, but showing this did not stop an unfriendly museum guard from shouting at us when we took photos. His solution for visitors who do not speak German was to come closer and shout louder!

Neues Schloss Hummelshain

Neues (New) Schloss Hummelshain was the last schloss to be built in Thuringia before the German monarchy fell. It was built between 1880 and 1885 by Duke Ernst I of Saxe-Altenburg (1826-1908). Like many other princes of his time, the duke was passionate about hunting. His Ernestine forbears had hunted at Hummelshain since the fifteenth century and there was already a hunting castle on the site. Altes (Old) Schloss Hummelshain (now holiday lets) was built in the 1660s by Duke Friedrich Wilhelm II *Posthumous* of Saxe-Altenburg Elder Branch (see chart 4 and page 22). One suggestion for building a second new schloss

9. Hummelshain was the last schloss to be built in Thuringia.

29

is that Ernst I wanted to entertain the German emperor for hunting at Hummelshain and did not consider the old schloss to be grand enough. Certainly, Kaiser Wilhelm II was his guest in the Neues Schloss for hunting parties in 1891 and 1894[32].

Ernst I was born in Hildburghausen on 16 September 1826, only a few weeks before his grandfather ceded Saxe-Hildburghausen to become the first duke of the Saxe-Altenburg Younger Branch (chart 10 is their family tree). His father Georg (1796-1853) was a younger son and when Ernst was born there may have been little expectation this baby would come to the throne. The heir was his father's elder brother Joseph who was married with a family of his own. Joseph (1789-1868) and his wife already had four daughters and would have hoped for future sons. Two more daughters were born but there were no sons, so Ernst kept his place in the line of succession. Ernst I's father unexpectedly became the duke in 1848 on the abdication of his elder brother Joseph. But by May 1853 Duke Georg was so seriously ill he handed over the government to

10. Ernst I was the longest reigning duke of Saxe-Altenburg Younger Branch.

his son and retired to Altes Schloss Hummelshain where he died on 3 August that year[33]. Ernst I became duke of Saxe-Altenburg at twenty-six years old.

Ernst I would reign for fifty-five years and be the longest-reigning duke of the Saxe-Altenburg Younger Branch. As heir to the throne he served in the Prussian army and he continued to follow a parallel military career. Ernst I saw active service in the Franco-Prussian War of 1870 and was present at the ceremony at Versailles Palace in January 1871 when the king of Prussia was proclaimed as German kaiser (emperor)[34]. He was a friend of the Prussian royal family and a life's ambition was to entertain them at Hummelshain. In 1873 Ernst I's only daughter, Marie, married Albrecht of Prussia (a nephew of Kaiser Wilhelm I).

Rather surprisingly, Ernst I engaged an unknown architect for Neues Schloss Hummelshain. It was Ernst Eberhard von Ihne's first important commission and it made his name. He went on to become a favoured architect of Kaiser Wilhelm II responsible for important projects in Berlin (such as the Berlin State Library on the Unter den Linden). Von Ihne also built Schloss Friedrichshof at Kronberg in Taunus as a retirement home for Kaiser Wilhelm II's mother, the widowed Victoria, Empress Friedrich III (see *Schloss*).

Von Ihne designed Neues Schloss Hummelshain in what is known as historicist style, a modern uptake on the architecture of the past. In Germany this period of architecture is alternatively called Wilhelmine reflecting the grandiose image portrayed by Kaiser Wilhelm II (reigned 1888 to 1918). In Britain we might say it was high Victorian, built during the last years of Queen Victoria's reign. Elaborately decorative and visually appealing, the Neues Schloss has elements of gothic, renaissance, and baroque. It was no surprise to find it popularly called *the Neuschwanstein of Thuringia*[35] (Neuschwanstein is the fairy-tale castle in the Bavarian Alps built by King Ludwig II of Bavaria and on which the Disney castle was based). Since the reunification of Germany, Neues Schloss Hummelshain has been used as a location for several feature films and television dramas[36].

The dominant feature of the schloss is is the tall tower over the entrance, reaching one hundred and forty feet in height and topped by a steeply pointed roof, four corner turrets, and an all-around covered balcony with arcades.

Von Ihne also designed the interior of the Neues Schloss, including the décor and the furniture. The layout comprised a central entertaining suite of dining room and ballroom with a wing to the west for Ernst I and a wing for his wife, Duchess Agnes, to the east. The south-facing ballroom opened out onto a broad terrace with steps leading to the schloss park and views down the hillside towards the village and the Altes Schloss. Ernst I's favourite place in his new schloss is said to have been the west-facing loggia (covered patio) off the reception room in his apartments where he could watch the setting sun[37]. The reception room in Duchess Agnes's suite featured a large Venetian mirror and is known as the Mirror Room. The duchess was a gifted artist and her rooms included a painting studio[38].

The Neues Schloss was emptied of furniture before ownership passed to the new Free State of Saxe-Altenburg after the monarchy fell in 1918. However, much of the elaborate and impressive decoration survives. The Festsaal (ballroom) has carved oak entrance doorways to the east and west wings, each with a minstrel's gallery above, and a coffered oak ceiling with sunken panels hung with intricately carved rosettes. A broad frieze running round the room below the ceiling

11. Much of the original decoration survives in the impressive ballroom.

shows historical hunting scenes and views of the Saxe-Altenburg ducal schlösser, including Altenburg and Fröhliche Wiederkunft.

In 1896, to commemorate Ernst I's seventieth birthday, a magnificent bronze statue of two stags was erected in the Hummelshain schloss park. There were years of loss ahead for him. Duchess Agnes, his wife of forty-four years, died in 1897 and their only daughter Marie in 1898. Ernst I's only son had died soon after birth in 1856 and when the duke died (in 1908) he was succeeded by his nephew, Ernst II. Ernst II was the last duke and abdicated on 13 November 1918.

12. The deer statue commemorates the seventieth birthday of Ernst I.

In 1920 the Free State sold Neues Schloss Hummelshain into private ownership. It was bought by a Thuringian businessman who used it as a private home and for business entertaining. In World War II the schloss was confiscated for use as a military hospital; in the GDR years it became a children's home and youth training facility. Ernst I's loggia was fitted with sports equipment and converted to a gymnasium. After the reunification of Germany the youth facility closed in 1992. Neues Schloss Hummelshain was up for sale by the state again and in 1998 it was acquired by another German businessman through his company. But the purchaser lacked sufficient financial resources to buy and restore the schloss and over the years criticism grew as even essential repairs were not carried out and it deteriorated further.

In an remarkable turn of events Neues Schloss Hummelshain is being rescued by its Friends Association (Förderverein Schloss Hummelshain). For more than twenty years a group of enthusiasts, historians and sponsors have tenaciously promoted the need to save this unique royal building. Their efforts have borne fruit. In 2017 Neues Schloss Hummelshain was declared a monument of national

13. View from the south with Duchess Agnes's wing on the right.

importance by the central Federal Government; in 2019 the Friends Association won the State of Thuringia Monument Protection Prize. By agreement with the owner, the Friends Association are carrying out a programme of critical renovation funded by the State and Federal governments. Work is underway in phases to repair the roof and make the building watertight and eliminate rampant dry rot. You can monitor progress in the construction diary on the Friends website (www.foerderverein-schloss-hummelshain.de).

But the future of Neues Schloss Hummelshain is still uncertain. The company that bought it in 1998 went bankrupt and its ownership is under litigation. Very likely the schloss will need to be sold again and continued restoration and future use depend on the new owners. The Friends Association run guided tours of the Neues Schloss and schloss park and there is a nice video tour on their website. Unfortunately, my scheduled visit had to be deferred due to the covid-19 pandemic. The schloss is high on my list when I can safely return to Thuringia. I am most grateful to the Friends Association for providing images and information for this book.

3.

SAXE-COBURG AND GOTHA

The name of Saxe-Coburg and Gotha resonates in British royal history. The high point of this dynasty's fortunes was undoubtedly when Prince Albert of Saxe-Coburg and Gotha married Queen Victoria of Great Britain in 1840. All our monarchs from Queen Victoria have been members of this royal house. The surname of the British royal family was 'Saxe-Coburg and Gotha' until George V changed it in 1917 (during World War I) to the much more English sounding 'Windsor' (taken from Windsor Castle near London). That same year heavy German 'Gotha' bombers were carrying out night-time bombing raids on London.

The double duchy of Saxe-Coburg and Gotha was made up of two Ernestine Line territories (Coburg and Gotha) linked together in 1826 and ruled separately by the same duke (called a personal union). This chapter includes schlösser in the Gotha part of the double duchy; Coburg (now part of Bavaria) is in *Schloss in Bavaria*. We start at the 'forgotten' ancestral schloss of the Saxe-Coburg and Gotha family, and end at the *Sleeping Beauty* schloss in the Thuringian forest where Queen Victoria stayed when she made her first visit to Albert's home country.

The last duke of Saxe-Coburg and Gotha was Victoria and Albert's grandson Karl Eduard (reigned from 1900). When revolution came to Gotha in early November 1918, Karl Eduard was away in Coburg where his wife was imminently expecting their fifth child. The duke was deposed in his absence and on 13 November his reign as duke officially came to an end[1].

Saalfeld

Saalfeld was the residence of Johann Ernst (1658-1729), first duke of Saxe-Saalfeld and founder of the house of Saxe-Coburg and Gotha. Queen Elizabeth II of Great Britain is his seven-times great-granddaughter. The extraordinary rise in prominence of his branch of the Ernestine Line during the nineteenth century is one of royal history's greatest stories. From relatively modest beginnings the Saxe-Coburg and Gotha family came to occupy numerous thrones. Saalfeld is known as *The Cradle of European Dynasties* because the kings or queens of fourteen European countries were members of this royal dynasty[2]. One tragic consequence was that the main protagonists in World War

14. Saalfeld is the ancestral schloss of the house of Saxe-Coburg and Gotha.

I were all related to each other by blood or marriage. Saalfeld has been government offices since the 1920s and much of the original interiors have been lost. But the dazzling early-eighteenth century chapel has survived and is rightly described as *Ein kleinod des Barock* (a jewel of the baroque)[3].

Johann Ernst was the youngest of the seven surviving sons of Duke Ernst *the Pious* of Saxe-Gotha-Altenburg (see chart 5). After their father died in 1675 the brothers ruled the duchy jointly, but each wanted their own grand residence. The second brother Albrecht (1648-1699) began building a new schloss at Saalfeld. The foundation stone was laid on 26 March 1677. But things changed in the government of the duchy. The arrangement to rule collectively proved unworkable and there were disputes between the brothers. Under an agreement of 1680 the inheritance was divided into seven. Johann Ernst was allocated the smallest piece of territory and became the first duke of Saxe-Saalfeld. His dwarf duchy had an area of only one hundred and seventy-five square miles (four hundred and fifty square kilometres) with a population of fourteen thousand[4]. Brother Albrecht got the more important territory of Saxe-Coburg. When Albrecht died childless in 1699, Johann Ernst laid claim to Coburg but this would be contested by his brothers and their heirs for more than three decades.

Duke Johann Ernst and his wife Sophie Hedwig of Saxe-Merseburg made their ceremonial entry into Saalfeld on 3 August 1680[5]. The schloss was still a building shell; the east wing with the ducal apartments would not be ready for occupation until 1691. By then Sophia Hedwig was dead and Johann Ernst had married for a second time to Charlotta Johanna of Waldeck. Their coats of arms still flank the grand staircase and the couple are enthroned together on a cloud in the ceiling painting. The smallness of his duchy seems to have spurred Johann Ernst to parade his princely status with greater signs of outward display. The schloss at Saalfeld was extended through two more building phases to form the classic baroque three-winged horseshoe shape around an open courtyard. The north wing with the chapel was completed in 1714; the south wing with the ballroom by around 1720. The building work was finally complete with the addition of the clock tower in 1726. On my first visit to Saalfeld we climbed this tower and stood on the balcony to admire the views of town and countryside.

15. The dazzling chapel is a jewel of the baroque.

In 2020 Saalfeld celebrated the three-hundred-year anniversary of the schloss chapel. Over the weekend of 7 to 9 February there was a programme of events in the chapel including a religious service, a concert of eighteenth-century music, and a presentation by Niels Fleck, author of an authoritative book on schloss chapels in Thuringia (unfortunately only available in German)[6]. It took ten years to complete the interior of the chapel after the shell of the north wing was built. Johann Ernst engaged well-known artists who had already worked for his brothers, including Bartolomeo and Carlo Luchese for the stuccowork and the painter Carol Ludovico Castelli for the frescos. When it was finished, the duke waited for a sufficiently grand occasion to launch his stunning work of art[7]. The chapel was finally inaugurated on 8 February 1720 at the wedding of Johann Ernst's daughter. Sophie Wilhelmine married Friedrich Anton, the reigning prince of the next-door royal state of Schwarzburg-Rudolstadt. This family connection was reinforced when three years later, on 2 January 1723, the bride's brother, Franz Josias of Saxe-Saalfeld, married the groom's sister, Anna Sophia of Schwarzburg-Rudolstadt.

I can only compare the chapel at Saalfeld to a beautiful wedding cake. Cherubs romp across the ceiling, paintings and intricate plasterwork cover the walls, and two tiers of Corinthian columns run around the room, supporting the layers of the 'cake'. The whole space is lit by windows on three sides at both levels. The focal point is the gorgeous grey alabaster altar by Thuringian sculptor Gottfried Gröninger, with an altarpiece painting of the Ascension by Bavarian artist Johann Murrer that reaches as high as the gallery. The pulpit is at gallery level above the altar and faces the duke's pew at the other end of the chapel. Rising above it all, behind the pulpit, is a magnificent silver organ that glitters in the sun. Saxe-Saalfeld may have been a tiny state but the schloss chapel rivals anything I have seen.

Both of Johann Ernst's wives died young – Sophie Hedwig in 1686, after only six years of marriage; and Charlotta Johanna in 1699, after eight. When the duke died in 1729 at the ripe old age (for those times) of seventy he left two surviving sons – Christian Ernst (1683-1745) from the first marriage and Franz Josias (1697-1764) from the second. Both had equal inheritance rights as duke, but Franz Josias challenged his older half-brother's eligibility on the grounds that Christian Ernst had made an unequal marriage. In 1724 Christian Ernst married Christiane Friederike von Koss, the daughter of an official at the Saalfeld court[8]. Franz Josias made a dynastic marriage (see above) and his eldest son Ernst Friedrich (1724-1800) was born that same year. This awkward situation between the brothers was ultimately only resolved because Christian Ernst and Christiane did not have children. In 1735 the acquisition of Coburg was finally confirmed and Saxe-Saalfeld became Saxe-Coburg-Saalfeld. Christian Ernst resided in the schloss in Saalfeld and Franz Josias relocated to Coburg, the capital of the newly named duchy. When Christian Ernst died in 1745 the importance of Saalfeld as the main residence of a royal duke came to an end. Franz Josias introduced primogeniture in 1747[9] and was succeeded on his death in 1764 by his eldest son, Ernst Friedrich. (For a family tree of the dukes of Saxe-Saalfeld and Saxe-Coburg-Saalfeld see chart 12.)

The double duchy of Saxe-Coburg and Gotha

The double duchy of Saxe-Coburg and Gotha consisted of two separate duchies linked together in a personal union ruled by the same duke. The double duchy came into being in 1826, on what would be the last major reorganisation of Ernestine Line lands in Thuringia.

The story of the double duchy begins in 1680 with a division between seven brothers. The eldest got Gotha as part of the duchy of Saxe-Gotha-Altenburg, the second son got Coburg, and the youngest son became duke of tiny Saxe-Saalfeld. After the second son died childless there was a reshuffle of his lands; and in 1735 Coburg was added to Saalfeld to become Saxe-Coburg-Saalfeld. In 1826, following the death (without a male heir) of the last duke of Saxe-Gotha-Altenburg and after protracted inheritance negotiations, the duke of Saxe-Coburg-Saalfeld was awarded Gotha and in turn ceded Saalfeld to Saxe-Meiningen (another Ernestine Line branch). Duke Ernst III of Saxe-Coburg-Saalfeld then became Duke Ernst I of Saxe-Coburg and Gotha (with his new title, the numbering started again).

Duke Ernst I now ruled a double duchy with two capitals (Coburg and Gotha) and two parliaments. The two parts of his double duchy were not contiguous or joined up. Coburg and Gotha are sixty miles apart and the court resided alternatively in each[10].

When almost ninety years later the monarchy fell, the separate history of the two duchies pulled them apart. In a referendum of 1919, the citizens of Coburg voted overwhelmingly to become part of the state of Bavaria, leaving Gotha as part of Thuringia. This had profound consequences after World War II when Thuringia (but not Bavaria) fell behind the Iron Curtain.

Saalfeld is proud of its place in the ancestry of the British royal family. In the nineteenth century two descendants of Duke Johann Ernst married into the British royal family. The first was in 1818 when Victoire of Saxe-Coburg-Saalfeld (the great-great-granddaughter of Johann Ernst) married Edward Duke of Kent, the fourth son of George III. Their only child was Queen Victoria. The second was in the next generation when on 10 February 1840 at the Chapel Royal, St James's Palace in London, Victoria

16. Victoire of Saxe-Coburg-Saalfeld with her daughter Princess Victoria (later Queen Victoria).

married her cousin Albert of Saxe-Coburg and Gotha (the son of her mother's brother, Ernst I). Albert was a direct descendant in the male line of Heinrich *the Illustrious* of the house of Wettin, who inherited Thuringia from the Ludowinger landgraves (see the Wartburg in chapter 5); of Johann Friedrich *the Noble*, who lost Saxony for his Protestant faith (see Fröhliche Wiederkunft, chapter 2); and of Johann Ernst, a seventh son who got the smallest piece of territory. But by now Saalfeld had been exchanged for Gotha and was no longer part of the family title. This is the reason why Saalfeld feels the 'forgotten schloss' whose role in the history of the British royal family is often overlooked.

The warm welcome at Saalfeld makes this a favourite schloss. On our first visit for an earlier book (*Schloss II*), we learned how the town celebrated the birth of Prince George of Cambridge in July 2013 as a new heir to the British throne descended from their historical royal

17. Saalfeld seen from the schloss park.

family. On our return home I wrote to the Duke and Duchess of Cambridge to tell them of the town's warm interest and received a letter of thanks for Saalfeld from Kensington Palace. The welcome at the schloss was equally warm on our return visit for this book. During a special day in Saalfeld we were privileged to meet the director of the Saalfeld brewery and see the brew kettle that brewed a special-edition *Prince George's beer* in honour of his birth.

Friedenstein

Friedenstein at Gotha was the only schloss to be built during the Thirty Years' War (1618-1648). In 1640 Duke Ernst I (1601-1675) inherited the duchy of Saxe-Gotha[11]. He found it in a pitiful condition. Thuringia had suffered the ravages of a terrible war with fire, famine, and plague caused by repeated troop movements through the area. In some parts the population was reduced to one tenth of pre-war levels[12]. Ernst I reigned for over thirty years and did much to rebuild Saxe-Gotha after the devastation of war. He proved a model ruler whose disciplined government, sober lifestyle, and strong faith earned him the epithet of Ernst *der Fromme* (the Pious). Ernst's one extravagance was to build the largest schloss in Thuringia as the physical manifestation of his majesty and power. His schloss is monumental but unadorned. The plain façade seems to reflect the stern principles of Ernst's Lutheran faith. He named it Friedenstein or Rock of Peace to reflect hope for the future rather than the failures of the past. Above the entrance are carved figures of Peace and Justice embracing in a sculpture known as *The Kiss of Peace*. 'Peace nourishes, strife devours' says the inscription[13].

The foundation stone for Friedenstein was laid on 26 October 1643 and the ducal family moved in to celebrate the birth of Ernst's son Friedrich (later Friedrich I) at the consecration of the schloss church on 17 September 1646. The floor plan of Friedenstein is enormous. The central wing is four stories high and one hundred and twenty yards in length (one hundred and ten metres). The two side wings are one hundred and fifty yards long (one hundred and forty metres) and each end in a massive square tower (the East and West Towers). One reason for the schloss's huge size is that Ernst I was a believer in centralisation. So church, armoury, mint, ducal archives, stables and all the other institutions and services of his duchy were under the same roof as his residence. The courtyard between its wings is big enough for a military parade ground or several football pitches!

18. Statue of Ernst *the Pious* outside his schloss.

Grimmenstein

Friedenstein (Rock of Peace) was built on the site of a previous castle at Gotha called Grimmenstein (Rock of Wrath). This was razed to the ground in 1567 on the orders of the Holy Roman emperor. Grimmenstein had been the residence of Duke Johann Friedrich II (1529-1595), the eldest son of Johann Friedrich I the Noble who was forced to sign over the electorate of Saxony to his cousin Moritz (see Fröhliche Wiederkunft in chapter 2). The son was no more fortunate than the father.

Johann Friedrich II hoped to regain his father's lost lands and title. He made the mistake of sheltering a known outlaw at Grimmenstein and refusing to give him up. He was placed under the Imperial Ban by the Emperor Maximilian II, which meant he lost all his rights and that his property could legally be taken from him by other princes. Grimmenstein was besieged and then destroyed by Elector Augustus of Saxony, the brother and successor of Elector Moritz who had dispossessed Johann Friedrich II's father. Johann Friedrich II spent the rest of his life (some twenty-eight years) in prison. His lands were awarded to his younger brother, Johann Wilhelm (1530-1572), the grandfather of Ernst the Pious.

In 1672 Ernst *the Pious* also inherited Altenburg by virtue of his wife Elisabeth Sophia (1619-1680), who was the last of the Saxe-Altenburg Elder Branch (chart 4). Ernst's territory increased in size and became the duchy of Saxe-Gotha-Altenburg. He and his wife had seventeen children, and when Ernst died in 1675 there were seven surviving sons. Ernst intended them to rule jointly, in a committee arrangement with the eldest as chairman[14]. But over time this proved unworkable with each brother claiming an inheritance. The dispute went on for several years until it was eventually referred to the Holy Roman emperor for arbitration. The emperor came down in favour of division and the father's lands were split into seven for the sons (chart 5). After all, it was in the emperor's interests to divide and rule and not to have powerful vassals[15]. The eldest son, Friedrich 1 (1646-1691) became duke of a smaller Saxe-Gotha-Altenburg, comprising around two-fifths of his father's territory. One of the first things he did was to introduce primogeniture (inheritance by the eldest surviving son)[16]. Chart 6 has the family tree for Friedrich I and the six dukes of Saxe-Gotha-Altenburg who followed him.

Today Friedenstein is home to the university library, state archives, and public records office, as well as several museums. We visited the schloss museum which itself is enormous. We followed the museum rundgang (suggested tour) with the help of an English audio-guide but were soon adrift in what seemed like an endless series of rooms. Our visit was saved by smiling museum attendants who patiently answered questions, untangled my audio-guide, suggested where to go next, and (best of all) helped to identify the family portraits. Friedrich I was more focused on court display than his father and created a suite of

19. Friedenstein is enormous –
the courtyard measures 120 by 150 yards!

state apartments on the second floor. Their highlight is the Banqueting Hall with magnificent stuccowork decoration. At each end of the room, huge stucco statues of the seasons flank buffet niches for displaying china; the ceiling is a riot of stucco gods and godesses among garlands of leaves, flowers and fruits.

The museum tour ended in the fascinating Ekhof theatre in the West Tower. This was opened with an opera performance to celebrate the birthday of Friedrich I's wife on 24 April 1683 and still has its original stage sets and machinery in working order! The Ekhof theatre is named after Konrad Ekhof, known as *the father of German acting* and hailed as the best actor and acting teacher of the eighteenth century[17]. Ekhof was artistic director at Gotha from 1775 until his death in 1778 under Friedrich I's great-grandson (Ernst II). Friedrich I was also responsible for an appealing quirk of the silhouette of Friedenstein. The roof shapes of the East and West towers do not match! When he rebuilt the East Tower after a fire in 1677 Friedrich I gave it a domed-shaped roof; the West Tower still has its original angular pitched roof.

20. View across the courtyard to the East Tower, rebuilt by Duke Friedrich I.

An excitement for me at Friedenstein was the connection with the British royal family. One princess of Saxe-Gotha-Altenburg was the mother of King George III and another the mother-in-law of Queen

Victoria! The stories of these two princesses are not well-known parts of British royal history and visiting Friedenstein helped me to find out more about them.

The first princess was Auguste (1719-1772) of Saxe-Gotha-Altenburg, the daughter of Duke Friedrich II. In 1736 she married Frederick Lewis Prince of Wales (1707-1751) the eldest son of George II. Frederick Lewis died before his father, so Auguste never became queen, but she was the ancestress of all our later monarchs. When the sixteen-year-old Auguste (Augusta in English) was reviewed on the shortlist of potential brides for Frederick Lewis she was not considered to be beautiful, intelligent, or well-educated. She was however assessed as fertile (she first menstruated at the early age of eleven) with a physique described as 'like the women who deliver robust children'[18]. Such reports were good enough for George II and Frederick Lewis was content to accept his father's choice. He was hoping that marriage would enable him to get more money out of the British parliament. Augusta did not speak English when she arrived in Britain as this accomplishment had not been considered necessary back in Gotha. Surely after twenty years of Hanoverians on the throne everyone in Britain would speak German[19]! She made a good start with her parents-in-law by prostrating herself on the ground as a sign of extreme respect. Her outwardly docile and submissive nature was highly valued by her husband. But the young bride stepped into a hostile family situation. Frederick Lewis hated his parents and was loathed by them in return.

When his grandfather suceeded to the British throne as George I in 1714, seven-year-old Frederick Lewis was left behind as the family representative in their home duchy of Hannover. He did not see his parents (George II and Queen Caroline) again for fourteen years! When Frederick Lewis eventually came to Britain he was viewed by his father as a potential rival. George II was relieved to find 'I think this is a son I need not be much afraid of'[20]. Queen Caroline was at first distressed to leave Frederick Lewis behind, but as the years went by she focused her love on her younger son William who was born in Britain[21]. She harboured hopes that Frederick Lewis was impotent so that the throne might descend through William[22]. But it was a vain hope: Frederick Lewis and Augusta had nine children, the last born postumously three months after his death.

When Augusta became pregnant with her first child, Queen Caroline was highly suspicious and determined to attend the birth and prevent any skullduggery. Frederick was equally resolved to thwart his parents wishes. The royal family were in summer residence at Hampton Court when Augusta's waters broke on the evening of 31 July 1737 and she went into labour earlier than expected. Despite the hazard to his wife and unborn child, Frederick Lewis insisted on travelling back to St James's Palace in London so that his mother could not be present at the birth. Fifteen miles in labour over bumpy roads in a horse-drawn carriage must have been a nightmare for Augusta. Nothing was ready for their arrival and she gave birth on a table cloth because there was no bed linen available[23]!

Frederick Lewis died aged forty-four in 1751, probably from a pulmonary embolism (blood clot on the lungs)[24]. He did not make much impression on history and is usually remembered only as 'Poor Fred' from the contemporary epigram

> Here lies poor Fred, who was alive and is dead,
> Had it been his father, I had much rather.
> ...
> But since tis only Fred, who was alive and is dead,
> There's no more to be said.[25]

The widowed Augusta was given custody of their children and designated as regent should her son come to the throne as a minor. She has attracted heavy criticism for the narrow and sheltered upbringing she provided for George III, and ridicule for her alleged relationship with the Earl of Bute whom she appointed as his tutor and who went on to become his prime minister. But it seems unlikely that Augusta and

Bute were lovers[26]. George III suceeded his grandfather (George II) in 1760 aged twenty-two; Augusta Dowager Princess of Wales died in 1772. She never became queen and is a little-remembered British royal.

The second princess from Friedenstein with a connection the British royal family is even less well-known. Luise of Saxe-Gotha-Altenburg (1800-1831) was the mother of Prince Consort Albert (husband of Queen Victoria). Luise was banished from her son's life while Albert was a child and never saw him grow up.

Luise was born at Friedenstein on 21 December 1800. Her mother died a few days after her birth and her father, Duke August (1772-1822), soon married again in the search for an heir. But there were no children from his

21. Prince Albert was the second son of Luise of Saxe-Gotha-Altenburg.

second marriage to Karoline Amalie of Hesse-Darmstadt (1771-1848) and Luise was an only child. She was married at Friedenstein on 31 July 1817 to Duke Ernst III of Saxe-Coburg-Saalfeld. He was a distant kinsman from another Ernestine Line branch (see Saalfeld above). It was an excellent match for Ernst because Luise brought a substantial dowry and had prospects for a major inheritance. After her father and her uncle, Luise was the last of the Saxe-Gotha-Altenburg branch of the Ernestine Line. For Luise's father, the marriage may have seemed desirable to keep the inheritance within the family. His younger brother, who succeeded him as Friedrich IV (1774-1825) in 1822, was unmarried and an invalid. But for sixteen-year-old Luise the marriage would turn out a disaster. Her thirty-three-year-old bridegroom was an established rake who had already fathered illegitimate children. He was not in love with Luise and would not prove a loving or faithful husband.

Ernst and Luise had two sons in quick succession while she was still a teenager – Ernst in 1818 and Albert in 1819. But the marriage was unhappy almost from the start. Luise was young, romantic, lonely, and badly treated by her husband. She began to enjoy flirtations with other men and there were rumours she too was unfaithful. We cannot know if the rumours were true, but it is possible Luise did have an affair; she certainly began to live openly with her suspected lover, Maximilian von Hanstein, soon after her separation. Ernst could not tolerate his wife's infidelity and in 1824 Luise was sent away. Her story has always angered me because of the double standards of the day. The terms of the separation were harsh. Luise was not permitted to see her sons and was given only an allowance while Ernst kept control of her fortune. He wanted to get his hands on her inheritance, so he waited until her uncle, Duke Friedrich IV, died in 1825 before starting divorce proceedings. In the reshuffle of Ernestine Line lands that followed the death of the last duke of Saxe-Gotha-Altenburg, Ernst was awarded Gotha in exchange for Saalfeld and Duke Ernst III of Saxe-Coburg-Saalfeld became Duke Ernst I of the twin duchies of Saxe-Coburg and Gotha.

Prince Albert's mother, Luise, disappeared from his life overnight when he was five-years-old, and he never saw her again. He did not forget her. When Victoria and Albert's fourth daughter was born in 1848 she was named Louise Caroline Alberta. Her first name was for Albert's mother and the second for his beloved step-grandmother, Dowager Duchess Karoline Amalie of Saxe-Gotha-Altenburg, who died that same year. After Luise was sent away the dowager duchess (her stepmother) played an important role in the upbringing of Luise's two young sons. The boys often stayed at Friedenstein during their childhood. When Queen Victoria and Prince Albert visited Gotha in 1845, they stayed at Schloss Friedrichsthal (illustration 22) in the grounds of Friedenstein; this was the Dowager Duchess Karoline's home.

Was Albert illegitimate?

Because of the suggestion that Duchess Luise had affairs during her marriage, the question has arisen as to whether Albert was illegitimate and Duke Ernst I of Saxe-Coburg and Gotha not his biological father. A fascinating book called 'The Coburg Conspiracy' by Richard Sotnick (see bibliography) suggests this is plausible for several reasons. It dates the breakdown of the marriage of Ernst and Luise to the time of her second pregnancy (with Albert); and argues that she would not have so meekly accepted the harsh terms of her separation had she not thought herself guilty of a terrible offence. It is also true that, as a man, Albert was quite different in character to his father and his elder brother.

However, Albert was always treated as the second son of Duke Ernst I and the rumours about his birth do not seem to have begun until after Queen Victoria's death. This does not of course put the matter beyond doubt; there are other cases where, to avoid scandal, a royal husband accepted paternity of his wife's children from an affair. The youngest daughter of Grand Duchess Wilhelmine of Hesse-Darmstadt, born in 1824, married the heir to the Russian throne. Officially her father was her mother's husband, the grand duke of Hesse-Darmstadt; in all likelihood her natural father was her mother's lover, Baron de Senarclens-Grancy (see Heiligenberg in 'Schloss III').

But while Albert grew up to be unlike his father, he did show many Saxe-Coburg and Gotha family traits, such as intelligence, astuteness, and purpose in life. These were also apparent in his redoubtable grandmother (Ernst I's mother) Duchess Augusta of Saxe-Coburg-Saalfeld (born Reuss-Ebersdorf – see Ebersdorf in chapter 6) and in his uncle Leopold, later king of the Belgians (Ernst I's younger brother). Which does leave an interesting possibility. At the time Albert would have been conceived, Leopold was on a visit home to his family in Coburg. He was a newly bereaved widower having lost his wife Princess Charlotte of Wales (only child of the prince regent, later George IV), with whom he was very much in love, a few months before. A grieving widower and a neglected, unhappy wife thrown in proximity ...?

22. Schloss Friedrichsthal was the home of Albert's step-grandmother.

On meeting the dowager for the first time, Victoria described Karoline in her journal.

She is a charming old Lady, so nice looking, & so erect & active, – for she is 74 but she is unfortunately very deaf; she is very little, being nearly a head shorter than me, & round & fat. She was so happy to see us, kissed me over & over again – & Albert, whom she adores – who is the dearest Being to her in the World, she was so over enchanted to see again, & kissed so kindly. It did one's heart good to see her joy[27].

After the divorce Luise married Maximilian von Hanstein and made a new life in St Wendel in the small principality of Lichtenberg in the Saarland (two hundred and fifty miles from Gotha near the French border). This had been awarded to Ernst at the Congress of Vienna in 1815 after the Napoleonic Wars. Her second marriage was happy but the couple did not have many years together. Luise died in 1831, aged thirty, from cancer of the uterus. Her ex-husband Ernst sold Lichtenberg to Prussia in 1834 on the grounds that it was too far away[28].

Molsdorf

Molsdorf near Erfurt was the country home of Graf Gustav Adolph von Gotter (1692-1762); described at the schloss as 'diplomat and playboy'[29]. Gotter was not born an aristocrat but achieved high rank and wealth through a mixture of talent as a diplomat, smart networking, and gambling. He won the jackpot in the lottery twice in 1726 (first in London and then in The Hague) and this enabled him to buy the old, moated castle at Molsdorf. But Gotter was a big spender who liked to live well and enjoy his pleasures to the full. He laid out a fortune to transform Molsdorf into a palatial country estate to compare with those of his royal patrons. Inscribed on a shield high in each corner of the Banqueting Hall is his favourite motto 'Vive La Joie'[30]. I might translate this in modern parlance as 'Let's all have a jolly good time!'. Graf Gotter lived beyond his means and debts forced him to sell the schloss only fifteen years after he bought it. The heyday of Molsdorf was short.

I went to Molsdorf with no expectations of the visit. I had not heard of Graf (count) von Gotter and simply picked the name of the schloss from a list published by the Thuringian state castles and gardens foundation[31]. But I have learned from experience never to pre-judge a visit. The most famous palaces may not live up to expectations, while lesser known schlösser can be the most exciting to visit. By chance, we happened to go on an 'open day' when entrance was free and there were more visitors than usual. The staff seemed taken aback to discover we were English, but rallied around and produced an English handout for the (German) guided tour.

The day was overcast and cold; it was gloomy inside the schloss with dark décor and the blinds drawn. To my dismay we were required to wear the old-fashioned felt overshoes that were once standard in GDR (East German) museums but are rarely seen nowadays. As the group of visitors shuffled along in coats and overshoes, I was reminded of prisoners in the gulag. But when we moved into the Banqueting Hall

(Bankettsaal) the whole mood changed. Our guide had a flair for the dramatic; she directed us to seats and then suddenly turned on the lights. Wow! This was theatre!

23. Molsdorf was the country estate of Graf Gustav Adolph von Gotter.

The Banqueting Hall is panelled from floor to ceiling in dark oak and hung with thirty-three imposing male portraits. This room has charisma. Above us the gods assembled in the ceiling painting; and from a painted balustrade around the edge lively and gesticulating figures in eighteenth-century costume looked down as we listened to the guide. The Banqueting Hall is Gotter's version of an ancestral portrait gallery but the portraits here are not of his forbears. Gotter was a parvenu, created baron by Emperor Karl VI in 1724 and raised to count in 1740. Instead, these portraits are the kings, princes, and generals with whom Gotter claimed a connection. They include Duke Friedrich II of Saxe-Gotha-Altenburg (1676-1732), who gave Gotter his first diplomatic posting and kick-started his spectacular career; King

Friedrich Wilhelm I of Prussia and his son King Friedrich II (Frederick the Great), who made him privy councillor and Prussian ambassador in Vienna; and the famed imperial general, Prince Eugene of Savoy, with whom Gotter formed a close friendship during his years at the Viennese court. The Banqueting Hall is a visual demonstration of Gotter's enhanced social position and a tribute to his networking skills.

The dramatic performance with the lights was repeated in the Silver Cabinet (Silbernes Kabinett) next door to the Banqueting Hall. Gotter hung this room with thirty-five female portraits he called the 'queens of his heart'[32]. They included empresses and queens such as Elisabeth Christine of Prussia (wife of Frederick the Great), Maria Theresa of Austria, and Catherine the Great of Russia. There were also less high-ranking ladies chosen for their intelligence and beauty[33]. In pride of place was the portrait of Duchess Luise Dorothea of Saxe-Gotha-Altenburg (1710-1767). She was the wife of Duke Friedrich III of Saxe-Gotha-Altenburg (1699-1772), son and successor of Gotter's first patron (Friedrich II). The authoritative 'who's who' on royalty called the *Almanac de Gotha* was first published in Gotha during Friedrich III's reign. Luise Dorothea was a stronger personality than her husband. Intelligent and well educated, she corresponded with the cultural giants of the day, including Voltaire who found a home in Gotha after he fell out with Frederick the Great and left Prussia. In 1739 Luise Dorothea and her husband set up a club for courtiers called *The Order of the Happy Hermits*. Their aim was to lead a joyful and carefree life. Gotter became a member and the order sometimes met at Molsdorf. Luise Dorothea wears the 'uniform' of the order in her portrait in the Silver Cabinet (brown taffeta dress and pink straw hat) and a ribbon pinned on her bodice with their motto (Vive La Joie)[34]. The Happy Hermits were each given a special name to reflect their characters; Gotter was Tourbillon or Whirlwind[35].

Despite his wealth and social success, Gotter never married. Perhaps his low-born origins meant he would not have been considered a suitable husband in the aristocratic circles to which he aspired.

Judging by the decoration in the Silver Cabinet, his attitude to women was ambivalent. Running around the ceiling, above the portraits, is a silver-plated stucco cornice incorporating the figures of small animals. Gotter indicated these symbolised characteristics of the female sex – the squirrel for a craving for sweet snacks, the monkey for an obsession with cleaning, the peacock for vanity, the bird of paradise for showing off, the dragon for vengefulness, the parrot for chattering, the falcon for cunning, the gryphon for inquisitiveness, and the Cupid with the bird on his hand for flattery[36]. I wonder if the great ladies of the portraits in the Silver Cabinet knew Gotter may have been mocking them?

Gustav Adolph von Gotter was born in Gotha in 1692. His father was an envoy at the imperial (Holy Roman Empire) court in Vienna and in 1715 Friedrich II of Saxe-Gotha-Altenburg sent the young Gotter there to assist his father. He soon acquired a reputation both as a skilled diplomat and as a bon vivant. This is an extract from his 1867 biography by August Beck, archivist and librarian at the Gotha court[37].

His house was one of the most resplendent in all Vienna. Its rooms were furnished in extravagant opulence. Magnificent carriages and horses were at his command, and a host of richly attired lackeys and runners waited on him hand and foot. In a word, his household was almost princely. But nothing cost him more than his lavishly set table, because he loved FINE DINING only too much and enjoyed gathering a large company at his table.

Gotter clearly enjoyed good living but he also used ostentatious display to make friends and influence people. Guests at his table would find gifts such as watches and jewellery hidden in their food.

The grandeur Gotter radiated and which not rarely outshone the wealth of the most respected envoys to Vienna was not always a mere effect of his love of fine things; very often, he projected this image deliberately for political reasons, for the purpose of gaining influence and achieving his goals, and only rarely did he fail to do so[38].

24. The statues were known as Graf Gotter's moneymen.

After Duke Friedrich II of Saxe-Gotha-Altenburg died in 1732, Gotter left the service of the Gotha court and, as a personal favour to Prince Eugene of Savoy, was appointed Prussian ambassador in Vienna by King Friedrich Wilhelm I of Prussia[39]. His track record and good connections enabled Gotter to negotiate a high salary. The statues on the gate posts at Molsdorf were known locally as *Graf Gotter's moneymen*. The story goes that they brought money from Prussia in the moneybags on their backs. They used to face towards the schloss but, when the money stopped coming, Gotter had them turned around to face away[40]. He was at the height of his career when he bought Molsdorf in 1734. He intended it to be his future retreat from the hurly-burly of diplomatic life where he could live in the high style he desired. But circumstances conspired against Gotter retiring to the schloss. He always lived above his income and debts forced him to return to diplomatic service. In 1748 Gotter had to sell Molsdorf against the right to reside there and a pension. He died in harness in Prussia in 1762 and is buried in Berlin rather than in his beloved Molsdorf.

Drei Gleichen

The Drei Gleichen (three of a kind) schlösser are three medieval hilltop castles within sight of each other not far from Molsdorf. These were the first schlösser I saw in Thuringia and for me they are the symbol of the state. As we drove east to west on the E40 motorway there they were on the stretch between Erfurt and Gotha – Burg Gleichen just to the north and Mühlburg to the south with Veste Wachsenburg slightly further away. Burg Gleichen and Mühlburg are ruined castles but Veste Wachsenburg was rebuilt and is a hotel.

Burg Gleichen was built in the eleventh century to protect the trade route from Franconia (Bavaria) to Thuringia. From 1139 until their line died out in 1631 the schloss belonged to the counts of Gleichen. There is a story that the bigamous Count Ernst von Gleichen lived in the Burg with both his wives! The already-married count was captured and imprisoned while taking part in the fifth crusade (1217-1221). The beautiful daughter of the sultan agreed to help him escape in return for his promise of marriage. The pope gave his blessing to the bigamy, and the count lived at Burg Gleichen with his two wives. Until 1813, visitors were shown their 'three-sleeper' bed. Perhaps it is a legend, although on his tombstone in Erfurt Cathedral Count Ernst is shown with two wives! The Burg became the property of Prussia on the breakup of the Holy Roman Empire.

Mühlburg (see illustration) is the oldest of the Drei Gleichen and first

mentioned in a deed of 704! This is the oldest documented schloss in Thuringia. In 1211 Count Meinhard III of Mühlburg was in the party accompanying four-year-old Princess Elisabeth of Hungary on her journey to the court of Landgrave Hermann I at the Wartburg (see chapter 5). The little girl would grow up to *become St Elisabeth of Thuringia. The most prominent feature of Mühlburg is its tower, built in 1903 as a lookout. Mühlburg also belonged to Prussia from the beginning of the nineteenth century.*

The foundation stone for Veste Wachsenburg was laid in 936. The schloss came to the Wettin in 1369 and to the duchy of Saxe-Gotha when it was created in 1640. Duke Ernst the Pious carried out extensive reconstruction work and dug a deep well (three hundred feet) to secure the water supply. Wachsenburg became a hostelry in the nineteenth century and in 1890 the schloss was rebuilt. In 1905 the Hohenlohe tower was added, the name reflecting that the Hohenlohe royal family once owned land in the area. When Prince Viktor Hohenlohe (a nephew of Queen Victoria) renounced his rights to marry the daughter of a British admiral in 1861, he was given the lessor title of Count Gleichen (see Langenburg in 'Schloss in Baden-Württemberg').

One aspect of history I find so interesting is that the interpretation of characters and events changes over time. Gotter acquired the reputation in history of a rapacious libertine. When Queen Victoria made a day trip to 'the fine old chateau of Molsdorff' during her stay in Gotha in 1845, she wrote in her journal that it

... belonged to a Count Gotter, who lived there with a number of friends who belonged to an order, whose Motto was: 'Vive la joie', & who led very licentious lives[41].

Twenty years later his biographer August Beck said he was '... indulgent in all sensual pleasures, emptying the drafts of joy down to the dregs, like a second Casanova'[42]. This view fitted with GDR perceptions about the old aristocracy when Molsdorf was restored and opened as a museum in the 1960s. It may also be why the *Erotica Collection* of books and pictures was established at the schloss in the early 1980s. But this perception of him is now questioned by the curator at Molsdorf based on her research into the diaries and letters of his contemporaries. She says Gotter was essentially an ambitious, capable, and busy person who climbed out of the middle classes by his own efforts. He made his fortune and then spent it. His story still resonates with us today[43].

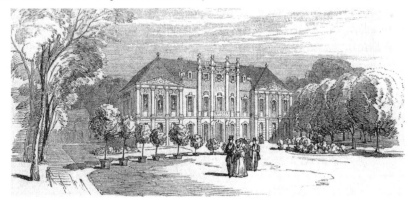

25. The Illustrated London News reporting Queen Victoria's visit to Molsdorf.

In the Intimate Cabinet (Geheimes Kabinett) at Molsdorf there is a portrait of Gotter with his niece, Friederike von Wangenheim (his sister's daughter). This is a copy of an original by Antoine Pesne, court painter to the Prussian royal family. To the modern eye it is a strange picture. Gotter has the round face and rosy cheeks of a bon vivant but carries a pilgrim's staff and wears the scallop shell (symbol of the pilgrim). Friederike looks over her uncle's shoulder and has her bodice undone to reveal her bosom. There are other breasts on display too. The Intimate Cabinet has a seductive portrait of an (unnamed) woman in the candlelight, unlacing the front of her dress.

I enjoyed my visit to Graf von Gotter's schloss enormously. Molsdorf is a dramatic-looking building with an interesting history and a guide who knew how to put this across, even to a non-German speaker. The last room on the tour was the Anteroom (Vorzimmer) with two portraits of Gotter at the end of his life. Our guide explained that he did not like how he looked in the first attempt so had a second, more flattering, version painted and persuaded the artist to give him a 'facelift'[44]. It seems Graf von Gotter was interested in appearances to the end.

Tenneberg

Tenneberg at Waltershausen near Gotha was a recommendation from the curator at another schloss. I have learned from experience that such recommendations are always worthwhile and so coming here was a must. The gate house was under renovation and a smiling workman on the scaffolding waved to direct us through the arch and into the cheerful courtyard. He set the friendly tone for our whole visit. The gentleman in the ticket office on the first floor was equally welcoming. He did not speak any English, but it is amazing how much can be communicated without a common language when there is good will on both sides. I think of Tenneberg as the friendly schloss!

Tenneberg dates to the landgraves of Thuringia and is first mentioned in a document of around 1176[45]. Schloss Tenneberg is located on the edge of the Thuringian Forest and served the Wettin landgraves of Thuringia and later dukes of Saxony as a hunting lodge. In 1640 it was allocated to the new duchy of Saxe-Gotha and Ernst *the Pious* initially resided at Tenneberg until Friedenstein was built. The last major remodelling of the schloss was carried out by his grandson, Duke Friedrich II from starting in 1714.

26. Schloss Tenneberg at Waltershausen.

Two magnificent rooms from this time survive (the ballroom and the chapel) and both have been recently restored. Friedrich II of Saxe-Gotha-Altenburg (1676-1732) refurbished Tenneberg as the future widow's residence for his wife, Magdalena Auguste of Anhalt-Zerbst (1679-1740). There is a portrait bust of Magdalena Auguste above the fireplace in the ballroom. The irony is that she did not like Tenneberg and never used it as a widow. When Friedrich II died in 1732, Magdalena Auguste chose to live at Altenburg and gave Tenneberg to her son[46].

There has been a museum at Tenneberg since 1929. Today there are two parts to this – a local history museum (including the ballroom and chapel) to one side of the ticket office and a famous doll museum to the other. We chose to see the historic rooms first and were on the way back through the ticket office when we bumped into the museum director. He spoke good English and we soon got chatting. Imagine our surprise and delight when he offered us a personal guided tour. 'You have seen the rooms through your own eyes;' he said, 'now see them through my spectacles.' What a privilege!

27. The magnificent Rittersaal with illusion ceiling painting.

The ballroom at Tenneberg is a hugely impressive space (illustration 27). It is called the Rittersaal which means 'Knight's Hall' but is in fact named after Johann Heinrich Ritter, artist to the Gotha court, who painted the ceiling. In modern buildings the ceilings are generally plain and unnoticeable but in historic rooms such as this they were an integral part of an overall work of art. This ceiling painting is an optical illusion cleverly designed by the artist to make it appear that the room extends upwards into another storey and then out into the open skies. In the centre Friedrich II and Magdalena Auguste are portrayed as Zeus and Hera (god and goddess) driving across the skies in a chariot pulled by giant doves. Wherever you move in this beautiful room the eyes of Friedrich II seem to follow you; stand in any corner and his chariot appears to be driving directly at you. Another fascinating feature of the Rittersaal is the statue busts of female figures that ring the room. Those along the long walls, on the piers between the windows, represent the signs of the zodiac. On the short walls are the four seasons (spring, summer, autumn, winter) and the four elements (air, fire, earth, water). The museum has researched the meaning of the small paintings above each statue. Each painting is on the same subject as its statue so, for example, the picture for autumn is a pumpkin. But the 'language' of some other pictures and how they relate to the subject of the statue is lost to the modern mind[47].

The ceiling painting in the chapel is also by Johann Heinrich Ritter. It was somewhat disconcerting to go down a flight of stairs from the Rittersaal to emerge on the first-floor gallery of the chapel. This is because the chapel was created by converting the old stables on a lower level of the hillside. The writing on the altarpiece is original to the time of Friedrich II and tells us the chapel was consecrated in 1721 to the glory of God and in honour of his grandfather Ernst *the Pious*. When this Lutheran chapel became a Catholic church in the 1920s the writing was covered with an altarpiece painting and was only rediscovered in the recent renovation. Friedrich II's magnificent organ did not survive the deprivations of the twentieth century. It was torn apart for the

28. The chapel was consecrated in 1721 in honour of Ernst *the Pious*.

metal in World War I, and for the wood to burn for heating after World War II when Tenneberg housed numerous families. The organ in the chapel now is new but constructed to the original eighteenth-century design. The golden sun in the centre of the pipes revolves when the organ is played.

The city of Waltershausen took ownership of Tenneberg when the GDR collapsed. The schloss was in a poor condition with major water damage from a leaking roof and riddled with dry rot. Our visit was shortly before a local government 'open house' day and a long line of storyboards in the Rittersaal charted the progress of the major restoration from 1998, detailing the work year by year with lots of before and after pictures.

The Rittersaal is now used in summer for weddings and events. It cannot be used in winter because much of the original decor is made of wood and heat would make the wood crack and distort. The statues in the Rittersaal are wood, painted to look like stone; the pillars in the chapel are wood, painted to look like marble. There are restrictions on the numbers of attendees for events as the entrance through the gatehouse is too narrow to admit a modern fire engine.

Our visit to Tenneberg concluded in the doll museum. Visitors come from all over the world to see this. During the nineteenth and twentieth centuries the town of Waltershausen was an important centre of doll manufacture. Dolls from Waltershausen won a Grand Prize medal (the

Friedrich the Bitten and his ride to Tenneberg

The legends of the early Wettin landgraves of Thuringia are illustrated on the walls of the Landgraves' Room at the Wartburg (chapter 5)[48]. One of these legends is the wild ride of Landgrave Friedrich the Bitten from the Wartburg to Tenneberg to have his new-born daughter baptised. Friedrich the Bitten (1257-1323) got his unusual epithet from an accident in childhood. His mother was running away from his cruel father (Albrecht the Unnatural) and in the anguish of parting from her son she inadvertently bit him on the cheek drawing blood and leaving a scar[49].

In 1306 Friedrich and his wife were under siege in the Wartburg when their daughter Elisabeth was born. There was no priest available at the Wartburg and Friedrich decided to take the baby to Tenneberg for christening by the Abbot of the nearby monastery of Reinhardsbrunn. A small party left the besieged Wartburg on horseback when Elisabeth was eight days old – Friedrich, the wet-nurse with the baby, and a guard of knights. Unfortunately, they were spotted by the besiegers and pursued.

Speed and stealth were essential to evade the pursuit, but as Friedrich's party were in full flight baby Elisabeth began to cry with hunger. Despite the danger Friedrich ordered a halt so the wet-nurse could breast feed his little daughter, nobly declaring her welfare must come first, even though it cost his kingdom. As the knights gathered round the wet-nurse to protect her and the baby, Friedrich could hear the horses' hooves of their pursuers. By an immense stroke of good fortune they were not discovered and, when the baby was fed, reached Tenneberg unharmed. After her baptism, Friedrich left baby Elisabeth with her wet-nurse in the safety of Tenneberg and went to help his wife, still besieged in the Wartburg[50].

top award) at the St Louis World Fair in 1904[51]. The last doll factory in Waltershausen did not close until after the fall of the GDR. The doll museum is full of display cases with dolls from across the history of manufacturing in Waltershausen. I particularly liked those from the 1960s when I was growing up.

29. The cheerful courtyard with excellent schloss café.

Tenneberg has everything to make a visit enjoyable, not least the excellent schloss café in the courtyard. There is even a ghostly lady in white who haunts the castle at midnight! The story of the ghost known as *The False Queen of England* begins in 1559 with the arrival of a noble lady at the court of Duke Johann Friedrich II in Schloss Grimmenstein (see Friedenstein). She claimed to be Anne of Cleves which, if true, would have been impressive! In 1540 Anne of Cleves became the fourth wife of Henry VIII and was briefly queen of England until the marriage was annulled a few months later. She was also Johann Friedrich II's aunt (the sister of his mother – see Fröhliche Wiederkunft in chapter 2). It was not long however before fears surfaced that the lady was an imposter, and she was sent for trial at Tenneberg where the court was held. Under torture the accused told conflicting stories – that she was Anne of Cleves or, if not, the chambermaid of Anne of Cleves, or, possibly, an illegitimate daughter of the duke of Cleves. The court held that her testimony was unreliable and condemned *The False Queen of England* to be imprisoned in a walled-in cell at Tenneberg. Only a small hole was left in the wall to pass through food and water. The prisoner did not long survive this treatment. A ghostly lady dressed in white was first seen walking through the castle a year after the prisoner's death and there have been sightings ever since[52].

Reinhardsbrunn

I followed in Queen Victoria's footsteps to Reinhardsbrunn. On the queen's first visit to her beloved husband's homeland in 1845, to see the well-remembered places of Albert's youth, they stayed at Reinhardsbrunn as the last overnight stop before Gotha. The schloss as Victoria found it had been recently rebuilt by her father-in-law, Duke Ernst I of Saxe-Coburg and Gotha. She described it in her journal as 'one of the most beautiful spots imaginable'[53]. When I first saw the schloss the beauty still shone through, but Reinhardsbrunn was abandoned and decaying. Built in gothic revival style with towers, turrets, and pointed arches, and surrounded by lush but overgrown gardens, it felt to me like the palace in *Sleeping Beauty* while still in the middle of its hundred years asleep. The story of this schloss goes back to the beginning of royal history in Thuringia. What Reinhardsbrunn needs now is a new beginning.

Reinhardsbrunn lies in the Thuringian forest near the small town of Friedrichroda. On our first visit we could not find the schloss, so called at the tourist information office to ask for directions. Here we learned the sorry story of the schloss's fate. After the reunification of Germany in 1990 Reinhardsbrunn passed through the hands of a series of investors but failed to find an owner willing to make the large investment needed to restore it. In 2006 it was sold for a ridiculously low figure to a Thuringian company. Two years later that company was acquired by Russian investors and heavily leveraged with debt of millions of euros. Perhaps it was money-laundering?[54]. In the meantime, Reinhardsbrunn was slowly mouldering away and the constant target of thieves and vandals. Not long before our visit they even took the bells from the tower. It was not possible to see inside the schloss, which was shuttered and barred, but on some afternoons in summer there are tours of the gardens. Volunteers cut the grass and clear the paths to maintain access. We had a fascinating afternoon walking the grounds with a knowledgeable guide who told us its history and showed pictures of how it all used to look.

30. Reinhardsbrunn in its heyday as a summer residence for the dukes of Saxe-Coburg and Gotha.

Reinhardsbrunn was built on the site of the monastery established by Count Ludwig *der Springer* (the Jumper or Leaper) of Thuringia in 1085. Ludwig the Jumper acquired his epithet by jumping out of a castle window into the river to escape his pursuers. He was an important figure in Thuringian history and founder of the iconic Wartburg castle (chapter 5). In 1085 Ludwig had recently married a young widow and the story goes that setting up a monastery was an act of atonement because he had been involved in the assassination of her first husband[55]. The name and location for his monastery were chosen after Ludwig met a man called Reinhard who lived near a brunnen (well or fountain). Reinhard was thought to be a visionary because he saw blue lights in the forest at night. Only hundreds of years later was it realised that these were natural gases from the mineral springs in the ground!

The Benedictine monastery at Reinhardsbrunn flourished and grew wealthy. This was the spiritual centre of Thuringia and the burial place of the Ludowinger dynasty of landgraves who descended from Ludwig *the Jumper* (chart 1 is their family tree). The monastery was stormed and looted by rebellious farmers during the Peasants Revolt of 1525. In 1543 it was secularised and Reinhardsbrunn passed into the ownership of the Ernestine Line. Friedrich Wilhelm I (chart 4) converted it to a hunting lodge and the widow of his younger brother Johann of Weimar (chart 3) built the schloss chapel where the tomb memorials of the Ludowinger landgraves were put on display[56]. They included Ludwig *the Jumper* (died 1123), his son Ludwig I (the first to hold the title of landgrave of Thuringia) who died in 1140, and Ludwig IV (died 1227) whose wife was canonised as St Elisabeth of Hungary. When Victoria stayed overnight at Reinhardsbrunn on 27 August 1845 she commented on 'the many curious Tomb-stones of the Landgraves of Thuringia' in 'the old chapel which is in decay'[57].

Reinhardsbrunn came into the ownership of Duke Ernst I of Saxe-Coburg and Gotha (1784-1844) in 1826 as part of the major reorganisation of the Ernestine Line when he ceded Saalfeld in return for Gotha. In 1827, almost as soon as he got the schloss, Ernst I began to rebuild it as a summer residence in the Gotha part of his new double duchy. He chose the romantic gothic revival or neo-gothic style that became popular in the nineteenth century. His new schloss incorporated parts of the monastery ruins and kept largely to the floor plan of the old hunting lodge.

Because of Ernst I's connections, much of Europe's royal circle came to Reinhardsbrunn in its heyday. He presided over an extraordinary reversal in the family fortunes. When Ernst I succeeded his father in 1806 their duchy had been invaded by Napoleon and the revenues sequestered. Before Ernst I died forty years later, his brother was the king of Belgium, his son was married to the queen of England, and his nephew to the queen of Portugal. The family's rise began with the marriages of Ernst I and his siblings. Behind these was the guiding hand of their mother, the formidable Duchess Augusta (born Reuss-Ebersdorf – see chapter 6). The marriage strategy of the house of Saxe-Coburg and Gotha became so successful that first minister Bismarck of Prussia would say that Coburg was *the stud farm of Europe*.

Victoria and Albert's visit to Reinhardsbrunn was in the year following his father's death and Albert's elder brother Ernst II (1818-

31. Queen Victoria at the time of her first visit to Reinhardsbrunn.

1893) was now duke of Saxe-Coburg and Gotha. They stayed in the duke and duchess's apartments on the second floor of the main wing (called the Hohes Haus or High House) where the central sitting room opened onto a balcony (illustration 33). Victoria praised her father-in-law's 'never failing exquisite taste', writing in her journal that 'the rooms are so beautifully furnished' and 'most tastefully painted'. She also commented on 'a large fine room with windows on both sides – our Ancestors painted round the ceiling'. This is the famous Ahnengalerie (Ancestral Gallery) at Reinhardsbrunn. High on the cornice are portraits of the forbears of the dukes of Saxe-Coburg and Gotha from Ludwig *the Jumper* to Ernst *the Pious*[58]. Painted on board and stuck to the wall, these were hard for thieves to take. Victoria was delighted with Reinhardsbrunn and 'miserable that we could not spend at least a week here'[59].

Queen Victoria's first visit to Saxe-Coburg and Gotha

On Saturday 9 August 1845 Queen Victoria left Buckingham Palace at the beginning of her first trip to Germany. It was something of a pilgrimage for Victoria. She longed to visit Albert's home country, but continual childbearing meant this was not possible earlier. In the five years since their marriage in 1840, four children had been born. Now she was excited at the prospect of seeing the scenes of Albert's childhood and meeting her German relatives.

The royal party travelled on the royal yacht, across the English Channel and up the River Scheldt to disembark at Antwerp in Belgium. From here they proceeded by train. At Mechelen (Malines) they were met by Victoria's uncle, King Leopold I of the Belgians. When they crossed the border into Germany at Aachen (Aix-La-Chapelle) they were greeted by King Friedrich Wilhelm IV of Prussia. Their holiday would start at his two beautiful schlösser on the Rhine – Augustusburg and Stolzenfels. Both are in 'Schloss III'.

From Stolzenfels Victoria and Albert travelled down the Rhine by boat to stay at the Hotel de L'Europe in Mainz. The rest of their journey was by carriage. After an overnight stop in Schloss Würzburg, Victoria arrived in Coburg on Tuesday 19 August, ten days after leaving home. Her official entry into the town was an emotional moment and it was only with difficulty that she resisted crying[60]. The extended Saxe-Coburg and Gotha family were gathered in Schloss Ehrenburg in honour of the occasion. (Ehrenburg is in 'Schloss in Bavaria'.)

After an eight-night stay at Schloss Rosenau in Coburg, Victoria and Albert left on Wednesday 27 August to travel on to Gotha. They stayed for one night in Reinhardsbrunn and then for a week (until Wednesday 3 September) in Schloss Friedrichsthal in the grounds of Friedenstein. During her stay Victoria visited Molsdorf and drove past Tenneberg. The Illustrated London News reported the trip and published pictures of both schlösser on 13 September 1845. The illustrations were said to be 'From His Royal Highness Prince Albert's drawing'. He owned many watercolours with views of his homeland and before leaving England had loaned some to the newspaper to assist their coverage of the royal visit[61].

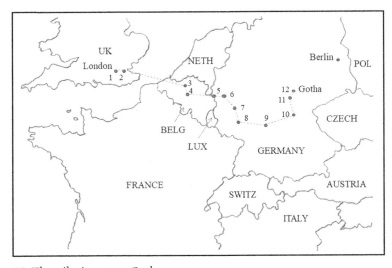

32. The pilgrimage to Gotha –
Victoria & Albert's journey from Buckingham Palace in August 1845.

1. Buckingham Palace	5. Aachen	9. Würzburg
2. Woolwich	6. Augustusburg	10. Coburg
3. Antwerp	7. Stolzenfels	11. Reinhardsbrunn
4. Mechelen	8. Mainz	12. Friedenstein

Victoria was back at Reinhardsbrunn a few days later, on her way to an outdoor entertainment that caused much criticism back in Britain. The queen's trip to Germany was not at all popular with her people. The 1840s have been called *the Hungry Forties* and there was tremendous disquiet that Victoria chose to take a lavish holiday abroad while many of her subjects were near starving. (King Juan Carlos of Spain was tarred with a similar brush when it was revealed he had gone on an elephant-hunting trip in 2012 while Spain suffered in deep recession.) There was also ongoing grumbling about the amount of British public money being paid out to the Saxe-Coburg and Gotha family. Ernst I's younger brother Leopold (now king of the Belgians) had drawn an annuity as the widower of Princess Charlotte of Wales for more than twenty years. Ernst I's sister, the duchess of Kent (Victoria's mother), also received substantial sums, and now Ernst's son Albert (Victoria's husband) was getting thirty thousand pounds a year. If the queen had to have a holiday, her critics argued, why could she not take it at home and spend the money in Britain?

The part of Victoria's overseas trip that caused most unhappiness back home was a deer drive near Reinhardsbrunn on 30 August 1845. Hundreds of local peasants spent days preparing the ground and fencing in a large clearing in the woods where the deer were to be slaughtered. The royal ladies, including Queen Victoria and her sister-in-law Duchess Alexandrine (the wife of Ernst II), were seated in a decorated pavilion in the centre of the clearing where they would have a good view of events. This pavilion was surrounded by a gallery for the shooters, including Albert and his brother. As refreshments were served to a crowd of spectators on the hillside and a band hidden in the trees began to play, the terrified deer were driven into the enclosure from which there was no escape and the killing began. It was not the English idea of sport!

> ... the contrast of the slaughter that was going on with the strains of light music had something shocking in it, and altogether was a scene no sportsman could bring himself to take part in ...[62]
> (*The Illustrated London News*)

The ladies passed along the line of dead on the way to their carriages. It was a wretched sight. The poor creatures arranged side by side – their dull, dim, dead eyes looking as ghastly as the wounds from which the clotted blood came oozing in black drops down the yet warm carcass. I had as lief see a knacker's yard.[63]
(*The Morning Chronicle*)

The queen and Prince Albert did not escape criticism. This lampoon by the magazine *Punch* is set to the tune of the nursery rhyme *Sing a Song of Sixpence*.

Sing a song of Gotha – a pocket full of rye,
Eight-and-forty timid deer driven into die;
When the sport was open'd, all bleeding they were seen –
Wasn't that a dainty dish to set before a queen?
The Queen sat in her easy chair, and look'd as sweet as honey;
The Prince was shooting at the deer, in weather bright and
sunny;
The bands were playing Polkas, dress'd in green and golden
clothes;
The Nobles cut the poor deer's throats; and that is all *Punch*
knows![64]

Victoria's journal reveals that while she clearly felt sorry for the
deer, '... fortunately they do not suffer long, tho' it is painful to see how
long they run after being wounded', she regarded it all as part of '... an
enchanting excursion, which I shall never be able to describe well, —
but which I shall ever remember'[65]. Sensibilities were very different in
those days! She would return to stay at Reinhardsbrunn in September
1862 as a grieving widow (Albert having died nine months before on
14 December 1861). You can read about this visit, when she was at
Reinhardsbrunn for a month, in *Schloss II*. As the holiday venue of
Queen Victoria in her happy days with Albert and a shelter in her early
widowhood, Reinhardsbrunn is a special place.

During World War II Reinhardsbrunn was taken over by the Nazis,
who planned to turn it into a stronghold headquarters for the führer.
When the Americans liberated Thuringia in early April 1945, they
discovered a horde of looted treasures in the tunnels of nearby salt
mines[66]. After the area was handed over to the Soviet occupying forces,
Reinhardsbrunn became a military hospital and then a training centre
for policemen and firefighters. The beautiful chapel (restored by Ernst
II after a fire in 1857) has been stripped out, leaving only rubble, but
the fireman's practice pole was still there when we visited. From 1961
Reinhardsbrunn was operated as a state-owned hotel. When the GDR

collapsed the hotel continued until it finally closed in 2001. Since then the schloss has been empty and deteriorating.

But the *Sleeping Beauty* palace is starting to wake up! By the time of our visit for this book things were moving in the right direction. After their approach to buy Reinhardsbrunn fell through, the State of Thuringia took legal proceedings against the Russian owners. In July 2018 Reinhardsbrunn was expropriated by court order under the Monuments Protection Act. This was the first ever action under such legislation in Germany. The creditors challenged the legality of the order, but the Supreme Court of Thuringia confirmed expropriation and held that the State of Thuringia is not liable for the mortgage debt on the schloss of some nine million euros. When the appeal process was exhausted, the schloss became State property in February 2021[67]. There is still a long way to go to save Reinhardsbrunn. The State of Thuringia has allocated monies for essential repairs but the full cost of restoration will be enormous, perhaps forty million euros or more. I hope so much that this beautiful schloss can be brought back to full glory and that I will visit Reinhardsbrunn again when it has been restored.

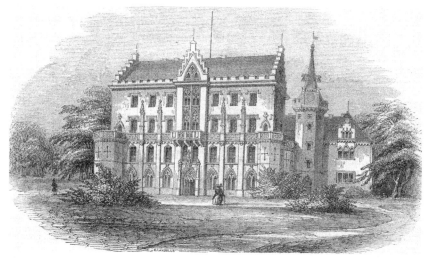

33. The High House with the rooms where Victoria stayed.

Two British schoolboys and the succession to Saxe-Coburg and Gotha

Duke Ernst II of Saxe-Coburg and Gotha died in 1893. Because his marriage was childless, the succession to the double duchy fell to the sons of his already-deceased younger brother, Prince Consort Albert. It would prove a poisoned chalice that uprooted two of Victoria's English grandsons and forced them to become German. (See chart 13 for the succession.)

The succession fell first on Victoria's second son Affie – Alfred, Duke of Edinburgh. Affie who had joined up at fourteen, was forced unwillingly to leave the Royal Navy. Awkward questions were raised in Britain about whether a German duke should sit in the House of Lords, and in Germany over on which side a retired British admiral would be in the event of war! Affie became more difficult, drank too much, and died from throat cancer in 1900. His only son, (also called Alfred and known as Young Affie), had died the year before him – aged twenty-four.

Young Affie was sent to Germany as a child to be educated for his role and saw his parents only occasionally. Perhaps this made him rootless and was a factor when he went off the rails as a young officer in the Prussian army. Affie caught syphilis, neglected his duties, and was forced to leave his regiment in disgrace. Syphilis was a shameful disease and his death was hushed up, allowing rumours to circulate. One story is that he tried to shoot himself, but it is more likely he died from his disease.

Young Affie's death reopened the problem of an heir to the double duchy. Next in line was Victoria's third son, Arthur, Duke of Connaught, but he renounced the succession for himself and his son. The choice fell on sixteen-year-old Charles Edward (Charlie) of Albany, the posthumous son of Leopold (Victoria's haemophiliac youngest son). Charlie was taken away from Eton and sent to Germany, and his name germanised to Karl Eduard. As a British prince succeeding to a German throne, poor Charlie was in a cleft stick. He was stripped of his British titles during World War I, while in Germany his English origins made him suspect. Perhaps he over-compensated by trying to become 'more German than the Germans'? In the 1930s Charlie joined the Nazi party and became a follower of Hitler.

4.

SAXE-MEININGEN

The duchy of Saxe-Meiningen dates from the division in 1680 by the sons of Ernst *the Pious*. Bernhard I (the third son) was allocated lands in south-west Thuringia and chose Meiningen as his capital. In 1826 the duchy doubled in size when his great-grandson Bernhard II added Hildburghausen and Saalfeld to his territory. The schloss at Hildburghausen is included in this chapter; Saalfeld is in chapter 3.

The history of Saxe-Meiningen illustrates the problems caused by royal family rules on inheritance – a struggle to introduce primogeniture followed by a paucity of sons. For the century between the death of Anton Ulrich in 1763 and the birth of Bernhard III in 1851 there was no, or only a single, male heir to the throne. Saxe-Meiningen is also memorable for producing one British queen and two respected female regents who steered the duchy through some of its most difficult years. Charlotte Amalie (1730-1801) repaired the ravages of forty years of family infighting and Luise Eleonore (1763-1837) ruled during the upheavals of the Napoleonic Wars. In the nineteenth century, Meiningen achieved fame for its ground-breaking theatre company. I enjoyed discovering the story of Duke Georg II, described as the first modern theatre director and known to history as *the Theatre Duke*.

The last duke of Saxe-Meiningen was Bernhard III; his reign coincided almost entirely with the years of World War I. Bernhard III came to the throne a few days before Archduke Franz Ferdinand was assassinated in Sarajevo and abdicated a day before the armistice.

Elisabethenburg

A plaque at the entrance records Elisabethenburg in Meiningen as the childhood home of Queen Adelaide of Great Britain (1792-1849). Adelaide is not a well-known British queen, and little has been written about her in English. But in Meiningen she is remembered as an important personality who followed the path of duty for the benefit of her country. Adelaide was the only princess of Saxe-Meiningen ever to become a queen. In 1818 she married William Duke of Clarence, later King William IV of Great Britain (reigned 1830-1837). My visit to Elisabethenburg made me want to find out more about Queen Adelaide's family background and her early life.

Elisabethenburg was built by the first duke of Saxe-Meiningen. Bernhard I (1649-1706) added two new wings to a medieval castle at

34. Elisabethenburg was the residence of the dukes of Saxe-Meiningen.

Meiningen to create the typical horseshoe-shaped baroque schloss. It was called Elisabethenburg after his wife, Elisabeth Eleonore of Brunswick-Wolfenbüttel. The foundation stone was laid in 1682 and the work completed ten years later with the inauguration of the schloss church. The exterior appearance was later altered when Queen Adelaide's brother, Bernhard II (1800-1882), added the dark red quoins and stonework window surrounds that are the dominating feature of the front elevation today. Bernhard II also remodelled the medieval wing in nineteenth century neo(mock)-medieval style.

Queen Adelaide's childhood home was hard to find. The front of Elisabethenburg is completely shut off from the town by a long semi-circular building (also built by Bernhard I) that connects the two side wings. On our first visit we were forced to call in at the tourist information office for directions to the schloss only to discover we had, without knowing, parked the car right next to the entrance with Queen Adelaide's plaque. The schloss museum is large and there were few visitors. The sense of space and emptiness was exaggerated by an energy-saving lighting system, triggered by movement as we entered a room. Looking to right and left down the long enfilade of darkened rooms was eerie! The tour began in the baroque schloss church of Bernhard I, where the pulpit is supported by a huge carved angel brandishing a palm branch. It ended in the suite of rooms redecorated by Georg II (1826-1914) for his third wife towards the end of the nineteenth century.

The Blue Corner Cabinet is dedicated as a memorial to Queen Adelaide. This delightfully pretty room is light and airy with turquoise panelling, accentuated with gold paint. It has been restored as it would have been during Adelaide's lifetime when used by her sister-in-law Marie (the wife of Bernhard II). It is likely that Adelaide saw it when she visited Meiningen during her widowhood[1]. On the wall is a copy of the large state portrait of Queen Adelaide by Sir William Beechey painted in 1831. In the window, looking out, stands Adelaide herself (a life-size mannequin) wearing a copy of the dress from her portrait.

Queen Adelaide

Princess Adelheid of Saxe-Meiningen (Adelaide is the English form of Adelheid) was born in Elisabethenburg in 1792. She was her parents' first child, after they had been married for nearly ten years, and they must have despaired of having children. Georg I (1761-1803) was a single thread in the line of succession and the Saxe-Meiningen branch of the Ernestine Line was in grave danger of dying out (chart 7). He and his wife Luise Eleonore of Hohenlohe-Langenburg had to wait eight more years after Adelaide for the birth of their only son, Bernhard II (1800-1882).

Adelaide's father wanted a good education for his two daughters, and she was much better educated than many German princesses. Adelaide was certainly better educated than her future husband, William of Clarence, who joined the Royal Navy at thirteen and was known to the British public as 'Silly Billy'. She learned Latin and Greek as well as foreign languages. When she arrived in England as a bride-to-be Adelaide spoke English reasonably well (although she never lost her heavy German accent)[2]. She also had powerful female role models in her family. Adelaide's father, Georg I, died in 1803 when she was eleven and her little brother, who became the next duke, only three. Their mother, Luise Eleonore, was appointed regent and ruled Saxe-Meiningen on his behalf until his majority in 1821. Adelaide's grandmother had performed the same role for Georg I when he succeeded his father at only a year old (see Altenstein). The example of her mother and grandmother influenced Adelaide to accept William's proposal when it came.

Adelaide was twenty-five when she received an offer of marriage from William, duke of Clarence, the third son of George III. Princesses were more often married in their teens and Adelaide may have thought she would be a spinster. William had not met Adelaide and there was no romance involved in his offer. He was under pressure from the British parliament to get married and father an heir to the throne following the death of Princess Charlotte of Wales a few months earlier (she died giving birth to a still-born son). William was middle-aged (fifty-two), unattractive, and with rough manners formed during his service in the Royal Navy. He badly needed the money he expected parliament to vote him on marriage to support his ten illegitimate children.

Adelaide was initially reluctant to consider William's offer but was persuaded to do her duty. She agreed to become William's wife in the interests of Saxe-Meiningen and to provide her brother with a close connection to the powerful British throne[3]. Neither of William's two elder brothers had an heir, so there was a good chance that Adelaide's child, if she had one, would succeed to the British throne. Adelaide knew that, should her child still be a minor (as was quite possible), she was well suited to be the regent.

William and Adelaide were married in July 1818. They became king and queen in 1830 and reigned until William's death in 1837. But, sadly, none of their babies survived. William's previous mistress, Mrs Dorothea Jordan, had given him ten illegitimate children with little difficulty, but Adelaide's experience of pregnancy was different. Two baby girls were born alive, but both died soon after and all her other pregnancies ended in miscarriage. Adelaide was a loving stepmother to William's children and a devoted aunt. She fostered her sister Ida's disabled eldest daughter Luise (1817-1832) who died as a teenager from a spine disease[4].

When Adelaide died, she left a cherished possession to her niece by marriage, Queen Victoria – a statue of her second baby daughter Elizabeth sleeping on a couch. Elizabeth was born six weeks prematurely on 10 December 1820. She would have been queen of Great Britain instead of Victoria had she lived, but she died in agony from convulsions on 4 March 1821. Victoria was fond of her Aunt Adelaide and asked the dowager queen to be godmother to her first child, the princess royal, born in November 1840 and christened Victoria Adelaide.

Queen Adelaide is remembered as a benefactor in the country of her birth. His sister's marriage brought Bernhard II close to the British court (he became a knight of the Garter) and her money helped to fund his building projects in Meiningen. These included a widow's residence for their mother called the Grosses Palais or Big Palace (now a medical centre); neo-gothic-style Schloss Landsberg (now empty but previously a luxury hotel); and the Meiningen Court Theatre building which his son, Georg II, would bring to international fame.

35. Queen Adelaide (left of the font) stands as godmother to the princess royal, first child of Queen Victoria and Prince Albert (right of the font).

For me, the schloss museum at Elisabethenburg most came to life with the history of the Meiningen Court Orchestra and Court Theatre. Music was always important here. The first duke, Bernhard I, enjoyed singing and music and founded the Meiningen Court Orchestra. His great-great-grandson Georg II (played piano) led the Meiningen Court Orchestra to its greatest years when they set new performance standards and toured Europe to great acclaim from 1880 until World War I. During this period, the music directors included piano virtuoso and star conductor Hans von Bülow (1880-1885); his protégé, composer Richard Strauss (1885-1886); and Fritz Steinbach (1886-1903), who was a leading interpreter of Johannes Brahms and made Meiningen into a Brahms centre. The composer conducted the premier of both his Third and Fourth Symphonies in Meiningen in the 1880s. The tradition of music at Elisabethenburg continues today. As well as the museum, the schloss is home to the Max Reger Music School (Reger was music director 1911-1914) and the Johannes Brahms Concert Hall.

Georg II was not fond of Elisabethenburg itself and used the schloss only for public duties and his work with the Court Orchestra and Theatre. He suffered from asthma and the river fogs in Meiningen aggravated his condition[5]. The duke accepted he would have little political influence in the new Germany led by Prussia and devoted his considerable artistic talents to music and the theatre. His greatest artistic love was the theatre. Under the leadership of *the Theatre Duke* the Saxe-Meiningen Court Theatre toured internationally from 1874 to 1890 and caused a sensation with their ground-breaking approach. Georg II introduced a new style of realism to acting and productions, personally designed costumes and scenery, and directed crowd scenes. It is claimed that the Royal Shakespeare Company was modelled on the Meiningen Court Theatre[6].

Georg II came to the throne in 1866 as a new German Empire was being forged by Bismarck's wars. From a young man, he took a different view on politics to his father. Bernard II believed in the old order and supported Austria for the leadership of Germany. Saxe-Meiningen was one of only two Thuringian states to side with Austria against Prussia in the Seven Weeks' War of 1866 (the other was the Reuss Elder Line – see Unteres Schloss Greiz). His son could better see which way the wind was blowing. Georg II served in the Prussian army and married a Prussian princess. Prussia quickly defeated Austria in the Seven Weeks' War and Prussian troops occupied Saxe-Meiningen. As the price of avoiding annexation, Bernhard II was forced to abdicate in favour of his son. It led to great bitterness on his part and a breach that would be exacerbated by Georg II's third marriage[7].

Chart 8 shows the three marriages of Georg II. In 1850 he married Charlotte of Prussia (1831-1855), a niece of the Prussian king. They were much in love and shared an interest in the arts. But their years of happiness were short. Their second son died as a toddler in 1855 and weeks later Charlotte died in childbirth with a baby boy who lived for only a day. Georg II was left a grieving widower with two small children – Bernhard III (aged four) and his younger sister. The children needed a new mother and in 1858 Georg II married Feodora of Hohenlohe-Langenburg (1839-1872), a niece of Queen Victoria. Queen Adelaide had arranged the marriage of Feodora's parents – Victoria's half-sister (Feodora of Leiningen) and Adelaide's cousin, Ernst of Hohenlohe-Langenburg (see Langenburg in *Schloss in Baden-Württemberg*). Georg II tried to develop his new wife's interests; and the correspondence

36. Georg II, *the Theatre Duke.*

between Queen Victoria and her half-sister records with approval that young Feodora was taking drawing lessons and listening to history lectures[8]. But his second marriage did not turn out so well as the first. The verdict is that Feodora was incapable of sharing his cultural and artistic tastes and Georg II had not got over his first wife's death[9]. Two sons were born (Ernst in 1859 and Friedrich in 1861), but after the birth and death of a third baby boy in 1865 (he lived for only a few days) the couple drifted apart. Georg began an affair with the actress Ellen Franz and threw himself into his work with the theatre; Feodora mostly stayed away. Despite their estrangement Georg II remained fond of his wife and was deeply upset when Feodora died from scarlet fever in 1872[10]. The children remembered her with affection too. When his own daughter was born in 1879, Bernhard III named her Feodora after his stepmother[11].

Ellen Franz (1839-1923) joined the Meiningen Court Theatre in 1867 and was described as a '... finely educated princess full of talent'[12]. Her relationship with the duke caused scandal and when Ellen became his third wife in 1873 she was forced to give up her career to allay public anger. The decision caused her great anguish, but it was completely unacceptable for the duke's wife to be on the stage[13].

The dukes of Saxe-Meiningen

In 1680 the seven sons of Duke Ernst the Pious of Saxe-Gotha-Altenburg divided their inheritance and Bernhard I (1649-1706) became the first duke of Saxe-Meiningen. There were eleven dukes before the monarchy came to an end in 1918 and chart 7 shows their family tree.

Bernhard I failed to change the rules of inheritance for the new duchy and the consequence was forty years of machinations between his sons. Primogeniture was eventually introduced by his grandson Georg I (1761-1803) at the end of the eighteenth century.

Bernard I had three surviving sons, but in later generations the succession looked far less secure. Duke Anton Ulrich (1687-1763) was sixty-seven when his heir was born; Georg I waited eighteen years of marriage for his only son, Bernhard II (1800-1882).

Saxe-Meiningen doubled in size during the reign of Bernhard II. In the last major reorganisation of Ernestine duchies in 1826 (following the death of the last duke of Saxe-Gotha-Altenburg), Bernhard II gained the territories of Saxe-Hildburghausen and Saxe-Saalfeld.

Bernhard II was the longest reigning duke of Saxe-Meiningen. He succeeded his father as a toddler and was on the throne for sixty-three years. It would have been longer, except that he was forced to abdicate in 1866 in favour of his only son, Georg II (1826-1914). This was the penalty for supporting the losing side (Austria) in the Seven Weeks' War.

The last duke of Saxe-Meiningen was Bernhard III (1851-1928), who was the son of Georg II. When a council of soldiers and workers came to Elisabethenburg to demand his abdication on 10 November 1918, Bernhard III was astonished since he always believed he was popular with his subjects[14]. He retired to Altenstein and he and his wife Charlotte (a sister of German Kaiser Wilhelm II) are buried there.

The head of house Saxe-Meiningen today is Friedrich Konrad born in 1952. He is the grandson of the youngest of Bernhard III's two half-brothers (see chart 8).

The third marriage of Georg II was morganatic, and Ellen never became the duchess of Saxe-Meiningen. Instead, on their wedding day, her husband gave her the title of Freifrau (baroness) Helene von Heldburg. This was taken from Schloss Heldburg (south of Meiningen near the border with Bavaria) that Georg II renovated and became a favourite home.

37. The mock-medieval style wing at Elisabethenburg.

Georg II's third marriage caused a storm in royal circles and things cannot have been easy for Helene. The kaiser was appalled that a reigning German prince should be married to an actress, and Queen Victoria was outraged over the treatment of her niece[15]. There were resignations at the Saxe-Meiningen court, the army refused to salute her, and her disgruntled father-in-law, Bernhard II, declined to meet Helene for several years. All the slights to his new wife made Georg II very angry. Helene continued to be involved in the Court Theatre and shared in its achievements. But her role was behind the scenes, as artistic director and acting coach, rather than centre stage. The consolation was a happy marriage that lasted for over forty years.

Georg II died in June 1914 as Europe spiralled into World War I. His funeral in Meiningen on 28 June was on the same day the fatal shots were fired in Sarajevo. He was succeeded by his son from his first marriage. Bernhard III (1851-1928) was a retired career officer in the Prussian army and the brother-in-law of Kaiser Wilhelm II. He left the government of Saxe-Meiningen to his wife Charlotte (sister of the kaiser) and went off to inspect troops at the front. He was the last duke of Saxe-Meiningen and abdicated in November 1918. Bernhard and Charlotte were the parents of an only daughter and he was succeeded as head of house by his half-brother Ernst (the elder of the two sons of Georg II by his second marriage).

Altenstein

Altenstein was the summer residence of the dukes of Saxe-Meiningen. The story of how it was spurned by the royal builder is my favourite schloss-building anecdote. When the sixteenth-century schloss on the site was destroyed by arson in April 1733, it was rebuilt by Duke Anton Ulrich of Saxe-Meiningen (1687-1763). He mostly lived away from Saxe-Meiningen and presumably did not visit before it was completed in 1736. When he did come, the official opening degenerated into disaster. An angry Anton Ulrich confronted the Italian architect (Alessandro Rossini) over how his instructions had been carried out. One version says Anton Ulrich had expected Altenstein to face south (it faces east)[16]; another that he was disgusted by the view because Rossini had failed to clear away a clutter of unsightly farm buildings and dung heaps[17]. Whatever the reason, the architect was forced to flee Saxe-Meiningen in disgrace and Anton Ulrich never went to Altenstein again. It was sixty years before the schloss was renovated by his son, Georg I (1761-1803), and used as his summer residence. Georg I was the father of Queen Adelaide of Great Britain. He liked Altenstein so much that he also founded the nearby spa town of Bad Liebenstein.

Altenstein has a lovely location on the edge of the Thuringian Forest, a half-hour by car north of Meiningen. The schloss is surrounded by an English landscape park first laid out by Georg I. I loved the

38. Altenstein was the Thuringian version of an English stately home.

sunken pergola garden with tremendous views across the Thuringian countryside and the tiny Ritterkapelle (Knight's Chapel), dating from 1799, perched precariously high on a sheer lump of rock. The name Altenstein translates as ancient or old stone and great chunks of rock are a natural feature of the park. In February 1982, the schloss was destroyed by fire again, leaving it a burnt-out and roofless shell. Restoration has been slow and is still underway, but visitors can glimpse the interior by guided tours of the Brahms museum. The composer Johannes Brahms stayed at Altenstein as the guest of Georg II of Saxe-Meiningen and his wife, the retired actress Ellen Franz. Because of the furore over their unequal marriage (see Elisabethenburg), the couple retreated from the royal scene. They found their friends in the world of music and theatre and entertained them at Altenstein. In the late 1880s Georg II remodelled Altenstein in what has been described as neo-renaissance English stately-home style. Looking at the theatrical concoction of gables, turrets, bay windows and tall chimneys it is hard to recognise Altenstein today as the same eighteenth-century baroque schloss built by Anton Ulrich.

Anton Ulrich was the youngest of the three sons of the first duke of Saxe-Meiningen. Bernhard I (1649-1706) had two surviving sons from his first marriage to Maria Hedwig of Hesse-Darmstadt and one

(Anton Ulrich) from his second to Elisabeth Eleonore of Brunswick-Wolfenbüttel. Anton Ulrich was named for his maternal grandfather Duke Anton Ulrich of Brunswick-Wolfenbüttel (1633-1714) who is one of my favourite characters in royal history (see Wolfenbüttel in *Schloss II*). Despite his own bad experience of sharing power with his brothers, Bernhard I did not introduce primogeniture for his new duchy. The provisions of his will decreed that Saxe-Meiningen should not be divided on his death but instead ruled jointly by his three sons. This was much the same arrangement as had already failed between Bernhard and his brothers (see Friedenstein.) It failed again and led to forty years of squabbling between his sons, much to the detriment of their poor country. Eventually, by virtue of living the longest, Anton Ulrich became the undisputed duke of Saxe-Meiningen in 1746. The tussle over rights to rule makes the succession to Saxe-Meiningen complicated for this period and I have tried to set it out in simplified form in chart 7.

When Bernhard I died in 1706, his eldest son, Ernst Ludwig I (1672-1724), set aside the provisions of his father's will in favour of primogeniture. He seems to have been successful in persuading his full brother to go along with this, at least within his own lifetime. Friedrich Wilhelm (1769-1746) has been described as slow-witted and easily led[18]. But his half-brother was a different character. Anton Ulrich was bitterly opposed and fought tenaciously for his rights.

Ernst Ludwig I died in 1724 leaving the throne to his eldest son, Ernst Ludwig II (1709-1729), who was still a minor. In the arrangements for a regency Ernst Ludwig I deliberately overlooked his half-brother Anton Ulrich. He named as regents his full brother Friedrich Wilhelm, plus (given Friedrich Wilhelm needed someone to take the lead) his cousin the duke of Saxe-Gotha-Altenburg[19]. Anton Ulrich challenged his exclusion and was successful in being reinstated as regent by the courts of the Holy Roman Empire. Relations between the surviving half-brothers became hostile in the extreme, with each side issuing conflicting decrees and causing chaos in the government of Saxe-Meiningen. The discord got so out of hand that an imperial commission was sent to Meiningen in 1729 to try to sort it out. Even an attempted arbitration by the king of Saxony was unsuccessful in restoring harmony[20]!

Ernst Ludwig II died from smallpox before reaching his majority and the regency continued for his younger brother Karl Friedrich (1712-1743). He was not much interested in the business of governing and mostly left things to his uncles even when he came of age in 1733. Karl Friedrich's interests are said to have been eating, drinking, and sleeping; he became so obese he could not walk and had to be wheeled around by servants on a trolley[21]! When Karl Friedrich died unmarried in 1743, the rule of primogeniture (that his father had struggled hard to introduce) died with him and the joint rule arrangements of Bernhard I were back in place. His uncles continued their dysfunctional joint rule until Friedrich Wilhelm died (also unmarried) in 1746. As the surviving male dynast in this royal tontine, Anton Ulrich was now the sole duke. He had always lived abroad and saw no reason to change things now. Anton Ulrich seldom visited Saxe-Meiningen and ruled the duchy from his residence in Frankfurt am Main, a hundred miles away.

But at fifty-eight years old, Anton Ulrich did not have an heir. The dukes of the other Ernestine Line duchies were rubbing their hands over a carve-up of Saxe-Meiningen on his death. In 1711, as a young man in military service, Anton Ulrich secretly married an officer's daughter called Philippine Elisabeth Caesar. When the marriage was made public a few years later it was declared morganatic so that his children did not have dynastic rights. Anton Ulrich fought against this family diktat using connections on his mother's side. His first cousin was Elisabeth Christine of Brunswick-Wolfenbüttel, wife of the Holy Roman Emperor Karl VI[22].

In 1727, after ten years of lobbying, Karl VI raised Anton Ulrich's wife to the rank of princess and declared their children to be princes and princesses of Saxe-Meiningen with rights of succession. But emperors come and go and, in a tough blow for Anton Ulrich, Karl VII reversed his predecessor's decisions in 1744. Philippine Elisabeth died the same year and her coffin lay unburied because Friedrich Wilhelm, the hated half-brother, refused to agree to interment in the royal crypt. When the chance came, Anton Ulrich got his revenge. For sixteen months after Friedrich Wilhelm died in 1746 his coffin lay above ground next to that of his despised sister-in-law Philippine Elisabeth before they were both buried in the royal crypt[23].

39. The entrance to Altenstein as it looked before World War II.

In 1750 Anton Ulrich made a late second marriage to Charlotte Amalie of Hesse-Philippsthal (1730-1801) who was forty-three years his junior. All future dukes of Saxe-Meiningen were descended from this marriage (chart 7). When her husband died in 1763, Charlotte Amalie was appointed regent of Saxe-Meiningen for the joint rule of their small sons, eight-year-old Karl August and nearly-two-year-old Georg I. She proved a benevolent and effective ruler who reformed the ducal finances and did much to rebuild a country burdened by debt and shattered by the Seven Years' War (1756-1763). The emperor was so impressed with her financial management skills he put Charlotte Amalie in charge of the imperial debt commission sent to sort out Saxe-Hildburghausen (see Hildburghausen below)[24]. Charlotte Amalie ruled Saxe-Meiningen for nineteen years until her younger son came of age in 1782. She was sole ruler as regent for both sons until Karl August reached his majority in 1775 and then joint ruler with him as regent for Georg I. Karl August (1754-1782) suffered poor health and died in 1782 leaving twenty-one-year-old Georg I (1761-1803) as the sole duke of Saxe-Meiningen. In 1800, Georg I finally changed the rules of inheritance for the duchy to primogeniture[25].

Altenstein is a mile or so from the health resort of Bad Liebenstein. This town owes its existence to Georg I. Like his elder brother, Georg I endured ill-health from childhood[26] and felt benefit from drinking the natural spring waters at Altenstein. In 1800, he bought up the land, laid a new road, and began to develop the facilities and accommodation needed to attract visitors to his new spa. When Georg I died from a lung infection on Christmas Eve 1803, his widow Luise Eleonore of Hohenlohe-Langenburg (1763-1837) went on with the development of Bad Liebenstein. In a repeat of the arrangements of a generation before, Luise Eleonore was the regent for their only son, three-year-old Bernhard II. She ruled Saxe-Meiningen for eighteen years and steered the duchy through the ravages of the Napoleonic Wars and the years of bad harvests that followed.

40. Queen Adelaide celebrated her birthday with a ball at Altenstein in 1834.

Between 1803 and 1806 Luise Eleonore built an elegant new schloss called the Royal Villa in Bad Liebenstein. Her daughter, Queen Adelaide, returned here for her health several times after her marriage. She was staying with her mother in the Royal Villa in 1819, to recover from the death of her first baby daughter, when she received the news of the birth of the princess who would become Queen Victoria[27].

Adelaide was at Bad Liebenstein for her birthday in 1834 and celebrated with a ball at Altenstein. The Royal Villa was later renamed the Palais Weimar after Adelaide's sister Ida, who inherited it from their mother and was married to Duke Bernhard of Saxe-Weimar-Eisenach (the younger son of Grand Duke Carl August (see Residenzschloss Weimar in chapter 5).

Today the Palais Weimar houses the town library and the tourist information office. On the first floor, underneath the central dome, visitors can see the grand room called the Kuppelsaal (domed hall), now a wedding venue and concert hall.

Like his grandfather (Anton Ulrich), Bernhard II (1800-1882) disliked the schloss building at Altenstein and wanted something more in keeping with the English landscape park laid out by his father (Georg I). Through the connections of his sister Queen Adelaide, Bernhard II engaged the English architect and garden designer Sir Jeffry Wyatville who had carried out a radical (and expensive) remodelling of Windsor Castle for King George IV. Wyatville was the architect for Schloss Landsberg in Meiningen built by Bernhard II in the 1830s. He also drew up plans for Altenstein but these were never realised.

After his forced abdication in 1866 Bernhard stayed on at Altenstein until his death in 1882, and then his widow lived there until she died in 1888. When their son got his hands on Altenstein things moved fast. Georg II (1826-1914) wanted his own version of a sixteenth-century English stately home and sent his architect, Albert Neumeister, sketches of Hatfield House in Hertfordshire and Knole in Kent to use as examples[28]. In the two years between 1888 and 1890 Altenstein was transformed – from the eighteenth-century baroque schloss of Anton Ulrich into the late nineteenth-century-imagined English stately home of Georg II.

Hildburghausen

The state of Saxe-Hildburghausen existed from 1680 (when the sons of Ernst *the Pious* split their inheritance) until 1826 when it was absorbed by neighbouring Saxe-Meiningen (in the last reorganisation of Ernestine Line lands in Thuringia)[29]. The royal house of Saxe-Hildburghausen is little-known today, but for a century and a half it ranked with Germany's other royal families and was connected to several European thrones. The beautiful Queen Therese of Bavaria, whose wedding began the tradition of the Oktoberfest in Munich, was born a princess of Saxe-Hildburghausen.

41. Hildburghausen before it was destroyed in World War II.

Chart 9 shows a family tree for the dukes of Saxe-Hildburghausen. The first duke was the sixth son of Ernst *the Pious*. Like other rulers of the small German courts, Ernst (1655-1715) wanted a grand residence where he could live in princely style – his own mini version of King Louis XIV of France's court at Versailles. The foundation stone for Hildburghausen was laid on 27 May 1685 and the schloss was officially inaugurated ten years later. The floorplan was in the shape of a letter E but the middle bar was demolished within Ernst's lifetime. The main wing and one side wing were three stories in height; but the third (stables) wing was lower and more modest in design. Plans to enhance it had to be shelved for financial reasons. Inside, the state rooms were decorated with stuccowork and frescos and the chapel (on the right in illustration 41) with paintings on canvas. The largest room was the ballroom and theatre on the second floor, above the chapel[30]. The costs of building the schloss and funding the duke's lifestyle were more than the revenues of his small state could bear; when he died in 1715, Duke Ernst left a heavy debt burden[31].

His successors carried on regardless. Their desire to compete with the larger courts in pomp and display would bring Saxe-Hildburghausen perilously close to bankruptcy. The second duke, Ernst Friedrich I (1681-1724), liquidated his wife's dowry, but spent the money on enhancing the schloss garden rather than to reduce the debt[32]! Duke Ernst had laid out a garden in the formal French style and surrounded it with a canal. His son, Ernst Friedrich I, developed this into an intricate pattern of avenues, paths, hedges, flower beds, water features, and garden structures (illustration 42). The idea behind such structured and artificial gardens (which were very costly to create and maintain) was to demonstrate man's mastery over nature and symbolise the duke's God-given right to rule.

The fourth duke, Ernst Friedrich III (1727-1780), added a new façade to the schloss in honour of his prestigious marriage to the king of Denmark's sister. Ernst Friedrich III considered his high and mighty status required he dine in public daily with a hundred guests[33]. The debt rose inexorably until it reached a staggering level equivalent to fifty-five times the annual tax revenues[34]. In 1769, the Holy Roman emperor called a halt and appointed an imperial commission to restructure the debt and cut the spending. From now on, the dukes were kept on a strictly reduced civil list. Ernst Friedrich III resisted the commission's remit and troops had to be called on from neighbouring principalities

42. Eighteenth-century plan of the schloss and baroque schloss garden.

to impose their orders. One of their economies was to alter the baroque schloss garden into an English landscape park. This newly fashionable and more naturalistic style of gardening, with sweeping lawns, meadows, lakes, and trees, required fewer gardeners and was less expensive to run. This fourteen-acre landscape park survives to this day, still surrounded by Duke Ernst's canal.

One member of the imperial debt commission appointed in 1769 was Prince Joseph Friedrich of Saxe-Hildburghausen (1702-1787). Joseph Friedrich is one of a multitude of minor royals whose colourful personal stories enliven the pages of royal history. As the younger son of Duke Ernst, Joseph Friedrich joined the imperial army when a teenager. Over a long military career, he served three Hapsburg Holy Roman emperors and took part in several wars. He became a well-known figure at the Viennese court; was made a knight of the Order of the Golden Fleece in 1739 (broadly equivalent to the British Order of the Garter); and promoted to field marshal in 1741. Joseph Friedrich has the reputation of being a curmudgeonly and unlikeable commander[35]. He lost more battles than he won, but there is no doubting his bravery and organisational abilities. His last battle (one he lost) was against Frederick the Great of Prussia at Rossbach in 1757 (during the Seven Years' War).

I first heard of Joseph Friedrich on a visit to Schloss Hof, the country estate of Prince Eugene of Savoy, east of Vienna and close to the border with Slovakia. Here the curator explained how Joseph Friedrich came to own the schloss through his unlikely marriage to Prince Eugene's heiress, Anna Viktoria of Savoy-Soissons (1683-1763). When Prince Eugene died in 1736, Anna Viktoria was fifty-two years old, unmarried, and living in a convent near Turin. She suddenly found herself to be one of the richest women in Europe. She quit the convent and in 1738 married the twenty-years-younger Joseph Friedrich of Saxe-Hildburghausen. Their age difference held the bride up to some ridicule at the time[36]. The marriage was not a success and when the couple separated in 1752, Joseph Friedrich kept Schloss Hof as part of his husband's dower. He adored hosting lavish parties there, but his extravagant lifestyle caught up with him and he needed to find a rich buyer to relieve his financial difficulties[37]. Joseph Friedrich hit on a brilliant marketing strategy. In September 1754, he hosted an amazing four-day house party at Schloss Hof in honour of Empress Maria Theresa of Austria. The cost was astronomical, but the ploy paid off. Maria Theresa bought Schloss Hof and presented it to her husband Emperor Franz Stefan of Lorraine.

In 1780 Joseph Friedrich, now aged seventy-eight, became the regent of Saxe-Hildburghausen on behalf of his great-great-nephew. Duke Friedrich (1763-1834) succeeded as a minor and was under his great-great uncle's regency until 1784. Friedrich was the last duke of Saxe-Hildburghausen and reigned for forty-six years before ceding Hildburghausen to Saxe-Meiningen in 1826 to become first duke of Saxe-Altenburg Younger Branch (see Altenburg in chapter 2). In 1785 Friedrich married fifteen-year-old Charlotte of Mecklenburg-Strelitz

(1769-1818) at Hildburghausen. A letter from Joseph Friedrich to the putative bride still survives, pleading his young relative's case[38]. Through this marriage, Saxe-Hildburghausen became connected to the British court – the bride's aunt (the sister of her father) was Queen Charlotte, wife of George III. Through the later marriage of Charlotte's younger sister, Duke Friedrich would also become brother-in-law to the king of Prussia.

Charlotte (born in 1769) was the eldest of four famous royal sisters celebrated for their beauty, grace, intelligence, and culture. Charlotte had a wonderful singing voice and was given the nicknames of *Sing-lotte*[39] or *Sing-sister*[40]. When the German writer Jean Paul visited the Hildburghausen court in May 1799, he described her as

> ... the heavenly duchess, with beautiful childlike eyes, her face full of love and attraction and youth, a glottis [vocal chords] like a nightingale and a mother's heart ...[41]

Charlotte's younger sisters were Therese (born in 1773), Luise (1776), and Friederike (1778). They visited her at Hildburghausen several times. Therese and Luise were part of the family party that accompanied Charlotte to her wedding there in September 1785. Luise and Friederike were at Hildburghausen with their father in December 1793 on the way to their own double wedding in Berlin[42]. Luise married the crown prince of Prussia (the future King Friedrich Wilhelm III) and Friederike his younger brother[43]. All three of Charlotte's sisters were staying with her when Jean Paul visited the Hildburghausen court in May 1799. The writer was entranced and dedicated his latest novel to 'four beautiful and noble sisters on the throne'[44].

Childbirth exacted a high cost on Charlotte and her sisters. Their mother had died in childbirth aged twenty-nine after bearing ten children in thirteen years. Charlotte gave birth to her first child nine months after her wedding and eleven more children followed over eighteen years.

43. Duke Friedrich and Duchess Charlotte of Saxe-Hildburghausen.

Charlotte's grandmother (her mother's mother) commented

... of all his duties, he [Duke Friedrich] only fulfils his marital duties with zeal. Charlotte, who never loved this man, is always pregnant.[45]

Charlotte's sister Luise died young (in 1810), aged only thirty-four, worn out by the stress of war and the strain on her health from ten pregnancies in fifteen years. As queen of Prussia during the Napoleonic Wars, Luise achieved legendary status for her attempt to intercede with Napoleon on behalf of her country (see Charlottenburg in *Schloss*). The memorial Charlotte erected to her sister in the schloss park at Hildburghausen in 1815 was the first memorial to Queen Luise outside Prussia[46].

In 1810, Friedrich and Charlotte's daughter Therese married the crown prince of Bavaria (later King Ludwig I). Therese had inherited her mother's good looks and was considered the most beautiful princess of her generation. The celebrations for her wedding on 12 October 1810 were the beginning of the famous annual Oktoberfest in Munich.

In 1826, Duke Friedrich left Hildburghausen to take up his new role as duke of Saxe-Altenburg. His wife Charlotte had died some years before. Hildburghausen ceased to be a royal residence and fell in importance. The chapel was deconsecrated for use as a courtroom; from 1867 the schloss was a military barracks. In the closing weeks of the war in Europe, Schloss Hildburghausen was destroyed by artillery fire as the American army advanced into Thuringia to liberate the town on 7 April 1945.

44. An old photo when the schloss housed an officer's mess.

Visitors to Hildburghausen today can stroll through the schloss park with the memorial to Queen Luise and explore the Stadtmuseum (town museum) where an exhibition sets out the history of the town from its medieval beginnings. A highlight is the section devoted to the century and a half when this was the capital of the state of Saxe-Hildburghausen and the dukes were in residence at the schloss. Unfortunately, a scheduled visit to Hildburghausen as part of the research for this book had to be deferred due to the covid-19 pandemic. I plan to reschedule it as soon as practicable. I want to thank the curator of the museum for his invaluable help in providing material and suggesting sources to enable me to write this piece.

5.

SAXE-WEIMAR-EISENACH

Saxe-Weimar-Eisenach was the largest of the eight royal states in Thuringia and the only one to carry the (higher) dignity of a grand duchy (as opposed to a mere duchy). It was formed in 1809 on the merger of the Ernestine Line duchies of Saxe-Weimar and Saxe-Eisenach and raised to a grand duchy in 1815. The name was later changed to the grand duchy of Saxony, but this official title was rarely used and for simplicity I have called it Saxe-Weimar-Eisenach throughout.

Saxe-Weimar-Eisenach rose in importance on the international stage during the reign of Grand Duke Carl August. As a young man Carl August formed an unlikely friendship with a commoner called Johann Wolfgang Goethe (later hailed as *the German Shakespeare*). Their fifty-year collaboration propelled the capital city of Weimar from little-known backwater to acknowledged cultural capital of Europe. The new respect brought his duchy powerful international connections. Carl August's son married a Russian grand duchess (sister of the Tsar Alexander I); his granddaughter became queen of Prussia and German empress. This chapter includes the stately residence schloss in Weimar built by Goethe on behalf of his royal patron, as well as the delightful out-of-town summer palace beloved by Carl August's Russian daughter-in-law because it reminded her of home. It ends at the iconic Wartburg castle where the royal story of Thuringia began.

The last grand duke of Saxe-Weimar-Eisenach was Wilhelm Ernst, the three times great-grandson of Carl August. By the time he came to the throne in 1901 the glory days of the grand duchy were long over. Wilhelm Ernst was an unsympathetic and unpopular ruler. He left Weimar after his abdication in November 1918 and severed relations with his former state.

Residenzschloss Weimar

In 1547, Duke Johann Friedrich I *the Noble* was defeated in battle and lost his title and lands as elector of Saxony. He chose Weimar as the capital for his remaining lands in Thuringia and the old castle became the residence (residenzschloss) of the senior branch of the Ernestine Line. The old castle (called Hornstein) was remodelled in renaissance style by the famous architect Nikolaus (Nickel) Gromann[1]. (Gromann also built Fröhliche Wiederkunft for Johann Friedrich I – chapter 2). His renaissance schloss at Weimar was later rebuilt in baroque style by Wilhelm IV of Saxe-Weimar (1598-1662) and its name changed to Wilhelmsburg in his honour.

Wilhelmsburg burned down in 1774 when an undetected kitchen chimney fire took hold[2] and the schloss was rebuilt again by Carl August (1757-1828), this time in classical style, under the direction of his friend Johann Wolfgang von Goethe. From now it was known as Residenzschloss (Residence Palace) Weimar or sometimes Stadtschloss (City Palace). During the long reign of Carl August, Weimar was transformed with Goethe's help into a much-admired cultural centre. This period of Weimar's heyday before the two friends died (Carl August in 1828 and Goethe in 1832) is known as *Weimar classicism*.

1775 was an important year for Duke Carl August of Saxe-Weimar and Eisenach. On 3 September that year (his eighteenth birthday) Carl August took over the government of the twin duchies from his

45. Residenzschloss Weimar with the oldest and newest parts of
the building – the fifteenth-century Bastille gatehouse building on the left
and twentieth-century south wing on the right.

mother, who had acted as the regent during his minority. It must have
been hard for the young Dowager Duchess Anna Amalia (1739-1807),
still only thirty-five, to hand over the reins after seventeen years in
charge. Relationships between mother and son had been tense for a
while. Carl August was a headstrong young man and his choice of the
Fürstenhaus (Princes' House) as his temporary residence after the fire
at Wilhelmsburg much irritated his mother who thought the building
unsuitable[3]. Anna Amalia also resented how courtiers were turning
away from her and towards Carl August as 'the rising sun'. She wanted
to hand over the regency a year early but was dissuaded from doing so[4].
Instead, Carl August was sent on a grand tour with his younger brother
to experience other European courts before settling down at home.
Two stops on the tour would have a profound influence on his future
life – Frankfurt, where on 11 December 1774 he met and was dazzled by

the young Goethe; and Karlsruhe, where a short time later he proposed to Luise of Hesse-Darmstadt (1757-1830), the bride picked out for him in childhood by his mother.

Carl August and Luise were married on 3 October 1775, exactly one month after Carl August took over the regency. The newly-weds began married life on affectionate terms but their relationship cooled. Carl August was confident, lively, and unconventional; he

resented the formality of court life and was inclined to break loose and go on the razzle with his friend Goethe. Luise on the other hand was reserved and diffident, insisting on etiquette and the deference due to royalty to boost her self-esteem. Luise was on strained terms with her mother-in-law Anna Amalia, who called her 'A lump of ice there is no thawing'[5]. Nor was Luise helped during her early years in Weimar by her failure to produce an heir. With the birth of their son Carl Friedrich in 1783, Carl August and Luise reached an accommodation, although he

46. Duchess Luise of Saxe-Weimar-Eisenach.

remained a womaniser who fathered many illegitimate children and she resented his affairs[6].

Luise's icy demeanour came into its own when, as his troops were plundering Weimar, Napoleon arrived at the Residenzschloss on 15 October 1806 fresh from his decisive victory at the battle of Jena-Auerstedt. The rest of the royal family had fled, but the brave and haughty duchess confronted the French emperor on the grand staircase and persuaded him to stop the looting[7].

The Grand Duchy of Saxe-Weimar-Eisenach

The first duke of Saxe-Weimar was Johann Wilhelm (1530-1573) who was the son of Johann Friedrich I the Noble. In 1640 Johann Wilhelm's grandsons carried out a division. Wilhelm IV (1598-1662) became duke of Saxe-Weimar (including Eisenach and Jena) and his younger brother, Ernst I the Pious (1601-1675), became duke of Saxe-Gotha (chart 3). Since Wilhelm IV was the elder brother, Saxe-Weimar-Eisenach (which descended from him) was the senior of the four surviving Ernestine Line duchies at World War I. The remaining three descended from Ernst the Pious.

In his will, Wilhelm IV (like his brother Ernst the Pious) decreed that Saxe-Weimar should not be divided after his death. His sons should rule jointly under the direction of the eldest, with each son allocated a residence schloss and income. Needless to say (as with the sons of Ernst the Pious) this solution proved unworkable and there was a division ten years after the father's death. The eldest son, Johann Ernst II (1627-1683), became duke of Saxe-Weimar and his younger brother duke of Saxe-Eisenach. (A third brother got Saxe-Jena, but his line died out within twenty years.) When the Eisenach sub-branch died out in 1741, Ernst August I of Saxe-Weimar inherited Saxe-Eisenach.

Ernst August I (1688-1748) ruled the duchies of Saxe-Weimar and Saxe-Eisenach in a personal union. The two were not merged to form Saxe-Weimar-Eisenach until 1809 during the reign of his grandson, Carl August (1757-1828). Carl August is the most well-known of the Saxe-Weimar and Eisenach dukes (chart 14 is their family tree). He was the first to hold the rank of grand duke conferred at the Congress of Vienna in 1815 at the end of the Napoleonic Wars.

The last grand duke was Wilhelm Ernst (1876-1923) who reigned from 1901 until his abdication on 9 November 1918. The head of house Saxe-Weimar-Eisenach today is Wilhelm Ernst's grandson Michael born in 1946. Michael has an only daughter and his heir as head of house is a (male) cousin also born in 1946. The two cousins are the last dynasts in the house, so it appears Saxe-Weimar-Eisenach will become extinct in the male line[8].

On 7 November 1775, just one month after Carl August's marriage, Johann Wolfgang Goethe (1749-1832) came to live in Weimar at the young duke's invitation. The twenty-six-year-old writer was already a literary celebrity following the publication a year before of his romantic novel *The Sorrows of Young Werther*. When Goethe arrived Weimar was a complete backwater, nothing more than a few hundred houses clustered around the blackened shell of the Wilhelmsburg schloss, burned down the year before. The story of its transformation to important cultural centre is that of the friendship between Carl August and Goethe. This was most unusual for the time because they came from different social classes. Goethe was a commoner who was later ennobled by the duke and given the right to use the prefix 'von'. *The Sorrows of Young Werther* triggered a Europe-wide craze for young men to dress in the style of Goethe's hero. Illustration 47 shows the two friends (Carl August on the left and Goethe on the right) wearing Werther's high boots, a long blue coat with brass buttons, yellow waistcoat, and pair of leather breeches[9] For Goethe the attraction of Weimar, as well as his growing friendship with the duke, was the opportunity to play an important role in the government. He would become the duke's adviser, a minister of state, and hold

47. Duke Carl August and Goethe dressed in the fashion started by Goethe's novel *The Sorrows of Young Werther*.

many senior positions including director of the ducal theatre and ducal library. He would also oversee the rebuilding of the Residenzschloss.

At the time of writing, the Residenzschloss in Weimar is closed for a major renovation that is not expected to be completed until 2030. I was fortunate enough to visit before the closure. There was much to interest lovers of royal history, including an amazing genealogical chart covering many hundred years of Wettin history – from the birth of the Ernestine Line to the death of the last grand duke of Saxe-Weimar-Eisenach. I was much taken with an arresting picture of the devastating fire of 6 May 1774 painted at the time by an unknown artist. The three wings of the schloss are ablaze, with smoke and flames billowing from the roofs and crowds of figures trying to save the contents. Only the tower and fifteenth-century Bastille gatehouse building escaped the conflagration. The gatehouse was mockingly christened the Bastille by the court ladies-in-waiting who lived there[10].

After the fire Carl August had no immediate plans to rebuild. Money was in short supply and it was not until 1789 that he set up a committee under the directorship of Goethe. Progress on the replacement schloss was slow, hampered by the wars with France and lack of funding. Over the years there were three architects in succession – the first lost interest when the project slowed, the second left after getting a better offer[11]. Goethe was always the driving force and Carl August left him to take the decisions. Eventually, after nearly thirty years away, the ducal family moved into the new Residenzschloss on 1 August 1803.

To save money, the Residenzschloss was rebuilt to the same three-winged floorplan as its baroque predecessor and incorporated the surviving stonework. But the new building was in the classical architectural style that was popular at the beginning of the nineteenth century. The ducal apartments of Carl August and Luise occupied the east wing facing the River Ilm with an elegant Festsaal (Ballroom) and imposing Treppenhaus (staircase).

My favourite rooms were the two hung with family portraits. The first displayed a series of beautiful portraits of Carl August, his wife

Luise, and their three children painted in the 1790s by Johann Friedrich August Tischbein. These are the earliest portraits painted from life, as everything in the ducal collection was destroyed in the fire of 1774.

The second room had a fascinating gallery of the duchesses of Saxe-Weimar-Eisenach, many painted long after their subjects were dead. These included a delightful portrait of Sybille of Kleve, wife of Johann Friedrich I *the Noble*, with her long red hair flowing in waves over her shoulders and a coronet of flowers. One portrait painted from life was of the most famous bride ever to come to Weimar. Carl August was most anxious to have the Residenzschloss finished in time for her arrival. In 1804 his eldest son Carl Friedrich married Grand Duchess Maria Pavlovna of Russia. She was immensely rich and one room in the Residenzschloss was devoted to her dowry. Carl Friedrich and Maria Pavlovna's rooms were in the west wing of the Residenzschloss. There she created the suite of four Dichterzimmer (Poets' Rooms) with murals illustrating works of the famous Weimar writers – Goethe, Schiller, Herder, and Wieland (see Wittumspalais below).

48. View of the Residenzschloss from the River Ilm.

Chart 14 is a family tree for the dukes and grand dukes of Saxe-Weimar-Eisenach. The two grand dukes after Carl August, (his son Carl Friedrich and grandson Carl Alexander) preserved the Residenzschloss as a memorial to the great days of *Weimar classicism*. But the last grand duke of Saxe-Weimar-Eisenach was less focused on his cultural heritage. Wilhelm Ernst (1876-1923) was more interested in hunting and the military and looked to the Prussian Kaiser Wilhelm II as his role model[12].

Between 1912 and 1914, immediately prior to World War I, Wilhelm Ernst added a fourth wing to the Residenzschloss. His new south wing enclosed the open courtyard between the three wings built by Goethe and shut off the schloss from the park and town. It was almost as if he turned his back on his inheritance. His father died when Wilhelm Ernst was a teenager and he was not close to his grandfather, Carl Alexander, whom he succeeded in 1901. The last grand duke was a difficult and irascible man, unpopular with his subjects and called 'the most hated prince in Germany'[13].

When the revolution came to Weimar, Wilhelm Ernst did not go gracefully and initially tried to resist demands for his abdication. The last grand duke signed the deed of abdication in the Residenzschloss on 9 November 1918 and left Weimar for his estate in Silesia[14]. The schloss became a museum in 1923.

A legacy of the brilliant period in its history known as *Weimar classicism* is that there is so much for the visitor to see in and around Weimar. The Residenzschloss is one of numerous sites connected with the great age of German literature that make up an UNESCO World Heritage Site[15]. As well as four schlösser in this chapter (Residenzschloss, Wittumspalais, Tiefurt, and Belvedere), the Classical Weimar World Heritage Site includes the Anna Amalia Library (see Wittumspalais), the ducal crypt with attached Russian Orthodox Chapel (burial place of Maria Pavlovna), the homes of Goethe and Schiller, and more. We enjoyed wandering the streets of the old city where history is evident everywhere.

Wittumspalais

The Wittumspalais (Widow's Palace or Dower House) in Weimar was the home of Dowager Duchess Anna Amalia of Saxe-Weimar and Eisenach (1739-1807). It is not a grand building and you could be forgiven for walking straight past without realising this was a royal palace. Anna Amalia's summer home just outside the city, Schloss Tiefurt, is also unostentatious. Anna Amalia was a remarkable woman who was widowed at eighteen, became one of the few princesses to govern a state in the Holy Roman Empire, and laid the foundations for Weimar as a cultural capital. The Wittumspalais was the venue for her weekly 'round table' social gatherings attended by the revered figures of classic German literature who made Weimar famous – Johann Wolfgang von Goethe, Friedrich Schiller, Christoph Martin Wieland, and Johann Gottfried Herder.

49. The Wittumspalais was the home of Dowager Duchess Anna Amalia.

Anna Amalia was born a princess of Brunswick-Wolfenbüttel. This royal house is renowned for the marriages of its daughters to emperors and kings. Anna Amalia's aunt (her father's sister) married

Frederick the Great and became queen of Prussia; her niece (her brother's daughter) married George Prince of Wales, later George IV, and was briefly queen of Great Britain. (For more on the marriages of princesses of Brunswick-Wolfenbüttel see *Schloss II*.) Neither of these two marriages turned out well – Frederick the Great was homosexual and bullied into marriage by his father; George IV loathed his bride at first sight and longed to be rid of her.

In 1756, when she was sixteen, Anna Amalia married Duke Ernst August II of Saxe-Weimar and Eisenach (1738-1758). Their first son (the future Grand Duke Carl August) was born the following year. Eight months later Ernst August II died of tuberculosis (TB) and Anna Amalia was widowed. There was another baby on the way and a second son (Constantin) was born three months after his father's death. The story of the short life of Ernst August II helped me to understand better why so many princes and princesses were married young, almost as soon as they reached puberty. Ernst August II succeeded his father at nine, was declared of age and fit to rule at seventeen and died before he was twenty. But he had already lived long enough to marry and father two sons of his own. Killer diseases such as smallpox and TB, and death in childbirth, were no respecter of rank, wealth, or age. Life might be short, but dynastic imperative meant the family line must go on.

Ernst August II was the son of Duke Ernst August I of Saxe-Weimar (1688-1748). He would not have been born at all had it not been for the early death of his older half-brother. Ernst August I was a middle-aged widower with no apparent inclination to marry for a second time when the only surviving son of his first marriage died in 1732. To secure the future of his line the duke was obliged to find a new young wife and breed again. He would have five sons from his two marriages but only Ernst August II, born when his father was forty-nine, survived childhood. The father showed little interest in his son other than as a dynastic asset. When his father inherited Saxe-Eisenach and moved his court to Eisenach, Ernst August II stayed behind in Weimar with his mother. She died in 1747, a few months before his father.

When his father died in January 1748, nine-year-old Ernst August II inherited the twin duchies of Saxe-Weimar and Saxe-Eisenach. No will was found and the Ernestine Line dukes bickered over the regency for nearly two years until a compromise was reached. In the end the regency was split between Saxe-Gotha-Altenburg (for Saxe-Eisenach) and Saxe-Coburg-Saalfeld (for Saxe-Weimar). The little duke became a ward of Friedrich III of Saxe-Gotha-Altenburg and spent the next few years at the Gotha court. Back in Weimar courtiers were most unhappy about this foreign influence and, to lure the duke home, he was declared of age early. Ernst August II took over the government in person in December 1755, when he was seventeen[16]. Three months later he married Anna Amalia of Brunswick-Wolfenbüttel. But he was already ill and died less than three years later.

When her husband died in May 1758 Anna Amalia was still a minor. Perhaps Ernst August II remembered the squabbles when his own father died because he left the regency to his father-in-law (Anna Amalia's father) and not to an Ernestine Line duke. Karl I of Brunswick-Wolfenbüttel petitioned the emperor, and in July 1758 Anna Amalia was declared of age and became regent for her baby son. She was eighteen years old, inexperienced, and heavily pregnant with her second child. She wrote in her recollections; 'Never did I pray with such devotion as I did in this my hour of need. I believe I might have become a saint'[17].

The political situation that confronted her was fraught with difficulty. The quid pro quo for the favour from the emperor was that Saxe-Weimar and Eisenach must support Austria in the ongoing war against Prussia (the Seven Years' War of 1756-1763)[18]. This was particularly tricky given that Frederick the Great of Prussia was Anna Amalia's uncle (her mother's brother) and he also expected her loyalty. In her first letter to the Prussian king as regent Anna Amalia stresses affection for her uncle and her submission to his orders but implores him to withdraw a Prussian requisition for army recruits from Saxe-Weimar. '...Your Royal Highness is too merciful to command me to do what would cause the ruin of the country over which I have to govern'[19].

50. Duke Ernst August II and Duchess Anna Amalia.

Anna Amalia was an intelligent and well-educated young woman, and she would prove a competent ruler. The young regent soon showed she had a mind of her own and declared she would personally attend meetings of the privy council and sign documents. Her brother said '... she has the courage and firmness of a man' and 'She listens to the advice of experience, but is a slave to no one.'[20] One of her early actions was to engineer the retirement of her husband's rather over-powerful first minister[21]. The twin duchies were heavily burdened with debt from the extravagance of her father-in-law. By dint of economies and cuts in court expenditure the debt was much reduced by the time Anna Amalia handed over the regency to her son in 1775, after a rule of seventeen years.

Anna Amalia had a strong interest in literature and the arts. She revived the Weimar court theatre and engaged the famous eighteenth-century actor Konrad Ekhof, known as *the father of German acting*. Had it not been for the devastating fire that destroyed the schloss with its theatre in 1774 he might have spent the rest of his career in Weimar rather than at Friedenstein (chapter 3). Anna Amalia saved the ducal library from the fire of 1774 because she had previously moved it to the Grünes Schloss (Green Palace). The library, which now bears her name (the Anna Amalia Bibliothek), is still in this building today. One of Anna Amalia's most important decisions for the future of Weimar was to appoint the professor of philosophy and poet Christoph Martin Wieland as tutor to her sons in 1772. Wieland's presence in Weimar was an incentive to the young Johann Wolfgang von Goethe when he was invited to the town by Anna Amalia's son a few years later. Goethe's presence would be the flame that attracted the poet Friedrich Schiller and the theologian and writer Johann Gottfried Herder. In retirement Anna Amalia continued to foster the cultural life of Weimar; visitors to the Wittumspalais can see the room where she held her weekly Friday 'round table' soirees with Goethe, Herder, Schiller, and Wieland.

51. Tiefurt was Anna Amalia's summer home.

The Wittumspalais was built between 1767 and 1769 by a minister at the Saxe-Weimar court. After the residenzschloss was destroyed Anna Amalia bought the Wittumspalais and lived there until her death in 1807. Her elder son, Carl August, moved into the Fürstenhaus (Princes' House) and her younger son, Constantin, to Schloss Tiefurt. The statue of Carl August on horseback outside the Fürstenhaus (now a music school) was put up in 1875 to commemorate the one-hundred-year anniversary of his taking over the rulership from Anna Amalia. Constantin was a disappointment to his mother and when he left Weimar in 1781 after a quarrel with his brother (over an unsuitable love affair[22]), she took over Tiefurt as her summer residence. The schloss is in the countryside and began life as a farmhouse; the exterior is plain and unadorned. Anna Amalia loved the simplicity and informality of life at Tiefurt in the summer months and this was her favourite home.

Schloss Kromsdorf

At Tiefurt we found a signpost to a walking path going to Schloss Kromsdorf. The idea to link up the two schlösser was that of Grand Duchess Maria Pavlovna when she and her husband were renovating Kromsdorf in the 1820s. Maria Pavlovna, born a grand duchess of Russia, was the wife of Grand Duke Carl Friedrich of Saxe-Weimar-Eisenach. It is well worth the walk (a mile and a half) to Kromsdorf to see a most curious garden feature. The seventeenth-century garden wall is inset with niches displaying statue busts of kings and emperors from around the world!

Kromsdorf was built around 1580 and takes its name from the family that first owned it. The unusual garden wall was built between 1664 and 1689 by a later owner. When Duke Wilhelm Ernst of Saxe-Weimar (1662-1728) acquired Kromsdorf in 1692 he developed the gardens as an outdoor summer entertainment venue and installed more statues in the wall.

There are sixty-four statues around the wall in total, placed in niches at regular intervals. The choice of subjects is amusing and eclectic. I loved ambling to explore the statues, almost each one more surprising than the last. There are contemporary monarchs of the time, including James II of England, Louis XIV of France, Sultan Mehmed IV of Turkey, and Wilhelm Ernst himself; more far-flung rulers from the centuries before such as Khan Tamerlane (fourteenth century), Aztec emperor Montezuma II (fifteenth), and Tsar Michael Romanov of Russia (seventeenth); and even imaginary Indian chiefs and emperors of Abyssinia and Japan.

115

Both Anna Amalia's schlösser are museums, with the interiors shown as when she lived there. It was a wet morning when we visited the Wittumspalais – umbrellas were up, and the pavements glistened. The schloss fronts directly onto the street (illustration 49) but in Anna Amalia's day there was a schloss garden she designed herself. After her death this was taken to create the square in front of the nearby German National Theatre. At Tiefurt we found the museum closed (despite saying on the website it would be open – very annoying) so explored the fifty acres of schloss park, with meandering paths and dotted with garden structures. The River Ilm runs through the park and on the bank is a monument Anna Amalia erected in memory of her son Constantin. He died from disease in 1793 on campaign during the French Revolutionary Wars.

Dornburger Schlösser

The Dornburger Schlösser are said to be on 'the balcony of Thuringia': three schlösser set out in a line on the edge of a steep limestone escarpment with a sheer drop to the river valley. We arrived first thing in the morning and were rewarded for an early start by warm pastries from the baker's van in Dornburg's picturesque market square. From here it was a short walk to the schlösser – the Altes Schloss, widow's residence for the first dukes of Saxe-Weimar; the Rococo Schloss, built by one of the most flamboyant princes of the eighteenth century; and the Renaissance Schloss dedicated as a memorial to the German literary giant who retreated here to mourn his royal patron. The Dornburger Schlösser are linked together by their gardens and share a stunning location four hundred feet above the wide valley of the River Saale. You can see for miles and, standing in the gardens of his schloss, I could well understand why Duke Ernst August I of Saxe-Weimar considered this the perfect location for a huge military display. The Rococo and Renaissance Schlösser are open to the public as museums; the Altes Schloss is a conference facility for the University

116

52. The Dornburger Schlösser 'on the balcony of Thuringia' – (left to right) the Renaissance Schloss, Rococo Schloss, and Altes Schloss.

of Jena but can be seen from the exterior. We spent a happy morning exploring the Dornburger Schlösser and their gardens.

There has been a schloss at Dornburg from the beginning of the Holy Roman Empire. The first emperor Otto I, crowned in 962, stayed at Dornburg in 965. Dornburg came into the possession of the Wettin on an exchange of lands with the Schwarzburg family in 1358; and to the house of Saxe-Weimar on its foundation. The first duke, Johann Wilhelm of Weimar (1530-1573), renovated the Altes Schloss as a widow's residence for his wife. His chosen architect was Nikolaus (Nickel) Gromann who was a firm favourite of his father. Johann Wilhelm was the son of Duke Johann Friedrich I *the Noble*, forebear of all Ernestine Line duchies in Thuringia (chart 3). The three Dornburger Schlösser all have alternative names and the Altes Schloss is sometimes known as Gromann Schloss.

The Rococo Schloss is alternatively called the Neues (New) Palais (it was the last of the Dornburger Schlösser to be built) and sometimes the Mittlere (Middle) Schloss (because of its location between the other two). It was built between 1736 and 1744 by Ernst August I of Saxe-Weimar and Eisenach (1688-1748). The duke was the archetypal eighteenth-century ruler of a small German court and considered it his birth-right to live in splendour. The resources of his small country were quite unable to support the duke's extravagance and Ernst August I resorted to various money-raising possibilities. One of the duke's schemes was to arrest wealthy subjects without cause and demand their fortunes as a ransom for release[23]. Another was to build up a large standing army that could be rented out to other countries[24].

53. The Rococo Schloss was built by Duke Ernst August I.

Ernst August I yearned to be seen as an important military leader. In 1730 Prince-elector Augustus II *the Strong* of neighbouring Saxony hosted a huge ceremonial army display that was hailed as 'the spectacle of the century'[25]. Ernst August I aspired to go one better and astonish his fellow princes by holding an even bigger and better display at Dornburg. In 1732, as part of the planning, he commissioned a new schloss on top of an escarpment twenty miles east of Weimar as the centrepiece of his military show. But plans for the event had to be abandoned for lack of money. This first version of the Rococo Schloss fell into disrepair and was demolished. When construction began afresh, this time on a new summer palace, Ernst August I chose a different architect. Gottfried Heinrich Krohne was a master of the baroque and rococo architectural styles. He also built gorgeous Belvedere at Weimar for Ernst August I (below); dramatic Molsdorf for Graf von Gotter (chapter 3); and created the fabulous ballroom at Heidecksburg (chapter 7). But the second effort at Dornburg was also doomed never to be completed; Ernst August I's attention had drifted away to yet another new schloss he was building[26]! Krohne's design shows how the Rococo Schloss is only the central wing of what he intended to be a long line of buildings down the site.

The architecture of the Rococo Schloss is full of surprises. From the garden side it appears as a one-story building with an attic floor. Steps up to the entrance lead directly into the vestibule to the ballroom. This elevation is multi-coloured (almost garish), painted in candy-floss pink, buttermilk yellow, and duck-egg blue. But the ground behind the schloss falls steeply away to the valley and at the rear the building has four floors. The rear elevation is painted a single colour and blends in with the surrounding landscape. Below the schloss on the valley side are a grotto, paved bastion, and terraces of vineyards – a spectacular outdoor setting for entertainment when Ernst August I was in summer residence. The footprint of the building is also quirky. The Rococo Schloss is small and each of the two floors of the museum has eight rooms arranged in the shape of a crown or a cluster of soap bubbles – two larger elongated bubbles in the centre, one on top of each other, with a semicircle of three smaller bubbles on either side. This rococo style is characterised by curves and there are few straight lines anywhere! A narrow spiral staircase, fitted into a space between the bubbles, connects the two floors. All very curious!

Ernst August I succeeded his father as duke of Saxe-Weimar in 1707 when he was nineteen years old. Saxe-Weimar did not then follow primogeniture and he had joint rulership rights with his uncle (his father's elder brother) Wilhelm Ernst (1662-1728)[27]. As the senior family member, Wilhelm Ernst assumed he would take the lead in the government of the duchy. This approach had worked tolerably well with his younger brother (Ernst August I's father), but his nephew was a different kettle of fish. Ernst August I was irascible, self-important, and hard to manage. As soon as he came of age, he began to assert his rights and challenge his uncle's decisions. Matters got so out of hand that Wilhelm Ernst was forced to seek an imperial order to protect the state officials who carried out his directions against revenge threats by his nephew. Ernst August I sacked them anyway after his uncle died[28]!

54. The Altes Schloss with glimpse of the panoramic river valley.

Wilhelm Ernst was childless and on his death in 1728 Ernst August I became sole duke of Saxe-Weimar. His twenty-year reign brought limited benefit to his state. The duke preferred hunting to the business of government and his decisions were often arbitrary or inconsistent. Ernst August I's passions for hunting and building new schlösser bled the treasury dry; his obsession with a large standing army (well out of proportion to the size of his state) brought Saxe-Weimar close to ruin. Expenditure on the military in the first years of his sole reign amounted to around ten times annual tax revenues! The duke blamed the mounting national debt on poor financial administration by his civil servants rather than his own profligacy[29]. In 1741 he also inherited the duchy of Saxe-Eisenach when this branch of the Ernestine Line died out. The twin duchies of Saxe-Weimar and Saxe-Eisenach were not amalgamated until the reign of his grandson, and Ernst August I ruled them separately in a personal union. He much preferred Saxe-Eisenach in the west of Thuringia, where the hunting was better, and moved his court and administration there. His wife stayed behind in Weimar and his young son and heir, Ernst August II born in 1738, never saw his father again[30].

Upstairs, on the entrance floor, the focus of the museum is on the building of the Rococo Schloss by Ernst August I and its renovation from 1816 by his grandson, Grand Duke Carl August (1757-1828). The largest room on this floor is the Marmorsaal (Marble Hall or ballroom) shown as originally designed by Krohne. The stucco marble was painted over by Carl August but revealed on a later restoration. On either side are the state apartments – the three rooms of the duke's apartments to the east and the duchess's to the west. Downstairs the story is the Rococo Schloss as *the birthday schloss* of Grand Duke Carl Alexander (1818-1901), the grandson of Carl August. His birthday was on 24 June and from childhood was celebrated almost every year when the court was in summer residence at Dornburg[31]. It was a special place for Carl Alexander and from 1870 he restored the three Dornburger Schlösser as a tribute to his ancestral house. The largest room on this floor is the Speisesaal (dining room) decorated in a heavenly colour scheme of peach, periwinkle blue, and white.

The Renaissance Schloss, at the far end of the escarpment, was built in the 1540s and takes its name from the architectural style. In 1824 it was purchased from non-royal owners by Grand Duke Carl August. Alternative names for this schloss are Stohmann Schloss, after the previous owner, and Goethe Schloss because of its connection with the famous German writer, Johann Wolfgang von Goethe. Goethe was fond of Dornburg from his stays there as a senior official in the Saxe-Weimar-Eisenach government. He recommended the purchase of the Renaissance Schloss to Carl August. The grand duke renovated the Renaissance Schloss and redesigned the gardens to link the three Dornburger Schlösser together in one overall concept.

55. Grand Duke Carl August in 1822.

When the grand duke died in June 1828, Goethe retreated to the quiet of the Renaissance Schloss to mourn his friend and patron of many years (see Residenzschloss Weimar). The elderly writer wrote to a friend how he could look out the window of his room to see flowers blooming in the well-kept gardens and grapes ripening in the vineyards planted by the grand duke[32].

When the monarchy fell in 1918 the Dornburger Schlösser passed into the ownership of the State of Thuringia. In 1922 the Rococo and Renaissance Schlösser were acquired by the Goethe Society; in 1928 the Renaissance Schloss opened as a memorial museum to Goethe. The museum includes the rooms where the famous writer lived for those weeks of mourning in summer 1828.

The mood in the Renaissance Schloss is calm and sober, quite different from the fun and frivolity of the Rococo Schloss. On the desk in the Bergstube (Mountain Room) is a facsimile copy of Goethe's melancholy poem 'Dem aufgehenden Vollmonde' (To the Rising Full Moon) written in the Renaissance Schloss on 25 August 1828.

> Wilt thou suddenly enshroud thee,
> Who this moment wert so nigh?
> Heavy rising masses cloud thee,
> Thou art hidden from mine eye.
> Yet my sadness thou well knowest,
> Gleaming sweetly as a star!
> That I'm loved, 'tis thou that showest,
> Though my loved one may be far.
> Upward mount then! Clearer, milder,
> Robed in splendour far more bright!
> Though my heart with grief throbs wilder,
> Fraught with rapture is the night![33]

Belvedere

Belvedere has a marvellous hilltop location with glorious views across the Thuringian countryside to Weimar in the distance. A long straight road called Belvederer Allee leads south-east from the city along the River Ilm to reach the schloss two miles away. Belvedere was a much-loved home of Grand Duchess Maria Pavlovna of Saxe-Weimar-Eisenach. She chose this as her widow's residence, and it is where she died in 1859. Maria Pavlovna was born a Romanov and her marriage to Grand Duke Carl Friedrich in 1804 brought wealth, glamour, and international connections to Saxe-Weimar-Eisenach. Perhaps one reason she loved Belvedere was that it reminded her of home. At one side of the schloss is the Russian Garden modelled on the Russian royal family's private garden at Pavlovsk, the perfect palace outside St Petersburg where she grew up. Maria Pavlovna wrote to her mother that she would '... spend most of my time in the little garden that has been laid out as an imitation of that in Pavlovsk; in some places it will be hard to tell the difference.'[34] Everything was right about our visit to this schloss – stunning building, welcoming and friendly staff, fascinating history. Even the sun broke through the rain clouds!

56. Belvedere was a favourite home of Grand Duchess Marie Pavlovna.

Belvedere was named after the summer palace of Prince Eugene of Savoy in Vienna. Its Thuringian namesake was built between 1724 and 1748 by Duke Ernst August I of Saxe-Weimar and Eisenach (1688-1748). The duke came across the site during a hunting trip and initially commissioned a new hunting lodge. But his plans changed when he visited Vienna and saw the newly completed Belvedere of Prince Eugene. Ernst August I disliked the residenzschloss in Weimar that he considered to be old-fashioned and gloomy[35]. So now he asked his favourite architect Gottfried Heinrich Krohne to change the hunting lodge to an elegant new summer palace, a Weimar version of the Viennese Belvedere. Krohne topped the hunting box with a lantern tower and added two oval-shaped side pavilions with pointed domes connected to the main building at first floor level. The beautifully proportioned and elegant front elevation he created is painted in soft and muted colours – pale apricot, dusty pink and white. The schloss is flanked by twin clock houses and twin cavalier houses (one of each on either side) and stands before a circular lawn with a fountain in the middle. Everything about Belvedere is harmonious and on the right scale; it seems to fit quite perfectly into its sylvan surroundings. Ernst August I much preferred Belvedere to the residenzschloss and stayed there when he was in the Weimar part of his double duchy.

After the death of Ernst August I the Belvedere became less important as a royal residence. His son Ernst August II and daughter-in-law Anna Amalia spent the first summer of their brief married life at Belvedere, but as a widow Anna Amalia preferred other summer homes such as Tiefurt (see Wittumspalais)[36]. Belvedere became down-at-heel and the baroque gardens laid out by Ernst August I, with a formal pattern of avenues radiating from the schloss, were wildly overgrown. Things only changed when Duke Carl August presented Belvedere to his son Carl Friedrich and daughter-in-law, Maria Pavlovna in 1811. The gift had been agreed at the time of their marriage in 1804, but the paperwork was held up by the disruption of the Napoleonic Wars[37]. With Carl Friedrich and Marie Pavlovna, the Belvedere came back to glory. The lost baroque garden parterres were transformed into a romantic landscape park bristling with exciting garden features. First came the Russian Garden in 1811, a Rose Arbour in 1815, the Scholar's Circle in 1818 (with busts of the four famous Weimar writers – Goethe, Schiller, Wieland, and Herder), a Hedge (outdoor) Theatre in 1823, the Maze in 1843, and more ... Traversing the schloss park is still Lindenallee, a long avenue of lime trees dating back to Ernst August I.

Maria Pavlovna (1786-1859) was the third of the five surviving daughters of Tsar Paul of Russia (a sixth daughter died in infancy). They were the trophy brides of their day and highly coveted on the royal marriage market. It was a spectacular coup for Saxe-Weimar-Eisenach when Carl August secured Maria Pavlovna for his son Carl Friedrich (1783-1853). The bride would bring not only an enormous dowry, but also close links with Russia that could help protect the duchy against Napoleon. At first sight the engagement might seem a surprise, given the disparity in wealth and power between their two countries. But there were longstanding links between the Saxe-Weimar-Eisenach and Russian royal families. Before her marriage, Duchess Luise (the wife of Carl August and mother of Carl Friedrich) had been vetted as a possible bride for Maria Pavlovna's father. In 1773 Luise was the youngest of three teenaged princesses of Hesse-Darmstadt invited to St Petersburg with their mother by Catherine the Great, on inspection for her son Grand Duke Paul (later Tsar Paul). Paul chose the middle sister, Wilhelmine, but was on friendly terms with his sister-in-law Luise. They kept in touch after Wilhelmine (now Grand Duchess Natalia Alexeievna) died an agonising death in childbirth less than three years after her wedding[38].

Maria Pavlovna and Carl Friedrich were married in a magnificent ceremony at the Winter Palace in St Petersburg on 3 August 1804. Negotiations for the marriage between their families began in 1799 when the bride-to-be was only thirteen. There were jitters in Weimar when Tsar Paul was assassinated in 1801[39] but the new tsar, Alexander I, kept to the arrangements made by his father. The lengthy engagement enabled the rebuilding of the Residenzschloss in Weimar to be completed, so that the new bride would have a home fit for her high station. When the young couple left St Petersburg two months after the wedding for their long journey to Weimar, they were followed by a baggage train carrying the bride's incredible dowry.

The ceremonial arrival of Maria Pavlovna in Weimar on 9 November 1804 was a red-letter day in the history of Saxe-Weimar-Eisenach. A painting in the museum at Residenzschloss Weimar records this history-in-the-making. The young couple are pictured as they arrive at the Bastille gatehouse of the Residenzschloss, sitting side-by-side in an open-topped wedding carriage (part of the bride's dowry) drawn by six beautifully groomed horses decked out in tassels and ribbons. They are greeted by young girls in white dresses with pink sashes carrying flowers and long green garlands. Maria Pavlovna wears evening dress with a dazzling tiara; Carl Friedrich is in military uniform with epaulettes and silk sash. Flags are flying; dense ranks of cheering crowds line the streets; and every window of the Bastille is packed with excited onlookers. This painting by Friedrich Preller the Elder was created forty years later (1849) and was part of a series commissioned by Carl Friedrich and Maria Pavlovna to commemorate important royal events.

57. Belvedere is set in a romantic landscape park.

Behind the wedding carriage in the painting is a glimpse of Maria Pavlovna's dowry baggage train – eighty carts stacked with crates of fabulous Russian treasures. Details of her awesome dowry were published in illustrated magazines across Europe. When the dowry itself was put on public show in Weimar, such a display of wealth stunned the local populace[40]. As well as the bride's lavish trousseau and amazing jewellery there was linen, silver and glassware, porcelain, chandeliers, furniture – everything of the very best Russian artistry and craftmanship. The centrepiece was a magnificent carved and gilded wedding bed topped by a canopy hung with luscious sky-blue velvet drapes. This wedding bed was on display in the dowry room of the Residenzschloss on our visit, although the drapes and the canopy crowned by the Russian eagle were missing. In the dowry crates were also religious icons and furnishings for Maria Pavlovna's personal chapel. Under the terms of her marriage contract it was agreed she could keep her Russian Orthodox faith. The Russians considered themselves a cut above other royal families and operated a double standard for their brides. Princesses marrying into the Russian royal family were expected to convert to Russian Orthodoxy but Russian princesses marrying out must never be required to change their religion.

Due to the powerful influence of Maria Pavlovna's brother (Tsar Alexander I) Saxe-Weimar-Eisenach prospered when the map of Europe was redrawn at the Congress of Vienna after the Napoleonic Wars. Her father-in-law was elevated from duke to the higher rank of grand duke (with the coveted address of 'royal highness' as opposed to the lessor 'serene highness') and his state almost doubled in size[41]. When Carl August died in 1828, Maria Pavlovna and her husband became the reigning grand duke and duchess. She was more intelligent and dynamic than her shy husband and her private wealth gave her a degree of independence[42]. Maria Pavlovna sponsored social initiatives, created public parks and libraries, endowed numerous charities from her private purse, and fostered the artistic and cultural life of the grand duchy. If Weimar had a *Golden Age* during the reign of Carl August, it enjoyed a second *Silver Age* under Carl Friedrich and Maria Pavlovna[43].

One sadness for the couple was the death of their first child. Carl was born a year after the wedding but died at seven months old. The birth of two daughters followed, Marie in 1808 and Auguste in 1811. Carl Friedrich and Maria Pavlovna had to wait until 1818 for the birth of their only other son, Carl Alexander. A portrait of Carl Alexander at Belvedere shows him as a child in the schloss gardens. In 1842 Carl Alexander brought another important bride to Weimar when he married his first cousin, Sophie of the Netherlands. Sophie was the only daughter of King Willem II and his wife Anna Pavlovna (a sister of Maria Pavlovna). Both Carl Alexander's sisters found husbands in the Prussian royal family. In 1827 Marie married Karl, the third son of King Friedrich Wilhelm III of Prussia; her younger sister Auguste married Karl's elder brother Wilhelm two years later. In the tight network of European royalty, the couples were already related by marriage. Wilhelm and Karl's sister was the wife of Maria Pavlovna's brother, Tsar Nikolai I of Russia.

58. Auguste of Saxe-Weimar-Eisenach with her husband Kaiser Wilhelm 1.

Auguste's Prussian husband was not an ardent bridegroom. Wilhelm was still deeply in love with his former childhood playmate Elise Radziwill. He had hoped to marry Elise, but after years of cruel deliberation and delay it was eventually decreed that she was not of equal royal blood. It seems a crazy decision, given that Elise's mother was a Prussian princess and a cousin of the Prussian king[44]. Wilhelm was second in line to the Prussian throne (after his elder brother) and accepted that he must make a dynastic marriage. But he made it clear that he could never love again; the most Auguste could hope for was respect and affection[45]. Wilhelm never forgot Elise and kept a picture of her on his desk until he died[46]. His lost love never married, and Elise died young thus always leaving a romantic image in Wilhelm's mind. His marriage to Auguste was long-lived and fractious; they quarrelled for fifty-eight years! Wilhelm and Auguste became king and queen of Prussia in 1861 after the death of his elder brother (Friedrich Wilhelm IV); and German emperor and empress ten years later when the new German Empire was proclaimed in 1871.

At the end of the monarchy Belvedere passed into state ownership, but without the contents, which by agreement remained the property of the ex-grand duke[47]. The schloss is a museum with eighteenth and early nineteenth century porcelain, glass, and furniture from the grand ducal collection. The beautiful items on display include St Petersburg porcelain that came to Weimar with Maria Pavlovna's dowry, and furniture that was part of the Dutch inheritance of her daughter-in-law Sophie. The main rooms on the first floor include the Festival Hall (Ballroom) with original décor, and magnificent views across the fountain garden to the city of Weimar. There are portraits of Ernst August I who built this exquisite schloss and of Maria Pavlovna who brought it back to life.

The Wartburg

The most famous castle in Thuringia is the Wartburg. A visit to this schloss is like walking through the pages of a history book. In the thirteenth century the Wartburg was home to Landgravine Elisabeth, canonised as St Elisabeth in 1235. In the sixteenth century, during the Reformation, the Wartburg is where Martin Luther was hidden after he was outlawed by the Holy Roman emperor. In the nineteenth century, soon after the Napoleonic Wars, the Wartburg was the scene of the first-ever democratic protest march in Germany. In the twentieth century this schloss, located on the border between East and West Germany after World War II, became the potent symbol of a divided nation. In the year after the Berlin Wall fell, more than one and three quarter million people came to see the Wartburg. When Dr Shephard Thomas Taylor wrote up the account of his tour of Thuringia in 1884, he devoted more pages to the Wartburg than any other place he visited. 'Most other ancient castles have to content themselves with one or two romantic incidents in their career;' he wrote 'but the history of the Wartburg seems to be one long tale of romance from beginning to end.'[48]

59. The Wartburg is the most famous castle in Thuringia.

The Wartburg was founded around 1067 by Ludwig *the Jumper* (died 1123)[49]. (He also founded the monastery at Reinhardsbrunn in chapter 3.) The Wartburg is situated on a steep spur of rock, more than a thousand feet above the town of Eisenach. The story goes that Ludwig *the Jumper* discovered the beautiful spot during a hunt and was so inspired that he claimed it as his own. 'Wart, Berg,' he is supposed to have exclaimed 'du sollst mir eine Burg werden!' ('Wait, mountain, you are going to become my castle!')[50]. This may be how the Wartburg got its name, but it is more likely it came from an even earlier watch tower (Warte) on the site[51]. The moment Ludwig *the Jumper* stands atop the rocky peak is one of the old legends of Thuringia depicted in the frescos of the Landgrafenzimmer (Landgrave's Room) at the Wartburg. (Another is Landgrave Friedrich *the Bitten*'s wild ride from the Wartburg to Tenneberg in chapter 3). According to the legend, Ludwig *the Jumper* did not own the land on which the Wartburg stands and resorted to a crafty ruse. Before starting to build he had earth from his own domains scattered on the site. He could then rightly assert to the emperor that the Wartburg was built on his own soil!

Ludwig *the Jumper* was the father of the Ludowinger landgraves of Thuringia (chart 1 is their family tree). In 1130 his son, Ludwig I (died 1140), was created the first landgrave of Thuringia by the Holy Roman Emperor Lothar in return for supporting his election as emperor[52]. Over the next century, until their line died out in 1247, the Ludowinger were a powerful and well-connected family with extensive lands in Thuringia and neighbouring Hesse. The Wartburg lay at the centre of their territories and was the most important residence. Ludwig II *the Iron* (died 1172), the son of Ludwig I, built the main wing of the Wartburg called the Palas. He married the sister of the Emperor Friedrich I Barbarossa. During the reign of Hermann I (died 1217), the Wartburg was a leading European centre of court culture, chivalry, and fine arts[53]. The famous Sängerkrieg (Singers' War), immortalised by the composer Richard Wagner in his wonderful opera Tannhäuser, was supposedly staged at the Wartburg in 1206. The Singer's War was a singing competition for minnesingers (minstrels), with execution by hanging as a booby prize for the loser[54]!

By the time of Hermann I, the Ludowinger dynasty had become so important that he could secure a king's daughter as a bride for his son. In 1221, Landgrave Ludwig IV (died 1227) married Princess Elisabeth of Hungary, the future St Elisabeth. The last male dynast in the family was Landgrave Heinrich Raspe IV (died 1247). He was the son of Hermann I and the younger brother of Ludwig IV. Heinrich Raspe IV briefly held the top position in the Holy Roman Empire when he was elected as a rival emperor or 'anti-king' in 1246 after the pope excommunicated Friedrich II (grandson of Friedrich I Barbarossa). It was a time of turmoil in the empire with competing factions. Heinrich Raspe IV died the following year from an arrow wound suffered on campaign. He had married three times, but all his marriages were childless. After his death there was a long war over the succession and ultimately the Ludowinger lands were split. Thuringia passed to the house of

60. St Elisabeth arrives as a child at the Wartburg.

Wettin through Heinrich *the Illustrious*, the son of Heinrich Raspe IV's sister Jutta (Judith). The lands in Hesse went to St Elisabeth's daughter Sophie who married the duke of Brabant and is the ancestress of the House of Hesse.

From 1257 the Wartburg was a favoured residence of the early Wettin landgraves of Thuringia. Albrecht *the Unnatural* (son of Heinrich *the Illustrious*) stayed here fifty-six times and his son, Friedrich *the Bitten*, chose the Wartburg as his retirement home[55]. As the house divided and re-divided, the Wartburg fell to the Ernestine Line and to the duchy of Saxe-Eisenach. After the Thirty Years' War (1618-1648) the schloss

133

ceased to be a royal residence and fell into dilapidation. The Wartburg was fortunate to be 'rediscovered' by Johann Wolfgang von Goethe who stayed there for several weeks in 1777 in his capacity as privy councillor to Duke Carl August of Saxe-Weimar and Eisenach. Goethe extolled the beauty and romanticism of the Wartburg in his poetry and drawings. But it would not be until after his death that his hopes for a renovation were realised.

Saint Elisabeth of Thuringia

Landgravine Elisabeth of Thuringia was the daughter of King András II and Queen Gertrude of Hungary. As a four-year-old she was sent to the court of Landgrave Hermann I of Thuringia in 1211 as the prospective bride of his son.

Elisabeth married Landgrave Ludwig IV in 1221 when she was thirteen. She was widowed only six years later, in 1227, when Ludwig IV died from disease in Italy on his way to the crusades. Their only son, Hermann II (died 1241), was still a child and his uncle (Ludwig IV's brother, Heinrich Raspe IV) took over the government. Elisabeth was forced out and left the Wartburg with her children in 1228.

From childhood Elisabeth never fitted the mould of a high-born medieval lady and attracted criticism for her ascetic way of life following the model of St Francis of Assisi. One picture in Elisabeth's Bower shows her laying down the Thuringian crown as a sign of Christian humility. After her expulsion from the Wartburg, Elisabeth moved to Marburg (part of the family's landholdings in Hesse), where she opened a hospital and personally cared for the poor and sick. This type of work was unheard of for a lady for hundreds of years to come. Elisabeth's life was short; she died in 1231 at the age of twenty-four and was canonised four years later.

The appeal of St Elisabeth has endured over the centuries and she remains a popular saint. Churches have been dedicated to her, hospitals and homes for the elderly called after her, and nursing orders established to carry on her work.

From 1839 to 1890 the Wartburg was restored and reconstructed as a national monument to German history by Grand Duke Carl Alexander of Saxe-Weimar-Eisenach (1818-1901). The grand duke and his wife Sophie of the Netherlands (1824-1897) were very conscious of the illustrious history of his ancestral house as the senior branch of the Ernestine Line. Carl Alexander also restored the three Dornburger Schlösser (see above) and Sophie set up the Goethe and Schiller Archive to preserve the legacy of these two great German writers in Weimar. The revival of the Wartburg was a headline project that attracted attention across Germany. It was financed entirely from the grand

61. Grand Duke Carl Alexander restored the Wartburg as a monument to German history.

duke's own resources[56]. After years of searching for the right architect a young university professor called Hugo von Ritgen was appointed to the role. Von Ritgen was so passionate about the Wartburg that, even before he got the job, he sent a one-hundred-and-forty-page treatise to the grand duke on the subject.

> The Wartburg: what a host of memories are associated with this name for every German! Where is the castle that is its equal in historical significance and poetic solemnity? The massive walls still stand ... high above Thuringia's woods and fields and, as faithful witnesses, remind us of the greatness of German heroes, of German strength and German poetry. With admiration Germany watches such a truly royal enterprise,[57]

Von Ritgen's programme of works included a complete overhaul and refurbishment of the twelfth century Palas (on the left in illustration 59) and the erection of new buildings on old foundations of those lost from the medieval period. The Bergfried or Keep (the tall tower in illustration 59) was completed in 1859 and the Neue Kemenate or New Fireplace Room (in front of it), the following year. Last to be built was a small bathhouse with a heated bath called the Knights' Bath, completed in 1890. The custom of bathing in warm waters was brought back to Europe by knights returning from the Crusades. The Wartburg became a royal residence again as the new buildings contained a lavish suite of apartments for Carl Alexander and his family. When the Wartburg underwent a 'de-restoration' in the 1950s, these ducal apartments were stripped out and became museum space. Only the grand duke's bedroom survives to give some idea of what they looked like.

The guided tour at the Wartburg takes visitors through the Palas, renovated by Carl Alexander in historicist style (a contemporary version of the architecture of the past). The rooms have medieval-sounding names – the Knights' Hall, the Landgrave's Room (with frescos of the old legends of Thuringia), the Hall of Minstrels (where, by tradition, the 1206 singing competition took place). A large fresco by Moritz von Schwind, romantic painter of idealised medieval knights and castles, dominates the Hall of Minstrels. It shows the scene at the climax of the Sängerkrieg (Singers' War). The minstrel who has lost the contest kneels at the feet of the landgravine (landgrave's wife) pleading for his life; the executioner looms nearby, with his hangman's rope looped over his shoulder[58].

Von Schwind also painted the frescos in the Landgrave's Room and in the narrow Elisabeth Gallery that leads to the Hall of Minstrels. This Gallery was the part of the Wartburg that fascinated me the most. The six frescos tell the life story of the most remarkable woman in the history of the schloss. This was Elisabeth, a royal princess, and landgravine of Thuringia, who was canonised in 1235 as St Elisabeth. The first fresco in the series (illustration 60) shows her being lifted down from the carriage when she arrives at the Wartburg as a small child. It is a charming picture – little Elisabeth's face is framed by a bonnet and she wears a blue coat trimmed with fur. The last picture in the cycle is both sombre and uplifting and shows the excavation of her remains a year after she was canonised. This was a great occasion in the presence of bishops and princes and the Holy Roman emperor.

62. An old postcard of the Elisabeth Bower
with stunning Byzantine style glass mosaic.

The Elisabeth Bower was part of the medieval women's quarters and may have been where Elisabeth lived. Between 1902 and 1906 the Bower was redecorated in Byzantine style with a stunning mosaic made up of over one million pieces of coloured glass[59]. The work was commissioned by Kaiser Wilhelm II in memory of Grand Duke Carl Alexander's achievements at the Wartburg (the grand duke died in 1901). Carl Alexander was related to the Prussian royal family and the kaiser was his great-nephew (grandson of his sister Auguste)[60]. The wall arches of the Elisabeth Bower are filled with luminous mosaic murals illustrating more scenes from the saint's life – the envoys of Hermann I arrive at the Hungarian court to plead for her hand; Ludwig IV journeys to the crusades (one of the knights in this picture has the features of Kaiser Wilhelm II)[61]; Elisabeth builds the hospital at Marburg after her expulsion from the Wartburg; ... Yet it was the patterned vaulted ceiling that was the star of this work of art for me. Lit by uplighters, the ceiling glittered and glowed in gold and bronze, and seemingly all the colours of the rainbow.

The last room on the guided tour was the Festsaal (or Grand Hall), completed in time for the eight-hundred-year jubilee of the Wartburg in 1867. This huge room takes up the whole of the second floor of the Palas and is decorated with paintings of the Ludowinger dynasty. When he visited, King Ludwig II of Bavaria (*the Dream King*) was so impressed with this room he had a copy made in his new fairy-tale castle of Neuschwanstein[62]. Over the central chimney piece hangs the student flag of Jena University (Thuringia), commemorating yet another important event in the Wartburg's history. On 18 October 1817, five hundred students from Jena and other German universities marched up the hill from Eisenach to the Wartburg in the first democratic protest rally in Germany. The students, called 'loveable hotheads' by Goethe[63], called for democratic freedoms and the unification of Germany. After the Napoleonic Wars, many Germans were bitterly disappointed that the old political order, with its patchwork of reactionary royal states, was restored at the Congress of Vienna. The student demonstration at the Wartburg was staged on the fourth anniversary of the decisive Battle of the Nations near Leipzig that brought about Napoleon's defeat. The German states responded by banning student organisations, but the black, red, and gold of the Jena student flag would eventually become the colours of the Weimar Republic and the German national flag.

The Wartburg is the last of the Ernestine schlösser in this book. The royal story of Thuringia began here with Ludwig *the Jumper* (father of the Ludowinger landgraves) in 1067 and ended eight hundred and fifty years later when the last grand duke of Saxe-Weimar-Eisenach abdicated. This schloss is a tumult of colourful images and royal stories and I will never tire of visiting. The Wartburg is the top tourist site in Thuringia and so important historically and architecturally that it is a UNESCO World Heritage Site.

Martin Luther at the Wartburg

On 31 October 1517, the religious reformer Martin Luther nailed to the door of the schloss church in Wittenberg, Saxony Anhalt, his ninety-five theses against the use of indulgences by the Catholic Church. This was the starting point of the Reformation and the beginning of the Protestant faith. Reformation Day is still celebrated with an annual public holiday in Thuringia. Luther was excommunicated by the pope and ordered by the Holy Roman emperor to appear in person at the imperial diet (parliament) in Worms in April 1521, to defend himself. When Luther refused to recant at the diet, the emperor placed him under the Imperial Ban which meant Luther became an outlaw and his personal safety was at risk. But in what may have been a signal he would connive in Luther's escape, the emperor granted him safe passage from the diet[64].

The hint was taken by Luther's patron, Elector Friedrich the Wise of Saxony (chart 2). He was the uncle of Johann Friedrich I with whom we began the story of the Ernestine line in Thuringia at Fröhliche Wiederkunft in chapter 2. Friedrich the Wise was Catholic, but the young monk Luther was a professor at his University in Wittenberg; and the elector loyally stood behind his man. On 4 May 1521, as Luther was on his way back from the diet, the elector staged a sham kidnapping not far from Altenstein in the Thuringian forest (chapter 4) and arranged for him to disappear. While his enemies thought him dead, Luther was hidden away at the Wartburg under the false name of Junker Jörg (Squire George).

Luther knew the Wartburg well since his parents came from the area and he went to school in Eisenach as a child[65]. His small room in the Vogtei (Bailiff's Lodge) is now famous as the Lutherstube (Luther Room), but had previously been part of a prison for knights. The Vogtei is in the part of the Wartburg called the Vorburg (front castle) as opposed to the Hofburg (main castle), where the Palas is located. During his ten months under house arrest at the Wartburg Luther grew his hair long and sported a beard as part of his disguise. He enjoyed a productive writing phase and the Wartburg is where Luther translated the New Testament of the Bible from Greek into German.

6.

REUSS ELDER LINE AND REUSS YOUNGER LINE

Two of the sovereign states in Thuringia in the time of the monarchy were ruled by branches of the royal house of Reuss. The larger of the two was the principality of Reuss Younger Line, ruled by Prince Heinrich XXVII (27). He was also regent of the smaller principality of Reuss Elder Line on behalf of its prince, Heinrich XXIV (24), who had suffered brain damage as a child and was deemed unfit to rule.

It is no coincidence that these two Reuss princes were both called Heinrich. The extraordinary thing about the Reuss family is that for hundreds of years all their male children were given the same first name of Heinrich. This makes their family history extremely difficult to follow notwithstanding that each individual Heinrich was given an identifying number at birth. The numbers are usually expressed as roman numerals and to assist the reader I have 'translated' these to the more familiar (arabic) numbers.

In this chapter we visit schlösser of both Reuss Elder Line and Reuss Younger Line. In what proved a recurring theme for the Thuringia royal families, both lines died out in the twentieth century. Notable personalities in royal history from the house of Reuss include

Augusta of Reuss-Ebersdorf, the grandmother of both Queen Victoria and Prince Albert (see Ebersdorf); and Hermine of Reuss Elder Line, whose father was adamantly anti-Prussian but who married Kaiser Wilhelm II (Unteres Schloss Greiz).

Unteres Schloss Greiz

The town of Greiz in south-east Thuringia, close to the border with the federal state of Saxony, was the capital of the principality of Reuss Elder Line (alternatively called Reuss-Greiz). Greiz has three fascinating but very different schlösser – the hilltop Oberes (Upper) Schloss which dominates the skyline and dates back to the twelfth century; the Unteres (Lower) Schloss in the town, built in the sixteenth century; and the gracious eighteenth-century Sommerpalais (Summer Palace) in the park along the river. They are all open to the public and our visit to Greiz was a very full day.

63. Unteres (Lower) Schloss Greiz with the hilltop
Oberes (Upper) Schloss in the background.

The House of Reuss and its sovereign territories

The first documented ancestor of the house of Reuss was Erkenbert I of Weida (around 1090-before 1143). The family's origins in Thuringia were as vogts on behalf of the Holy Roman emperor. Vogt is a difficult term to translate into English and I have seen it described variously as bailiff, steward, sheriff, reeve, and lord protector. The area around Weida, Greiz and Gera is still known as the Thuringian Vogtland. The family name of Reuss (or Russe) dates to around 1290 as a nickname for Heinrich I 'Der Reusse' Vogt of Plauen and was derived from the Russian ancestry of his wife.

The house of Reuss divided and reorganised their lands numerous times over the centuries. A division between brothers in 1564 resulted in two lasting lines – Reuss Elder Line and Reuss Younger Line. Both lines were later divided into branches with smaller states, many of which died out over time. The two remaining sub-states of the Elder Line were united as Reuss Elder Line (or Reuss-Greiz) in 1768 under Heinrich XI (11) of Reuss-Obergreiz (1722-1800). He was promoted from count to prince in 1778.

Consolidation of the four remaining sub-states in the Younger Line took place in the first half of the nineteenth century. The Reuss-Gera branch died out in 1802 and Reuss-Lobenstein in 1824. In 1848, the last prince of Reuss-Ebersdorf abdicated and Heinrich LXII (62) of Reuss-Schleiz (1785-1854) became sovereign of the new state of Reuss Younger Line (or Reuss-Gera). The counts of the Younger Line became princes between 1790 and 1806.

On 10 November 1918, Heinrich XXVII (27) (1858-1928) abdicated as ruling prince of Reuss Younger Line. The following day, as regent, he also abdicated on behalf of the incapacitated Heinrich XXIV (24) of Reuss Elder Line (1878-1927). Heinrich (27) became head of the entire house of Reuss in 1927 when the Elder Line became extinct on the death of Heinrich (24). From 1930 the designation 'Younger Line' was no longer used. However, Heinrich (27)'s branch of the house died out in turn when his son, Heinrich XLV (45), went missing in 1945 and was later declared dead. The headship of house then passed to the distant (non-ruling) Reuss-Köstritz branch. The head of house today is Heinrich XIV (14) Prince Reuss born in 1955.

We started at the Unteres (Lower) Schloss on the bank of the White Elster river. A disastrous fire swept through the town of Greiz in April 1802 and the sixteenth-century renaissance schloss burned down. It was rebuilt in classical style by Heinrich XIII (13) (1747-1817) and became the main residence of the princes of Reuss Elder Line. Heinrich (13)'s new building is on the left in illustration 63. The last major reconstruction of the Unteres Schloss took place in the 1880s when Heinrich XXII (22) (1846-1902) built a new south wing and called it the Ida Palace after his wife, born Princess Ida of Schaumberg-Lippe (1852-1891). The Ida Palace is the building with the onion dome on the right in illustration 63. Chart 15 provides a family tree for the princes of Reuss Elder Line; Heinrich (22) was the grandson of Heinrich (13).

64. The Blue Salon in the Ida Palace.

A spectacular spiral staircase leads to the main rooms on the first floor of the Ida Palace that now form part of the museum. My favourite rooms were here – Princess Ida's bedroom, dressing room, and the Blue Salon. There is little remaining of the original furnishings, but an excellent exhibition, with display boards and photographs, tells the story of Prince Heinrich (22), his wife Ida, and their children. Some of this information is translated in the English audio-guide.

Heinrich (22) was born on 28 March 1846. He was still a minor (thirteen years old) when his father died in 1859 and his mother, Karoline of Hesse-Homburg (1819-1872), became regent on his behalf. Like her husband, Karoline was anti-Prussian and supported Austria (the losing side) in the Seven Weeks' War of 1866[1]. Reuss Elder Line was occupied by Prussian troops and suffered a heavy war indemnity. When Heinrich (22) reached his majority and took over the reins of government, he continued his parents' conservative policies and anti-Prussian stance. Throughout his reign he never accepted the superior status of Prussia to the other German royal states.

As the young ruler of Reuss Elder Line, Heinrich (22) was a somewhat solitary young man[2]. His mother died from pneumonia in the Unteres Schloss after a short illness in January 1872. His two brothers died as children and Heinrich (22) was the last male standing in the Reuss Elder Line. There was a feeling that he ought to get married and father an heir as soon as possible. In August 1872, Heinrich (22) became engaged to Princess Ida of Schaumburg-Lippe during a holiday in the spa town of Karlsbad in Bohemia (now Karlovy Vary in the Czech Republic). They were married at her home in Schloss Bückeburg (in *Schloss II*) on 8 October 1872. It would be a happy marriage, although not free from tragedy.

Reuss Elder Line needed an heir, but Heinrich (22) and Ida had to wait five years for their first child. On 20 March 1878, to great jubilation in Reuss Elder Line, their son Heinrich XXIV (24) was born. The town of Greiz celebrated with a torchlight procession although, according to one report, this soon turned into a 'wobble' procession due to the free supplies of beer[3]! For his first five years, Heinrich (24) was a normal, healthy, child but then he suffered a terrible accident. This was initially kept secret, giving rise to all sorts of rumours about what happened. One version (later repeated by his younger sister in her memoirs) is a botched eye operation when the little boy struggled so much that the surgeon's knife slipped and penetrated his brain[4]. Another, as told to me at the Unteres Schloss – and perhaps more likely – is that Heinrich (24) was playing, climbed onto a box or table, fell heavily, and banged his head[5]. Whatever the cause the little boy was brain damaged and lost his speech. His parents tried all sorts of cures and remedies to no avail. Heinrich (24) would never have the mental capacity to rule. Heinrich (22) decided that his son should be educated within his abilities with a focus on physical fitness and good behaviour.

Heinrich (22) and Ida had more children, but one after another they were all girls. Princess Emma was born on 17 January 1881, Marie

on 26 March 1882, Karoline on 13 July 1884, and Hermine on 17 December 1887. Ida suffered from heart disease and her health deteriorated. In the spring of 1891 she was pregnant again, but she was also dying. Ida spent the summer weeks in the Sommerpalais Greiz (see later in this chapter) where she lay in a tent on the terrace or was wheeled around the gardens in a wheelchair[6]. On 4 September 1891 she gave birth to her last child – another daughter whom they called Ida after her mother. When his wife died on 28 September 1891 the grieving

65. Heinrich XXII (22) and family in 1890.

widower said, 'The sun of my earthly happiness in life went down ...'[7]. One can hardly imagine his desolation. His wife was dead; his only son was not fit to rule; and he would never have another son. Heinrich

(22) was the last prince of Reuss Elder Line to rule over his state. He died in middle age from heart disease on 19 April 1902 leaving six orphaned children – five daughters aged between ten and twenty-one and his twenty-four-year-old disabled son. Heinrich (24) (1878-1927) succeeded his father, but his reign was subject to a regency[8]. He never married and was the last of the Reuss Elder Line (chart 15). When the monarchy came to an end, Heinrich (24) was given the right to stay on in the Unteres Schloss and after he died there in 1927 the schloss became a museum.

The five Reuss-Greiz sisters all found husbands in the years after their father's death. The Oval Hall in the Unteres Schloss features huge storyboards about their weddings. First to marry, on 30 April 1903, was the middle sister of the five, eighteen-year-old Karoline (1884-1905). Her bridegroom was Grand Duke

66. Princess Karoline with her husband, Grand Duke Wilhelm Ernst of Saxe-Weimar-Eisenach.

Wilhelm Ernst of Saxe-Weimar-Eisenach (see Residenzschloss Weimar in chapter 5). At the Unteres Schloss Karoline was described as graceful, pretty, and sensitive[9]. She did not want to marry Wilhelm Ernst and tried to back out before the wedding[10]. She was urged into it by her uncle (her mother's brother), Duke Georg of Schaumburg-Lippe. He became the children's guardian after their father's death and arranged the match. Wilhelm Ernst was considered a great dynastic catch; he was a reigning prince and cousin to the kaiser. The new bride was welcomed by the people of Saxe-Weimar-Eisenach but her marriage to

Wilhelm Ernst was a torture for Karoline. She barely ate and became depressed; photos taken during her short, married life show Karoline as thin and downcast. She ran away to Switzerland, but Wilhelm Ernst followed and persuaded her to return[11]. When she caught pneumonia, Karoline did not have the will to fight it off and died on 17 January 1905 aged only twenty[12]. She had harboured thoughts of suicide and this led to many rumours about how she died[13].

Karoline's widower Wilhelm Ernst considered marrying her next younger sister, Hermine (1887-1947). They were briefly engaged in summer 1906 but it was quickly broken off[14]. On 7 January 1907, at the Unteres Schloss, Hermine married Prince Johann Georg of Schönaich-Carolath (1873-1920) who came from an old Prussian aristocratic family. They were happy together and five children were born (three boys and two girls) between 1907 and 1918. But only a year into the marriage, Johann Georg was found to be suffering from the lung disease tuberculosis (TB) and Hermine's role became that of nurse to an invalid. Johann Georg died in a sanitorium in April 1920 at the age of forty-six. Two years later Hermine remarried, and her second husband was a surprise to everyone!

In June 1922, the widowed Hermine arrived to stay at Huis (House) Doorn in the Netherlands, the home in exile of ex-Kaiser Wilhelm II of Germany (1859-1941). Hermine knew Wilhelm from court circles before World War I, but the invitation to visit came after her young son had spontaneously written the ex-kaiser a fan letter! After the death in April 1921 of ex-Kaiserin Auguste Viktoria (his wife of forty years), Wilhelm had become isolated and reclusive. His personal doctor encouraged him to seek more feminine company. Nevertheless, those around him were astonished when Wilhelm invited Hermine to Huis Doorn, and even more astonished when they became engaged just days after her arrival. Wilhelm and Hermine were married at Huis Doorn on 5 November 1922. Reaction from the ex-kaiser's entourage and family was hostile in the extreme. Hermine was young enough to be his daughter; came with the baggage of five children (the youngest Henriette not yet four);

and was regarded as a schemer who only wanted to marry the ex-kaiser so she would be empress if he was restored as emperor.

Wilhelm was clearly smitten with his 'Hermo', writing to a friend

So, I have found a woman's heart after all, a German princess, an adorable, clever young widow has decided to bring sunshine into my lonely house and to help share my solitude and make it beautiful with her warm devoted love. ... My happiness knows no bounds.[15]

There was also an element of calculation in his choice as he believed marrying a princess of equal 'blood' could only improve his chances of reclaiming the throne.

Wilhelm and Hermine were together for nineteen years. Probably it was a case of the adage 'Marry in haste, repent at leisure'. Hermine was never truly welcome in her husband's stultifying small court in exile and spent a lot of time away from Huis Doorn, on her first husband's estates at Schloss Saabor in Silesia (now part of Poland), or lobbying Hitler and senior Nazi leaders in Berlin for her second husband's restoration. World War II brought the final disillusionment of their hopes for a triumphal return to Germany. Wilhelm was probably disappointed that Hermine did not provide the unstinting devotion he craved. He also disliked her children except for the youngest, little Henriette, whom he jokingly nicknamed *the General!* The last happy occasion celebrated at Huis Doorn was the wedding of Henriette to Wilhelm's grandson Karl Franz (the son of his youngest son Joachim) in October 1940[16].

67. Princess Hermine married ex-Kaiser Wilhelm II.

The state of Thuringia

The federal state of Thuringia came into existence on 1 May 1920 as a combination of all the small free states in Thuringia. When the reigning princes abdicated in November 1918 and a German republic was declared, each of the eight royal duchies and principalities in Thuringia became a free state of the same name. So, as examples, the principality of Reuss Elder Line became the Free State of Reuss Elder Line and the duchy of Saxe-Altenburg the Free State of Saxe-Altenburg. Over the following months there was some reshuffling. The Free States of Reuss Elder Line and Reuss Younger Line combined to form the People's State of Reuss, whilst the union between Saxe-Coburg and Gotha was dissolved to form two separate free states of Saxe-Coburg and Saxe-Gotha. All the free states joined the new state of Thuringia when it was created, except Saxe-Coburg where the citizens voted to become instead part of the new state of Bavaria. The capital city of the new state of Thuringia was Weimar.

At the end of World War II, the state of Thuringia became part of the Soviet Zone of Occupation in July 1945. The boundaries of the state were expanded to encompass previously 'stranded' territories and the capital moved from Weimar to Erfurt, which had been part of a Prussian enclave. In 1952 Thuringia and the other states which made up the new German Democratic Republic (GDR or East Germany) were disbanded and replaced with more numerous administrative districts.

Today Thuringia is one of sixteen regional states (called länder) that make up the Federal Republic of Germany. On reunification in 1990, the ten existing states of West Germany were joined by five reconstituted states from the GDR (East Germany), including Thuringia. The sixteenth state is the city of Berlin. The capital of the modern-day state of Thuringia is Erfurt.

After Wilhelm's death in June 1941, Hermine returned to live at Schloss Saabor until forced to leave by the advancing Soviet army in January 1945. She fled to the home of her sister Ida at Rossla (just over the border with Thuringia in Saxony-Anhalt) where she was interviewed by American journalists in April 1945[17]. Hermine was warned the Americans were going to hand over the area, but refused to believe it and was stranded when the Soviet occupying forces took over in July. She was placed under house arrest and died in the town of Frankfurt an der Oder (on the border with Poland) on 7 August 1947, aged fifty-nine.

The Ida Palace at Unteres Schloss Greiz was named by Heinrich (22) in honour of his beloved wife. The rooms are full of memories of the prince and his family: of the sad story of his son, Heinrich (24), the last of the Reuss Elder line; of his daughter Karoline, forced into an uncongenial marriage; and of Hermine, who became an empress but only in exile.

Oberes Schloss Greiz

After our visit to the Unteres Schloss we walked up the steep castle hill to Oberes (Upper) Schloss Greiz. As can be seen from illustration 63, the two schlösser are within sight of each other. Their proximity reflects that for two centuries the town of Greiz was divided into two territories. When the Reuss lands were split in 1564, one brother received Obergreiz (Upper Greiz) and another Untergreiz (Lower Greiz). (A third brother got Gera and was the founder of the Reuss Younger Line.) The ancestral hilltop schloss (the Oberes Schloss) became part of Obergreiz. The new lord of Untergreiz had no residence and built the Unteres Schloss just a short distance away in the town on the bank of the White Elster river.

Obergreiz and Untergreiz were reunited in 1768 when the last count of Untergreiz died a bachelor and Heinrich XI (11) of Obergreiz (1722-1800) became ruler of the combined territories of Reuss Elder Line (also sometimes called Reuss-Greiz). He continued to use the Oberes Schloss as his residence and the Unteres Schloss became offices for civil servants. There is an appealing portrait of Heinrich (11) as a young man in the portrait gallery of the Oberes Schloss, wearing a curled and powdered wig tied in the nape of his neck with a ribbon. He was an important figure in the history of the Reuss Elder Line and the first of the Reuss counts to be promoted to the rank of prince. There were six princes of Reuss Elder Line before the monarchy came to an end in 1918; chart 15 shows their family tree.

68. Oberes (Upper) Schloss at Greiz on top of castle hill.

A narrow, cobbled, road climbs past the east wing of the Oberes Schloss with its distinctive renaissance gables (on the right in illustration 68), through the gatehouse, and into the lower courtyard. This was built in the 1740s when Heinrich (11) enhanced and extended the Oberes Schloss as part of his long campaign to be elevated to a prince. Prior to this the main entrance was higher up the hill by the Stelzentor (Stilt Gate) through the prison tower. The Oberes Schloss is a complex of buildings, some of which were in good condition and others in dire need of restoration. In the lower courtyard, the Treasury building (home of the City Archive) was newly painted in bright colours with a coat-of-arms on the gable and the initials of Heinrich (11) over the central window. However, next door the Cavalier House appeared to be in private occupation and looked dilapidated.

There is a nice story that the favourite horse of Heinrich VI (6) of Obergreiz (1649-1697) was buried near the lower courtyard under an oak tree. The Elder Line had a long history of loyalty to the Austrian Holy Roman emperors and Heinrich (6) was a field marshal in the imperial army. He died a hero's death at the battle of Zenta in 1697. This battle was Prince Eugene of Savoy's great victory over the Turks. Despite its own wounds, his faithful horse carried the dying Heinrich (6) from the battlefield. His master's last wish in return was for his horse to be taken home to Greiz and cared for. There it was so well looked after that it lived on in the Oberes Schloss for almost thirty years[18].

From the lower courtyard the road turns back on itself, narrows further, and climbs again, through the Stelzentor and into the upper courtyard. This is the oldest part of

69. The Stelzentor (Stilt Gate).

the schloss, dating originally to the twelfth century. The buildings were altered and re-altered over the centuries and display three architectural styles – romanesque, renaissance and baroque. The corps de logis (main wing) was remodelled to its present appearance by Heinrich (11) at the same time as the lower courtyard was built. It houses a museum packed with information on Reuss royal history. The curators gave us a friendly welcome and took time to explain how the exhibition was organised.

153

The name of Heinrich

A unique feature of the house of Reuss is that all male children are given the same first name of Heinrich. As a consequence, they are sometimes called the 'Heinrichinger'. The family custom on name is believed to have been set about 1200 by Heinrich II (2) of Weida (around 1150-1209), known as 'the Rich'. He wanted to show his devotion to the Holy Roman Emperor Heinrich VI in gratitude for the grant of preferments.

To distinguish between them, each Heinrich was also given an identifying number at birth, usually expressed as a roman numeral. This family numbering system was codified in 1688 and the numbers began again (at 1). The system then operated differently in each line of the house. In the Elder Line the numbers ran consecutively by order of birth in a single sequence until this line died out in 1927 on the death of Heinrich XXIV (24). In the more prolific Younger Line, the numbers also run consecutively by birth, but a new sequence begins again (at 1) at the beginning of each century. The current head of house, Heinrich XIV (14), Prince Reuss (born in 1955), was thus the fourteenth Heinrich born in the twentieth century.

The numbering system does not entirely overcome the confusion caused by using a single first name. It is important to remember that the sovereign princes of Reuss were known by their family number rather than their reign number. In Great Britain we had George I, George II, George III, and George IV in succession followed, after a gap, by George V and (after a shorter gap) George VI. In the Reuss Younger Line, Heinrich LXVII (67) (1789-1867) was followed by Heinrich XIV (14) (1832-1913) and then by Heinrich XXVII (27) (1858-1928). This apparent oddity is explained as follows. Between Heinrich (67), born 1789, and his son Heinrich (14), born 1832, there was a new century and the numbers in the Younger Line were reset (at 1) for boys born from 1801. And between the births of Heinrich (14), born 1832, and his son, Heinrich (27), born 1858, another twelve boys were born; one in their branch of the Younger Line (see chart 16) and eleven in other branches.

(Got it?)

The layout of the museum follows a timeline from the Reuss family's twelfth-century beginnings in Thuringia up to the Napoleonic Wars, when the Elder Line moved their residence from the Oberes to the Unteres Schloss. We began in the cellars, with the medieval brickwork of a romanesque double chapel, and worked our way up through the floors past the ballroom (called the Fürstensaal or Prince's Hall) to the rooms of Heinrich (11) and his son Heinrich XIII (13) (1747-1817). Heinrich (13) was the last prince of Reuss Elder Line to live in the Oberes Schloss. When the renovation of the Unteres Schloss was completed in 1809 (following the fire that destroyed much of Greiz in 1802) he moved down the hill. The Oberes Schloss was relegated to secondary status and used as government offices.

Heinrich (13) was born in the Oberes Schloss in 1747. He was the second son of Heinrich (11), but his elder brother died at a year old. Following in the family tradition, Heinrich (13) entered Austrian

70. Portrait of Heinrich XI (11) (left) in the Oberes Schloss; to the right his sons, Heinrich XIII (13) and Heinrich XV (15).

71. The corps de logis houses a museum on Reuss royal history.

military service in 1766 and rose from the rank of first lieutenant under Empress Maria Theresa to field marshal under her son Joseph II. In the 1780s he was Austrian envoy at the court of King Frederick the Great of Prussia[19]. The portraits of Heinrich (13) and his brother Heinrich XV (15) in the gallery at the Oberes Schloss show them in military uniform with stern expressions. Heinrich (13) saw active service against the French in the French Revolutionary and Napoleonic Wars. It must have been a bitter blow when he was forced by political necessity to resign from Austrian service in 1807 and take Reuss Elder Line into Napoleon's grouping of German states, called the Confederation of the Rhine. Fortunately, Heinrich (13) lived long enough to see Napoleon defeated and he returned to the Austrian military after the Battle of the Nations in 1813. The sovereignty of Reuss Elder Line was confirmed at the Congress of Vienna in 1815 and it joined the new German Confederation under Austrian presidency.

The Oberes Schloss holds a mine of information about the house of Reuss. Although none of it was translated into English, large parts of the display were visual making this museum accessible even for a non-German speaker. I enjoyed the gallery of large and colourful family portraits for the Elder Line and applauded a series of maps showing the composition of all the Reuss states and sub-states at different dates. This is such an effective way of explaining a complicated situation. Most remarkable were large charts on each landing of the stairwell, with timelines setting the history of Greiz and the Reuss Elder Line in the context of the Holy Roman Empire and wider European history.

At the end of the museum tour, visitors are invited to stay a while and enjoy the marvellous views of Greiz from the Kleiner Fürstensaal (Small Prince's Hall). Please make the time (as we did) and the friendly curators may make you a cup of coffee.

Sommerpalais Greiz

Sommerpalais (summer palace) Greiz is situated in Princes Park at the base of castle hill. The beginnings of this park were as a kitchen garden for the Oberes (Upper) Schloss that towers above it. When the young Count Heinrich XI (11) of Obergreiz (Upper Greiz) returned from his grand tour of Europe, his head was full of the glories of French art and architecture. He decided to build a Sommerpalais and baroque garden there, as his idyllic summer retreat. The French words *Maison de belle retraite* (beautiful retreat house) are inscribed on the grand gable front. Heinrich (11) also came home with the habits of a collector and continued acquiring books and engravings during his long reign. These became a founding pillar of the Greiz State Books and Engravings Collection housed in the Sommerpalais since 1922. Another pillar of their collection is more surprising – the books and engravings of an English princess!

Heinrich (11) (1722-1800) became the count of Obergreiz when he was one day short of his first birthday. He was the youngest of the four sons of Heinrich II (2) of Obergreiz (1696-1722). Two of these died before their father as small children and when Heinrich (2) died in 1722, he was succeeded by the oldest of his two surviving sons, Heinrich IX (9), born in 1718. The little boy reigned for four months before he too died, aged four[20]. The new one-year-old count, Heinrich (11), proved more robust and reigned for seventy-seven years.

Heinrich (11) was a bright little boy who received an excellent education from his guardian, Heinrich XXIV (24) of Reuss-Köstritz (a non-ruling branch of Reuss Younger Line). To finish off his education, as was customary for young princes, Heinrich (11) undertook the grand

72. Greiz Sommerpalais – the Garden Hall stretches
the full length of the ground floor.

tour of Europe between 1740 and 1742, visiting France, Italy, and
Germany. He was particularly influenced by a long stay in France where
he imbibed French culture and the ideas of the Enlightenment. Back
home in Upper-Greiz he came of age in 1743 to marry the daughter of
his guardian and take over the government of his state[21]. His domains
increased further when he inherited Untergreiz (Lower Greiz) in 1768
and the territories of Reuss Elder Line were reunited in a single state.
But Heinrich (11) was dissatisfied with his rank and aspired to princely
status. For years he persistently lobbied the emperor for this much-
desired title, providing soldiers for the imperial armies and paying
large sums into the imperial treasury[22]. Building the Sommerpalais was
partly to demonstrate that his lifestyle was befitting of a prince. On 12
May 1778, the ambition of Heinrich (11) was achieved when Emperor
Joseph II created him first prince of the Reuss Elder Line. To reflect his
new status, Heinrich (11) continued to further embellish and enhance
his Sommerpalais.

It was a short walk along the riverbank from the Unteres Schloss
to Sommerpalais Greiz in Princes Park. This park has been in public

ownership since the monarchy fell and in the GDR time was known as Lenin Park. Heinrich (11) surrounded the Sommerpalais with a French-style baroque garden, but after this was swamped in a major flood of 1799 the formal gardens were gradually redeveloped in the new English landscape style. When there were plans to put a railway line to Greiz along the riverbank, Heinrich XXII (22) (1846-1902) saved the park by rerouting the line through castle hill (a tremendous feat of engineering). With over a hundred acres, Greiz Princes Park has a large lake, monuments, curving walks, groves of trees, flower gardens, and a pinetum (rare conifers). There are fine views of the Oberes Schloss on top of castle hill. The Sommerpalais was completely restored between 2005 and 2011 and is in excellent condition. An elegant and beautifully proportioned building, surrounded by green lawns, it sparkled in the afternoon sun. This was my favourite of the three schlösser in Greiz.

The interior was just as delightful as the exterior with charming décor and an unusual layout. What is different is that the ground floor of the Sommerpalais is mostly taken up by one large, long, room. The Gartensaal (Garden Hall) stretches the entire length of the building with floor to ceiling windows on three sides. Doors on the fourth side lead to a corridor that runs behind the hall with access to the staircase and the service rooms on the north side of the building. The Garden Hall faces south and was used for entertainment and concerts when the prince was in summer residence. It is decorated with fluted pilasters and delicate stuccowork in motifs of flowers, garden tools and musical instruments. The date 1783 over the mirror above the fireplace shows when the work was completed[23]. Everything (walls, ceiling, columns, plasterwork) is painted in a monochrome shade of white and this adds to the airiness and lightness of the room. The Garden Hall was cluttered with display boards when we visited for an exhibition of the museum's collection of satirical cartons and caricatures, but nothing could disguise the stunning beauty of this space.

On the first floor, above the Garden Hall, is the enfilade of state rooms with the Festsaal (Ballroom) in the centre, the prince's apartments to one side and those of his wife to the other. The Ballroom (as the Garden Hall) is painted a single muted colour and relies entirely on the exquisite plasterwork for embellishment. To either side of it the rooms become more colourful and lavishly decorated as the enfilade unfolds, culminating in the Rotes Eckkabinett (Red Corner Cabinet) on the prince's side with bright pink walls, garlands of plasterwork, and lashings of golden gilding[24]. There are portraits of both wives of Heinrich (11) in the room called the Elizabeth Gallery in the prince's apartments (he married again after the death of his first wife); and that of his childhood tutor in the Cabinet with the Green Fireplace (named after the colour of the marble fireplace). The tutor was a big influence on Heinrich (11) and accompanied the young count on his grand tour[25]. In the princess's apartment, the Cabinet with the Red Fireplace has brightly coloured wallpaper with vivid flower baskets and paintings whose subjects represent the arts. Her side of the enfilade ends in the Grünes Eckkabinett (Green Corner Cabinet) where gilded niches on the panelling show this room was used to display porcelain.

73. The lake of the Sommerpalais in Greiz Princes Park
with a view of the Oberes (Upper) Schloss.

Sommerpalais Greiz was used as a royal summer home until World War I and became the property of the state after the last prince gave up his throne[26]. By an agreement of 1921, the library of books and engravings of the Reuss Elder Line was also transferred to the State of Thuringia[27]. The Sommerpalais was fitted out with display shelves and bookcases and opened as a museum to display this collection on 27 August 1922. Quite unexpectedly and very kindly, the curator presented us with a book on the collection at the end of the visit. One major part of the 1921 bequest was the books and engravings of Heinrich (11); another originated with a British royal – Princess Elisabeth of Great Britain and Ireland (1770-1840). I am frequently astonished by the close links forged by intermarriage between Europe's royal families. Elizabeth's books and pictures came to Greiz through her marriage in 1818 to a German prince and the marriage of her husband's niece in 1839 to Heinrich XX (20) of Reuss Elder Line, the grandson of Heinrich (11).

Elizabeth was the third of the six daughters of King George III and Queen Charlotte. Their daughters did not follow the usual path of a teenage marriage to a foreign prince, arranged for dynastic reasons. Their parents did not seem at all keen to marry them off. Elizabeth was intelligent, well-educated, an accomplished artist, and a collector. She became immensely frustrated with her spinster life at home under the close supervision of her mother. Eventually, when she was almost forty-eight, Elizabeth married Landgrave Friedrich VI of Hesse-Homburg. Her story is told at Schloss Bad Homburg in *Schloss*. On her death in 1840, Elizabeth willed her books and prints to her niece by marriage (the daughter of her husband's younger brother), Karoline of Hesse-Homburg (1819-1872). Karoline was the wife of Heinrich XX (20) of Reuss Elder Line and the mother of Heinrich XXII (22). She ruled Reuss Elder Line as regent between the death of her husband in 1859 and her son's majority in 1867 (see Unteres Schloss Greiz).

Sommerpalais Greiz had a narrow escape during World War II. The National Socialist (Nazi) government planned to convert the schloss into a hotel and restaurant but as the war began to go against Germany these plans had to be shelved (thank goodness)[28]. The schloss was used instead as a military hospital and after the war it reopened as a museum. The Sommerpalais and its park remain a public amenity for everyone to enjoy.

Osterstein

Osterstein is built on a mountain spur above the town of Gera in eastern Thuringia, twenty miles north of Greiz. The heyday of Osterstein was during the rule of Heinrich I (1) of Reuss-Gera (1572-1635), known as *Posthumous* because he was born two months after his father's death. He was the son of Heinrich XVI (16) (1530-1572), the founder of the Younger Line when the house of Reuss divided in 1564 (see the text box on page 143). Heinrich *Posthumous* liked to keep a flamboyant court and Osterstein was the scene of many celebrations, tournaments, and banquets. When his youngest daughter Ernestine was christened here in 1618, the guests drank over five thousand bottles of wine and fifteen thousand pints of beer[29]. After his death, the surviving sons of Heinrich *Posthumous* divided the Younger Line in 1647 and the eldest became ruler of a reduced-in-size Reuss-Gera. When this branch died out in 1802, Osterstein fell in importance.

A fresh lease of life for Osterstein began when the territories of the Younger Line were consolidated in 1848 and Heinrich LXII (62) became the first prince of a new sovereign state called Reuss Younger Line (or alternatively Reuss-Gera). (It is important here to distinguish between the term Younger Line used to encompass all the branches descended from Heinrich (16) on the split of 1564; and the name of the new state established in 1848 called Reuss Younger Line.) Gera was the capital of the new state and over the next sixty-five years the princes of Reuss Younger Line developed Osterstein as their grand residence. When Princess Eleonore of Reuss-Köstritz (a non-ruling branch of the Younger Line) made a dynastic marriage to Tsar Ferdinand of Bulgaria in March 1908 the wedding was at Osterstein. But there is little left of

74. Osterstein at Gera before it was destroyed by bombing in 1945.

the schloss today. Osterstein was destroyed during World War II in an allied bombing raid on Gera on 6 April 1945.

A family tree for the princes of Reuss Younger Line is set out in chart 16. The first prince, Heinrich (62) (1785-1854) was born a count of Reuss-Schleiz. This was another ruling branch of the Younger Line dating from the 1647 division by the sons of Heinrich *Posthumous*. Heinrich (62) was one of six sons, four of whom died as children[30]. He succeeded his father in Reuss-Schleiz in 1818 and became prince of the newly created state of Reuss Younger Line on its foundation in 1848. Heinrich (62) never married and was succeeded in 1854 by his sole surviving brother, Heinrich LXVII (67) (1789-1867). Heinrich (67) came to the throne at the relatively late age of sixty-four. He was a career general in the Prussian cavalry and sided with Prussia against Austria in the Seven Weeks' War of 1866. Reuss Younger Line therefore avoided the same fate as Reuss Elder Line which supported Austria and suffered Prussian occupation and a heavy indemnity. Heinrich (67) had five sons, four of whom died as children, and was followed by his sole surviving son, Heinrich XIV (14) (1832-1913)[31].

Tinz

Wasserschloss Tinz (Tinz water castle) is located on the outskirts of Gera. It was built in the 1740s by Heinrich XXV (25) (1681-1748) of Reuss-Gera. After the last count of this branch of the Younger Line died in 1802, his

widow stayed on in Tinz as her dower house[32]. But after her death in 1829 the schloss was never again used as a royal residence and its fortunes declined. In the Franco-Prussian War of 1870 Tinz was a camp for French prisoners of war.

When the monarchy fell in 1918 the Reuss family kept ownership of Osterstein but ceded Tinz to the state. It was a military hospital during both World Wars; from 1960 it was used by the National People's Army of the GDR. The fabric of the schloss was altered and degraded; the canals (which were such a feature of the garden) were filled in; and a major road was put through the grounds in 1936.

Today Schloss Tinz is in excellent condition and looks very much as in the old photo dating from 1945 (see illustration). The schloss was restored from 2012 to become a library and part of the local educational college. We visited over the weekend when the college was closed and so were not able to see inside. The schloss is flanked by modern blocks, but it is great to see this historic building cared for and put to good use.

Like his father, Heinrich (14) served in the Prussian army and followed a pro-Prussian policy. He had one son from his first marriage to a duchess of Württemberg. After her death he married again but, as this was morganatic, any sons were not eligible for the succession. Heinrich (14) enjoyed a long reign and from 1902 was also regent of Reuss Elder Line on behalf of its mentally incapacitated prince (see Unteres Schloss Greiz). Declining health in his last years forced Heinrich (14) to hand over the government of both states to his son in 1908 (a few years before his death in 1913). Heinrich XXVII (27) (1858-1928) was the fourth and last reigning prince of Reuss

75. Prince Heinrich XIV (14) of Reuss Younger Line.

Younger Line. When the revolution came to Gera at the end of World War I, he issued his abdication document from Osterstein on 10 November 1918. On the death of the last prince of Reuss Elder Line in 1927, Heinrich (27) became head of the entire house of Reuss.

Illustration 74 (kindly provided by Gera City Archive) shows how Osterstein looked before World War II. The most prominent feature to survive the bombing was the tower or keep, called the Bergfried. This is the oldest part of the schloss, dating to the thirteenth century, with walls up to twelve feet thick. Osterstein was built around two courtyards – the inner courtyard (to the left in the picture) and the outer courtyard (to the right). The inner courtyard was the more important, with buildings from across the centuries. The north and east wings dated back to Heinrich (16), founder of the Younger Line, and his son Heinrich *Posthumous*. Heinrich XVIII (18) of Reuss-Gera (1677-1735) created the Ahnensaal (Ancestral Hall) of family portraits in the east wing[33]. Following the establishment of the new state of Reuss Elder Line, Heinrich (67) built a south wing in 1859 to provide family accommodation; and Heinrich (27) the west wing between 1911 and 1913. This had entertaining rooms including the Tapestry Hall, music room and a library. The bombing raid on 6 April 1945 left the inner courtyard in ruins. What remained was blown up for safety reasons on 9 December 1962 and an ugly modern café built on the site.

76. The Ahnensaal or Ancestral Hall with family portraits.

The outer courtyard dated to the eighteenth-century and housed stables, farm buildings, offices, and accommodation for servants. This courtyard became the main entrance to the schloss; you can still see the bricked-up remains of an elaborate stone arch that led to the inner courtyard. The outer courtyard suffered less damage in the bombing and was restored and modernised during the 1960s. Some of its buildings served as homes during the GDR years. On our visit we found a gallery with an exhibition of modern art.

The site of Osterstein commands a superb hill-top position. It was a clear autumn day and there were stunning views over the sports stadium and town of Gera. The schloss is a popular spot with the locals: we met walkers on the path (once a defensive ditch) leading up to the Bergfried.

In the summer season there is a beer garden and music festival called *Sommer am Schloss* (Summer at the Schloss) in what was the inner courtyard. Part of the schloss garden (out of sight on the right in illustration 74) has been restored and was a pleasant place to sit in the sun.

77. Osterstein in the eighteenth century.

After the death of the last reigning prince in 1928 his only surviving son, Heinrich XLV (45) (1895-date not known), became the head of house. He was sometimes referred to affectionately by the citizens of Gera as *Ix-el-vau* (the German pronunciation of his roman numeral)[34]. When Thuringia became part of the Soviet occupation zone at the end of World War II, Heinrich (45) chose to stay and not to flee west. This was a big mistake. He was arrested at Schloss Ebersdorf in August 1945, taken to Buchenwald concentration camp, and never heard of again. He is thought to have died in the camp of starvation, probably in 1945[35]. On 5 January 1962 Heinrich (45) was declared legally dead[36]. He was unmarried and the last male of his branch of the Younger Line.

In 1935, Heinrich (45) had adopted Heinrich I (1) of Reuss-Köstritz (1910-1982) from another Younger Line branch. But this adoption did not apply to the succession as head of the house of Reuss. The headship passed to Heinrich IV (4) (1919-2012) from the Reuss-Köstritz branch whose family home is Schloss Ernstbrunn in Austria. The current head of house Reuss is his son, Heinrich XIV (14), born in 1955.

Osterburg

Osterburg at Weida (midway between Greiz and Gera) is known as The Cradle of the Vogtland. This is the ancestral schloss of the Reuss family. It was built from 1163 by Heinrich I Vogt of Weida and Gera (around 1122-1193). He was the son of Erkenbert I, the earliest documented member of the house of Reuss. The legendary Holy Roman Emperor Friedrich I Barbarossa (Red Beard) sent the first vogts (stewards or sheriffs) to pacify and rule lands in the east of his imperial domains. This is how their castle at Weida later became called Osterburg or Easterly Castle.

The symbol of Osterburg is its huge tower, fifty feet in diameter, one hundred and seventy-five feet high, and with walls up to eighteen feet thick. It has such a distinctive shape that Osterburg is instantly recognisable. The tower rises in three stepped tiers rather like an expanding telescope. Two tiers are topped by crenelated battlements and the third by a stone crown. The tower was built in the fourteenth century, but inside the base the original tower of Heinrich I survives; the new one was built around it.

The tower now hosts an exhibition about its building history, and a film projected through three hundred and sixty degrees around its circular walls telling the story of the Vogtland and the Reuss family.

From 1427 the ancestral schloss of the Reuss family belonged to the house of Wettin. In the 1485 division it was allocated to the (junior) Albertine line who remodelled Osterburg in renaissance style between 1537 and 1543. This was an early project for the famous architect Nikolaus (Nickel) Gromann who went on to build Fröhliche Wiederkunft (see chapter 2). After being destroyed by fire in 1633 (during the Thirty Years' War) Osterburg was rebuilt between 1667 and 1670 by Duke Moritz of Saxe-Zeitz (1619-1681) and its appearance has altered little since. The duchy of Saxe-Zeitz was a sub-branch of the Albertine line.

In the early eighteenth century Osterburg was at the centre of a scandal. In April 1717 Duke Moritz Wilhelm of Saxe-Zeitz (1664-1718), the son of Moritz, announced publicly his conversion to Catholicism. This caused outrage among his subjects and he was forced to leave his capital of Zeitz and retreat to Osterburg[37]. Europe watched with fascination as a Lutheran professor called August Hermann Francke arrived at Osterburg to tussle with the duke for his soul[38]. The professor won the battle; Moritz Wilhelm renounced Catholicism to become Protestant again just weeks before he died at Osterburg in November 1718.

After the Napoleonic Wars, Osterburg passed to the Ernestine line and the dukes of Saxe-Weimar-Eisenach. Grand Duchess Maria Pavlovna (see Belvedere in chapter 5) had a picture of Osterburg painted in 1859 as part of a series of the duchy's schlösser to hang in Residenzschloss Weimar[39]. The artist depicted a romantic scene. Osterburg stands on a steep rocky ridge, highlighted against the backdrop of a cloudy sky. At the base of the ridge the town of Weida nestles amid the trees and, in the foreground, some peasants tend the sheep in the fields. I loved this picture and bought a poster to bring home.

It was a steep climb up to see Osterburg, but worth the effort. At the top we found a café with a view, and a museum whose enthusiastic curator was willing to spend time with us and share her passion.

Ebersdorf

I was familiar with the name of Reuss-Ebersdorf long before I started to write about German schlösser. My interest in royal history began with Queen Victoria and studying her colourful life story led me naturally to take an interest in her many German relatives. Victoria's grandmother (on her mother's side) was born Augusta of Reuss-Ebersdorf (1757-1831). As the widow of the duke of Saxe-Coburg-Saalfeld, she became the doughty matriarch of the Saxe-Coburg clan. I wanted to go to Ebersdorf to see Augusta's childhood home.

78. Ebersdorf was the residence of the princes of Reuss-Ebersdorf.

The state of Reuss-Ebersdorf was founded in 1678 on a subdivision of the Younger Line. The family tree for its rulers is shown in chart 17. The first count of Reuss-Ebersdorf was Heinrich X (10) (1662-1711), who was still a minor and under the guardianship of a relative. In 1682 his guardian purchased the old, moated manor house at Ebersdorf as the new count's residence. But when he reached his majority and took over the government, Heinrich (10) did not think the manor house good enough for his status. To his mind it did not compare favourably with the residence schlösser of other Reuss branches. So, Heinrich (10) had the manor house demolished and built a baroque schloss in its place. Only when this was completed in 1694 did he feel sufficiently established to get married and move in[40]. Heinrich (10) and his wife were devout and under his reign Ebersdorf became a centre of Pietism in Thuringia. This was a religious movement that began in the seventeenth century and put great emphasis on personal piety and living a Christian life. Their son, Heinrich XXIX (29) (1699-1747), founded a religious community at the schloss under which the whole village worshiped together in the ballroom; master and servants on equal terms[41].

Somewhat disappointingly, there was not a great deal to see at Ebersdorf when we visited. The schloss has been empty and shuttered for many years. The road runs close to the south wing, but this part of the building looked so unprepossessing we drove right past without realising what it was. Only a glimpse through the trees of a grander elevation caused us to stop and explore. This was the west front with classical pediment and pillars (see illustration 80) remodelled from 1788 by Heinrich LI (51) (1761-1822). He was the fourth ruler of Reuss-Ebersdorf and the first to hold the rank of prince (from 1806).

Queen Victoria's grandmother, Augusta of Reuss-Ebersdorf, was the sister of Heinrich (51). She was married at Ebersdorf on 13 June 1777 to Franz Friedrich Anton (1750-1806), heir to the duchy of Saxe-Coburg-Saalfeld (see chapter 3). Augusta was his second wife. Franz Friedrich Anton's first wife died the previous October after just a few months of marriage[42]. Augusta was a determined young woman with a strong character. A contemporary said she '... united all the softness of her own sex with the firmness of the other. Undaunted by the storms of fate she never lost sight for a moment of her destination [destiny?] as a wife and mother.' [43]. Franz Friedrich Anton was an amiable and cultured man who enjoyed the good things in life. Augusta was always devoted to him even though he was flagrantly unfaithful[44]. Between 1778 and 1792 the couple had ten children of whom seven survived to adulthood.

Augusta always fondly remembered her childhood days at Ebersdorf. Years later on a visit to the schloss she wrote in her diary

... sweet memories came to me as I drove through the well remembered countryside. Memories of my early childhood and youth. ... The long years seemed to have vanished, and I felt myself a child again, with all the joys of life in front of me. That Ebersdorf should have changed so little is a real happiness to me.[45]

Fortunately, I was able to read Duchess Augusta's words in English. A book of extracts from her private diaries (translated into English) was published in 1941 by her great granddaughter (Queen Victoria's youngest daughter) Princess Beatrice. Called 'In Napoleonic Days' the extracts cover the turbulent years of the Napoleonic Wars and Beatrice felt they had some resonance in the dark days of World War II. When the book opens in April 1806 the French have defeated Austria at the battle of Austerlitz and the Holy Roman empire is breaking up. Later in the year French soldiers were billeted in Ebersdorf and Napoleon himself stayed overnight in the schloss prior to the battle at nearby Schleiz on 9 October[46]. Augusta was not far away at Saalfeld (chapter 3) where she witnessed the battle of Saalfeld on 10 October from the schloss windows. Her diary is a compelling account of the horrors

79. Augusta of Reuss-Ebersdorf, matriarch of the Saxe-Coburg clan.

of living in a war zone – of the unburied bodies of men and horses lying on the battlefield; the sacked and burning villages and destitute population; and the local men and boys conscripted to fight for Napoleon who never returned home. Even tiny Reuss-Ebersdorf had to provide a quota of soldiers for Napoleon's armies. Augusta records personal tragedy too as, after his duchy of Saxe-Coburg-Saalfeld was invaded and the revenues sequestered by Napoleon, Augusta's husband died in December 1806 broken by the shock of events.

With his crushing victory over the Prussians at the battle of Jena-Auerstedt (in Thuringia) on 14 October 1806, Napoleon was the dominant force in Germany. Of necessity, Augusta's brother, Heinrich (51), with the other Thuringian princes, abandoned the centuries-old allegiance to the Austrian Holy Roman emperor. They jumped ship to join the French emperor's new political grouping of German states called the Confederation of the Rhine. But as soon as it became clear that the tide had turned against Napoleon at the Battle of the Nations in October 1813, they again jumped ship to the winning side! Heinrich (51) was part of the delegation of Reuss princes who welcomed the Austrian emperor to Gera a few days after the battle[47]. As a result of this timely political manoeuvring, Reuss-Ebersdorf with all the other Thuringian royal states survived to be reinstated at the Congress of Vienna in 1815 and become members of the new German Confederation.

After she was widowed in 1806 at the relatively young age of forty-nine, Augusta focused her considerable powers on advancing the interests of her children. She would have been a role model for her granddaughter Queen Victoria, who was widowed at forty-two and became the stern matriarch of an enormous family. In later years Augusta's diaries record happier events, including the marriages of her children that were the foundation of the family's great rise in fortunes. Chart 18 has a list of Augusta's children, their marriages, and the thrones descended from them. For more on their incredibly successful Saxe-Coburg and Gotha marriage policy see Callenberg in *Schloss in Bavaria*.

The last prince of Reuss-Ebersdorf, Heinrich LXXII (72) (1797-1853), was Augusta's nephew (the son of her brother) and thus a first cousin (once-removed) of Queen Victoria. Heinrich (72) is remembered for a brief tangle in summer 1843 with the notorious femme fatale, Lola Montez. The middle-aged bachelor prince met Lola on a visit to London, where she had just caused a sensation with her debut on the stage as a Spanish dancer. Heinrich (72) paid off Lola's debts and invited her to Ebersdorf[48]. It was her first foray into continental Europe. The visit was short-lived and a disaster; Lola was rude, boorish, and generally behaved badly. Heinrich (72) soon lost patience and paid her to leave[49]. She travelled around Europe and in October 1846 turned up in Munich where her affair with King Ludwig I would be a disaster and contribute to his loss of the throne (see Nymphenburg in *Schloss in Bavaria*).

Heinrich (72) was responsible for a new word entering the German language – 'Prinzipienreiter' which translates as 'principles rider', or more broadly as a man obsessed with principles. In 1844 the prince became incensed by what he saw as lack of respect to state officials. He issued a decree insisting they be addressed by their correct titles and stating this was 'a principle he had ridden for twenty years'[50]. It conjures up a comic mind picture!

1848 was the year of revolutions across Europe and like rulers of other German states, Heinrich (72) faced demands for representative government, freedom of the press, and other reforms. He gave way but it did not calm the unrest. On 1 October 1848, Heinrich (72) abdicated and Reuss-Ebersdorf was absorbed into the new state of Reuss Younger Line. The last prince went to Dresden in exile and never returned to his old homeland. He died unmarried in 1853 and was the last of the Reuss-Ebersdorf branch of the Younger Line.

Ebersdorf remained a much-loved Reuss family home until it was expropriated by the Soviet occupying forces after World War II. Princess Woizlawa-Feodora Reuss (1918-2019) always remembered it as her favourite schloss. The princess was born just a month after the German monarchy fell and lived to see the centenary of the republic.

80. The west front at Ebersdorf, remodelled by Heinrich LI (51).

She was the niece of Heinrich XLV (45) of Reuss Younger Line (her mother was his sister) and in 1939 she married his adopted son, Heinrich I (1) of Reuss-Köstritz. Osterstein in Gera (see above) was their home. When Osterstein was bombed in the closing weeks of war, the family fled to Ebersdorf and this is where Heinrich (45) was arrested by the Soviets. Princess Woizlawa-Feodora and her husband fled to Bavaria in the west[51]. After the reunification of Germany, the princess returned to live in Gera close to her old home at Osterstein[52].

During the GDR years, Ebersdorf was converted for use as an old people's home. This closed in 2000 and since then the schloss has been empty and unused. The building is reported to be suffering from dry rot and the cost of restoration is expected to be enormous. But there is the glimmer of a better future for Ebersdorf. In December 2017, the schloss and park were sold by the local government to the house of Reuss for the nominal figure of one hundred thousand euros. The intention is to restore the schloss as a home for a cousin of the current head of house, Heinrich XIX (19) (born 1976)[53]. The sale was not without controversy as critics hoped it might be restored as a museum and local amenity[54].

7.

SCHWARZBURG-SONDERSHAUSEN AND SCHWARZBURG-RUDOLSTADT

The royal house of Schwarzburg is the oldest noble family in Thuringia. Division of the house in the sixteenth century created two lasting branches that survived as sovereign territories until the monarchy fell – Schwarzburg-Sondershausen (with the capital at Sondershausen in the north of Thuringia) and Schwarzburg-Rudolstadt (with the capital at Rudolstadt in the south). This chapter includes fascinating schlösser from both principalities.

The colourful stories of the Schwarzburg princes echo two themes that run throughout this book – the problems caused by family rules on inheritance, and the failure of so many royal houses to produce sons. At Sondershausen we meet Heinrich I (called *the Diamond Prince* after his passion for collecting the raw stones). He was a second son who refused to accept his father's right to disinherit him by bringing in primogeniture. At Heidecksburg in Rudolstadt I first heard of Prince Sizzo – a reigning prince's only son, but who could not succeed his father because his mother was adopted and not born royal. Bachelor princes and childless marriages led to the house of Schwarzburg running out of eligible male heirs.

The last prince of Schwarzburg was Günther Viktor who reigned in Schwarzburg-Rudolstadt from 1890 and also in Schwarzburg-Sondershausen from 1909. He was the last of all the German princes to abdicate when the monarchy fell. The life story of his wife, Anna Luise, as told to me by the curator at Schwarzburg was some of the history I most enjoyed discovering for this book.

Sondershausen

Sondershausen came into the ownership of the house of Schwarzburg by inheritance in 1356 and was a Schwarzburg residence for six hundred years. Princess Anna Luise (widow of the last reigning Schwarzburg prince) died there in 1951. Over the centuries the Schwarzburg counts and princes rebuilt, remodelled, and extended Sondershausen with the result that is a quirky mix of architectural styles. In the literature the schloss is described as an 'irregular four-wing complex', but this hardly does justice to its most unusual shape (see illustration 81). My visit to Sondershausen was exciting and enormously enjoyable, due to the quick-thinking staff who improvised and found a way to help me unravel its history. Sondershausen is a favourite schloss in this book.

We like to beat the crowds and always aim to arrive early, ready for opening time. At Sondershausen we were the first visitors of the day and the staff were still having their early morning meeting in the grand room that houses the ticket office. The arrival of English visitors asking about the family history caused something of a flurry and they went into a German-speaking huddle. When the huddle broke up, we were taken to see the Blauersaal (Blue Room) in the West Wing built in the 1760s by Prince Christian Günther of Schwarzburg-Sondershausen. This lively and joyous concert hall, decorated in intense sky-blue with white highlights and gilding (blue and white were the national colours of Schwarzburg-Sondershausen[1]), is all curves and waves, lightness, and clarity. We did not realise until our return to the ticket office that the suggestion to see it was a delaying tactic while one of the staff messaged her son to come to the schloss. This helpful young man kindly gave up his morning to accompany us on a personal tour with the curator and translate the German commentary. Thank you, Paul!

81. Sondershausen with (clockwise from the right) the west wing, new north wing (extending into old north wing), tower, east wing, and south wing.

Our tour began in the ancestral gallery where the story of Sondershausen and its princes is told in a memorable way through a collection of family portraits. I am a firm believer in the adage 'A picture tells a thousand words'. I love looking at portraits because they fix the characters in my mind and help me to remember their stories. The portrait gallery at Sondershausen is housed in a long enfilade of rooms, organised chronologically.

The House of Schwarzburg

The earliest likely ancestor of the house of Schwarzburg was Gundhareus (or Günther) mentioned in a papal document of 722[2]. The first to use the name of Schwarzburg (taken from Schloss Schwarzburg – see below), and from whom descent can be more reliably traced, was Graf (count) Sizzo of Schwarzburg (around 1090-1160).

In 1571, the four sons of Günther XL (40) (1499-1552) divided their inheritance. Johann Günther I (1532-1586) became the first count of Schwarzburg-Sondershausen and Albrecht VII (1537-1605) of Schwarzburg-Rudolstadt. When the two other sons died without heirs, their lands were reabsorbed on a further reorganisation of 1599. The two states of Schwarzburg-Sondershausen and Schwarzburg-Rudolstadt then endured until the end of the monarchy in 1918. Each had lands in both the north and south of Thuringia. The counts of Schwarzburg-Sondershausen were elevated to the rank of prince in 1697 and the counts of Schwarzburg-Rudolstadt in 1710. (Anton Albrecht of Schwarzburg-Rudolstadt (1641-1710) had declined the promotion in 1697, but accepted it in 1710).

In 1713 Christian Wilhelm of Schwarzburg-Sondershausen (1647-1721) and Ludwig Friedrich I of Schwarzburg-Rudolstadt (1667-1718) made an agreement on the house rules for inheritance. This confirmed the right of primogeniture (introduced in Rudolstadt in 1710 and Sondershausen in 1713) and provided that should either side of the house became extinct in the male line the other would inherit. This provision kicked in two hundred years later on the death of Karl Günther of Schwarzburg-Sondershausen (1830-1909) when the house of Schwarzburg was reunited under Günther Viktor of Schwarzburg-Rudolstadt (1852-1925). Günther Viktor used the title 'prince of Schwarzburg' but the two principalities remained separate and he ruled both in a personal union. Revolution came peacefully to the Schwarzburg principalities. Günter Viktor was the only German prince to abdicate by special law passed by the democratic parliaments of both his states[3]. He was also the last reigning prince to go, signing the documents for Rudolstadt on 23 November 1918 and for Sondershausen two days later.

As we progressed slowly down the enfilade from room to room the curator pointed out key characters and provided pen-pictures. In the first room were pictures of early members of the house, including Günther XXI (21) of Schwarzburg-Blankenburg (1304-1349). Günther (21) is the most famous Schwarzburg because in 1349 he briefly held the title of Holy Roman emperor. He was not a notable emperor and abdicated after only a few weeks, but they are proud of him in Thuringia. From the first room there was an enticing view down the enfilade to the portrait of Günther Viktor (1852-1925) at the other end. Günther Viktor was the last reigning prince of Schwarzburg and abdicated when the monarchy fell. In the centuries between Günther (21) and Günther Viktor were many colourful counts and princes who played a role in the family story and the building of Sondershausen.

82. The west wing houses the joyous Blauersaal (Blue Room).

Günther XL (40) (1499-1552) spent his childhood in the old medieval castle at Sondershausen. After this was damaged in the Peasants' War of 1525, he rebuilt it as a renaissance palace starting in 1534. His new schloss had three wings (the east, south, and old north wings) and incorporated the tower of the medieval castle (built around 1300). The Vault room in the tower survives and is part of the museum tour. Günther (40) is known to history as Günther *the Rich* because he was lucky enough to benefit from the early deaths of his brother and cousin to consolidate much of the Schwarzburg lands and wealth[4]. His other epithet is more difficult to fathom – Günther *with the Fat Mouth*! After his death, the sons of Günther (40) divided and re-divided their inheritance to create the principalities of Schwarzburg-Sondershausen and Schwarzburg-Rudolstadt.

Chart 19 gives a family tree for the princes of Schwarzburg-Sondershausen. The first prince, Christian Wilhelm (1647-1721), gave Sondershausen a makeover in the baroque architectural style, starting in the 1690s. You need a separate ticket to see his thrilling ballroom which takes up the entire second floor of the south wing. Named the Riesensaal (Giants' Hall) after sixteen larger-than-life stucco statues of Greek gods, this was my favourite room. It was inaugurated with a performance of opera and ballet to celebrate the fifty-fifth birthday of Christian Wilhelm in 1702[5]. Christian Wilhelm is an important figure in the family history who reigned in Schwarzburg-Sondershausen for more than fifty years. He ruled jointly with his brother, Anton Günther II (1653-1716), until they divided Schwarzburg-Sondershausen in 1681 to create Schwarzburg-Arnstadt for Anton Günther II (see Arnstadt below). In 1697 Christian Wilhelm achieved the coveted promotion to the rank of prince of the Holy Roman Empire.

Christian Wilhelm's decision to change the rules of inheritance to primogeniture fractured the relationship between his sons. The prince was married twice and had six sons – one from his first marriage and five from the second. The son of his first marriage, Günther I (1678-1740), benefited from the change to rule alone, but the younger sons (from Christian Wilhelm's second marriage) lost out and had to make do with a lower status and fixed incomes. (With the promotion to princes the numbering system began again, otherwise Prince Günther I would have been Count Günther XLIII (43)). Because of the family tension over inheritance, the ailing Christian Wilhelm decided to hand over the government before he died and abdicated in favour of his eldest son in 1720.

83. View from the marketplace with the Prinzenpalais on the right.

Günther I built the Prinzenpalais (Princes' Palace) at Sondershausen between 1721 and 1729 to provide for his younger half-brothers[6]. The eldest half-brother, Heinrich I (1689-1758), felt himself to be very badly treated and refused to accept the new rule. He carried on a feud with his elder brother (Günther I), who preceded him on the throne, and tried to disinherit the nephew (Christian Günther, son of his younger brother August), who succeeded him. Heinrich I even went so far as to leave his personal fortune away from the family and instead to the heir to the duchy of Saxe-Coburg-Saalfeld[7]. This led to a lengthy lawsuit between the two principalities after his death[8].

Heinrich I may be the least admirable of the Schwarzburg-Sondershausen princes, but he is certainly one of the most interesting. He is known as *the Diamond Prince* due to a penchant for collecting raw diamonds. He loved to travel and spent time in the Netherlands where he had contacts in the diamond trade[9]. Heinrich I was more focused on acquiring wealth and having a good time than on state affairs, or benefiting his country. He raised money by deplorable means, including illegally selling state offices[10]. His more upright and thrifty nephew Christian Günther was later forced to investigate and negate many of these transactions. As well as diamonds, Heinrich I collected horse carriages. Around 1738 he purchased *Die Goldene Kutsche* (the Golden Carriage) from France and brought it to Sondershausen where it has been ever since. This is Heinrich I's glittering legacy to the schloss, rather than any building project. According to the rules of royal etiquette of the day, the prince of Schwarzburg-Sondershausen was entitled to have his state carriage pulled by six horses[11]. The Golden Carriage is displayed in the coach house being drawn by six full-size model white horses. It is an astonishing work of art!

The Golden Carriage is a grand carrosse or type of state carriage developed in the reign of King Louis XIV. This was the ultimate status symbol for the prince of a small German court wanting to emulate *the Sun King* of France. Today the carriage is the sole example in Germany and one of only four worldwide. It is huge – twenty feet long, six and a half feet wide, and weighing two tons[12]. The two pairs of horses nearest the coach took the weight and the front pair did the steering. The coach has built-in suspension for the comfort of royal passengers. The gilded and delicately painted cabin is hung above the chassis on leather straps and a footman walked on either side to prevent it from swaying.

Soon after he followed his uncle to the throne in 1758, Christian Günther (1736-1794) embarked on major building works at Sondershausen, doubling the length of the old north wing (with an extension called the new north wing) and adding the west wing at an acute angle to this (see illustration 81). The historic rooms on show dating from this era include the Blauersaal (Blue Room) in the centre of the west wing, where we began our visit; and the Steinzimmer (Stone Room) in the new north wing clad in tiles of beautiful, polished limestone.

Günther Friedrich Karl I (1760-1837) was the reigning prince during the tricky times of the Napoleonic Wars. The curator pointed out graffiti in the chapel left by soldiers from the battle of Jena-Auerstedt in October 1806. Troops from Schwarzburg-Sondershausen fought for Napoleon in the battle, but the prince himself was not a military man.

It is thought that Günther Friedrich Karl I may have helped the defeated Prussian king escape the battlefield[13]. He was a jovial personality who liked to spend time hunting and with his many mistresses. His wife took their children and went to live separately in Arnstadt[14]. But his arch-conservative style of government was out of step with the growing pressure for reform. In 1835 he was ousted in a palace coup led by his son and forced to abdicate[15].

Günther Friedrich Karl II (1801-1889) swept away a group of buildings in front of the east wing of Sondershausen between 1837 and 1839 to create a grand new entrance in the classical style with a broad terrace and steps down to a new guard house in the marketplace next to the Prinzenpalais. Günther Friedrich Karl II had three sons from his two marriages (two from his first and one from his second) but it was not enough to secure the succession and his line died out in the next generation. (For how the princes of Schwarzburg-Sondershausen ran out of sons see chart 20). Towards the end of his life Günther Friedrich Karl II suffered from eye problems and abdicated in favour of his son in 1880.

Karl Günther (1830-1909) was the last prince of the Schwarzburg-Sondershausen line. He married in 1869 but there were no children. Neither of his younger brothers ever married, although both had illegitimate offspring[16]. Karl Günther was reported to have come to blows with his brother Leopold (1832-1906) in 1890 over the urgent need for him to marry and perpetuate the line[17].

84. Karl Günther was the last prince of Schwarzburg-Sondershausen.

Karl Günther suffered a serious hunting accident in 1906 and spent the last years of his life as an invalid. When he died in 1909 the Schwarzburg-Sondershausen line came to an end. Under the family agreement of 1713, the house of Schwarzburg was reunited (for the first time since 1571) under Günther Viktor of Schwarzburg-Rudolstadt. Karl Günther and Günther Viktor were first cousins (Karl Günther's mother was the sister of Günther Viktor's father). As we discover at Heidecksburg later in this chapter, the family agreement made two hundred years before did not solve the house of Schwarzburg succession crisis.

Neues Palais Arnstadt

Arnstadt was the second city in the principality of Schwarzburg-Sondershausen. At one time it was considered even more desirable as a noble residence than Sondershausen. When the four sons of Günther XL (40) divided their inheritance in 1571, the eldest son, Günther XLI (41) took Arnstadt and the second son got Sondershausen. Günther (41) rebuilt the old, moated castle at Arnstadt (called Schloss Neideck) as a renaissance palace just as his father had done before him with the castle at Sondershausen[18]. By the eighteenth century there were two more schlösser in and around the town – Augustenburg built by Anton Gunther II between 1699 and 1710 as a widow's residence for his wife, Auguste Dorothea; and the Neues Palais built between 1729 and 1735 by Günther I as a widow's residence for his, Elisabeth Albertine. Only the Neues Palais is still standing today, but treasures from all three schlösser have been preserved and are on display in its museum. These include the sixteenth-century Brussels tapestries from Neideck, the porcelain cabinet created by Günther I and Elisabeth Albertine at the Neues Palais, and (most amazing of all) the doll collection of Auguste Dorothea from Augustenburg.

Günther (41) (1529-1583) is historically the most important member of the house of Schwarzburg after Günther XXI (21), the Holy Roman

85. Neues Palais Arnstadt was built by Günther I of Schwarzburg-Sondershausen as a widow's residence for his wife.

emperor. Günther (41) is called *the Belligerent* because he spent most of his time away from home fighting in the imperial armies. He was held in high regard at the Hapsburg court and was able to rebuild Neideck using financial rewards from the emperor[19]. As a young man, Günther (41) did military training at the court of Nassau-Dillenburg where he became a close friend of Willem I of Orange (1533-1584), later stadtholder of Holland and leader of the Dutch revolt against Hapsburg rule. Willem was born a count of Nassau-Dillenburg and, as a child, inherited the title of prince of Orange from a cousin. In 1560, Willem was a guest at Neideck for the wedding of his sister Katharina to Günther (41). The royal guests and their entourages ate their way through a feast of one thousand sheep, two hundred and forty-five suckling pigs, eight hundred and forty rabbits, and three hundred partridges[20]! The Brussels tapestries of Günther (41) date to 1530 and were probably already in Neideck at this time. Günther (41) and

Katharina had no children and when he died Arnstadt was absorbed back into Schwarzburg-Sondershausen.

The sub-state of Schwarzburg-Arnstadt was recreated in 1681 for Anton Günther II (1653-1716). He was the younger brother of Christian Wilhelm of Schwarzburg-Sondershausen (1647-1721). Anton Günther II renovated Neideck as his residence and built a new schloss in Arnstadt called Augustenburg as a widow's residence for his wife, Auguste Dorothea. Anton Günther II was promoted to the rank of prince in 1697, at the same time as his older brother at Sondershausen, but delayed using the title for some years for fear of adverse reaction from the powerful house of Wettin. He was right to be concerned – the duke of Saxe-Weimar claimed sovereignty and occupied Arnstadt for a time in 1711[21]. Fortunately, Anton Günther II's wife was the aunt of Empress Elisabeth Christine (wife of Emperor Karl VI), so he had good connections to plead his case at the imperial court[22].

In 1684 Anton Günther II married Auguste Dorothea of Braunschweig-Wolfenbüttel (1666-1751). I was not surprised to learn

86. Auguste Dorothea of Schwarzburg-Arnstadt.

that Auguste Dorothea was a passionate art collector. She was the daughter of Anton Ulrich of Braunschweig-Wolfenbüttel whose fabulous art collection was the foundation of the Duke Anton Ulrich Museum in Braunschweig (see Wolfenbüttel in *Schloss II*). Auguste Dorothea established a pottery factory at Arnstadt with specialists from her father's factory in Braunschweig and created an amazing doll collection which she called *Mon Plaisir* (My Delight). After her husband's death, she lived on at

Augustenburg as a widow for thirty-five years until her own death in 1751. When the schloss was demolished just a few years later (in 1762) the doll collection came to the Neues Palais. No trace of Augustenburg remains today – only an old painting in the Neues Palais museum.

87. The ballroom in the historic rooms at Neues Palais Arnstadt.

The amazing Mon Plaisir doll museum at the Neues Palais was the life's work of Auguste Dorothea. Over fifty years the princess put together a collection of four hundred hand-made dolls, staged in eighty-two scenes of eighteenth-century royal life, and involving more than two-and-a-half thousand miniature items of furniture, household utensils, and other artefacts[23]. In a scene labelled 'Hofküche' (court kitchen) a team of cooks prepare food in a fully-equipped kitchen. There is a bustling market scene complete with stall holders, porter, and horse and cart. The musicians on stage in the court theatre play their miniature instruments to an audience of courtiers in the boxes. In 'Evening Entertainment' two elderly gentlemen sit at table playing cards while couples dance and the dancing master beats time with his stick. My favourite scene was 'Audience with the Princess'. The princess doll (Auguste Dorothea?) perches on the throne with her pet monkeys playing around her feet. Auguste Dorothea collaborated with her ladies-in-waiting, servants, and local craftsmen to create this incredible collection. Two clergymen fashioned the wax heads and hands of the dolls. Even the display cases are still original to Auguste Dorothea and the collection must be shown in dimmed light to preserve it.

When Prince Christian Wilhelm of Schwarzburg-Sondershausen introduced primogeniture for the principality in 1713, his younger brother Anton Günther II signed up to the agreement. His marriage to Auguste Dorothea was childless and on his death in 1716 Arnstadt reverted to Schwarzburg-Sondershausen. Nevertheless, there was still trouble: his nephew, Heinrich I (1689-1758), claimed Schwarzburg-Arnstadt by right as the second son of Christian Wilhelm (see chart 19). Heinrich I did not accept the new inheritance rule and decamped to Saxe-Weimar (his mother's home court) to drum up support to fight against it[24]. His aggrieved attitude led to a long-running family feud which continued even after he succeeded his elder brother (Günther I) in Schwarzburg-Sondershausen in 1740, and led to a lawsuit after his death in 1758 (see Sondershausen).

Günther I (1678-1740) preferred living in Arnstadt to Sondershausen. Unusually for royal circles, his marriage to Elisabeth Albertine of Anhalt-Bernburg (1693-1774) was a love match. Given the hostility of his brother Heinrich I, who was also his heir, Günther I was anxious to secure Elisabeth Albertine's financial position as a widow. He built the Neues Palais in Arnstadt for his wife and filled it with state treasures filched from Sondershausen to keep them out of the hands of Heinrich I[25]. The Neues Palais was located on a site next door to Neideck. The older schloss was the official residence in Arnstadt, but Günther I and Elisabeth Albertine were more likely to be found at the Neues Palais. After his death in 1740 Elisabeth Albertine spent her widowhood in the Neues Palais, dying there in 1774. After this the focus shifted away from Arnstadt and back to Sondershausen. Neideck became neglected and fell into ruins; following a part collapse, local people treated it as a quarry and took the stones for other building projects. Only the tower was secured and renovated; it is still there today.

88. The porcelain cabinet created by Günther I and Elisabeth Albertine.

The entrance to the Neues Palais is rather unusual. A narrow carriage drive runs all the way through the building flanked on either side by raised galleries with statue busts of emperors of the Roman Empire. Steps to the gallery on the right take visitors to the ticket office and shop; those on the left lead to the doll museum. The historic rooms on the first floor include a beautiful ballroom in the centre (called Der Grosse Speisesaal or large dining room) with large portraits of Günther I and Elisabeth Albertine and of his parents Christian Wilhelm and Antonie Sibille (illustration 87). The consecration of the Neues Palais took place in this room on 10 November 1734. Günther I and Elisabeth Albertine made a collection of Chinese and Japanese porcelain and I liked their delicious Porcelain Cabinet 'wallpapered' with items of porcelain displayed on special niches. We regard 'china' as a mundane household item of crockery to be used every day. But when the prince and his wife were collecting, porcelain was a hugely expensive luxury item affordable only by princes and intended as a work of art for display.

We ended our visit to Arnstadt at the *Bach in Arnstadt* exhibition on the second floor of the Neues Palais. In 1703, the eighteen-year-old Johann Sebastian Bach came to the town at the beginning of his musical career. He was employed as organist in the town church until 1707. Johann Sebastian came from a large family of professional musicians in Thuringia and was born in Eisenach where his father was director of music in the town. Arnstadt is often called *Bach Town* because four generations of the extended Bach family lived and worked here from 1620 to 1739[26]. The centrepiece of the exhibition is the organ keyboard from the church, commissioned in 1703, on which Johann Sebastian Bach played.

Heidecksburg

Heidecksburg at Rudolstadt was the residence of the princes of Schwarzburg-Rudolstadt. On the night of 26 to 27 July 1735, a huge fire raged through the schloss destroying much of the north and west wings. Friedrich Anton of Schwarzburg-Rudolstadt (1692-1744) decided to rebuild in imposing style as befitted his family's newly elevated status as princes of the Holy Roman Empire. His son, Johann Friedrich (1721-1767), fitted out the state rooms in the new west wing in my favourite architectural style. If I had to pick the perfect venue for the ball where Cinderella meets Prince Charming in the fairy-tale, it would be the exuberant rococo ballroom at Heidecksburg.

Chart 21 shows the family tree of the princes of Schwarzburg-Rudolstadt. Friedrich Anton followed his father to the throne in 1718, when he was twenty-six years old. From his father he also inherited a dispute over the high levels of taxation. The *Bulisius Controversy* (named after the lawyer who led the unrest) was a twenty-five-year campaign of civil disobedience which saw his subjects take the prince of Schwarzburg-Rudolstadt to the supreme court of the Holy Roman Empire to try and reduce the tax burden. The court eventually decided in favour of Friedrich Anton in 1731, but the long running dispute did not exactly make him popular in the country. Also, there was tension in Friedrich Anton's family over his younger brother's refusal to accept the new rule of primogeniture[27]. Wilhelm Ludwig (1696-1757) repeatedly ran up debts and had to be bailed out by his elder brother[28].

89. Heidecksburg was the residence of the princes of Schwarzburg-Rudolstadt.

Friedrich Anton engaged the Saxony court architect Johann Christoph Knöffel for the rebuilding of the west wing. The shell of the building went up quickly, but then the project ran into the sand. Knöffel was busy with other jobs in Dresden and did not have time to supervise the work at Heidecksburg. Progress slowed, costs escalated, and structural defects became apparent. In 1741 Friedrich Anton was forced to set up a building commission under the leadership of his son to oversee the work and sort out the problems. Johann Friedrich had good connections at the Saxe-Weimar court and engineered the appointment of the Weimar court architect, Gottfried Heinrich Krohne, to replace Knöffel. Krohne had already worked on the building of two delightful schlösser in this book for Duke Ernst August I of Saxe-Weimar and Eisenach (Belvedere at Weimar and Dornburger

Rococo Schloss – see chapter 5). The duke was soon to become Johann Friedrich's father-in-law; in 1744 he married Bernhardine Christine of Saxe-Weimar and Eisenach (1724-1757). Krohne retained much of his predecessor's plans at Heidecksburg but did make some important changes. One was to alter the decoration of the state rooms. Instead of the cool and simple décor Knöffel had intended, Krohne decided to use the more flamboyant and newly fashionable rococo style.

90. The exuberant rococo ballroom was a highlight of my visits to Thuringia.

The amazing suite of rococo state rooms commissioned by Johann Friedrich were a highlight of my visits to Thuringia. The rococo style is characterised by elaborate but delicate decoration and the use of curves, light colours, gold, and mirrors to create a feeling of elegance, lightness, and informality. The Marmorgalerie (Marble Gallery) leading into the Festsaal (Ballroom) has twelve fantasy landscapes showing people from all around the world. These are not real people or real landscape views; the paintings are part of the rococo decoration. I do not think I have ever been in a room that more assaults the senses (in a positive way) than the ballroom at Heidecksburg. It glitters and glistens with crystal chandeliers, china, mirrors, and the little pieces of marble embedded in the stuccoed walls. Decorative plasterwork shaped in curves and flourishes is enhanced by golden gilding. There are just no straight lines anywhere – even the walls wave in and out. I found it easy to imagine musicians playing on the golden balcony as Prince Charming whisks Cinderella in a dance around the room.

The Ballroom is flanked on either side by matching state apartments for the prince and princess – the Red Hall and Red Corner Cabinet on the south side (for the prince) and the Green Hall and Green Corner Cabinet to the north (for the princess.) Portraits of Johann Friedrich and his wife hang in the Green Hall. Bernhardine Christine died before her rooms were finished, aged only thirty-three. Johann Friedrich was left with four daughters but no son. He was succeeded as prince of Schwarzburg-Rudolstadt by his father's youngest brother Ludwig Günther (1708-1790). (The troublesome Wilhelm Ludwig was already dead.)

Johann Friedrich's eldest daughter married Ludwig Günther's only son and the future princes of Schwarzburg-Rudolstadt descended from this couple. A charming 1780 portrait of their five children playing together hangs in the Green Corner Chamber[29]. The elder boy Ludwig Friedrich II has a book in his hand while his younger brother Karl Günther builds a house out of playing cards. One sister sits at the keyboard and two younger girls are playing with their toys. This portrait tells a story as both sons would be important to the future succession. More than a century later, when the house of Schwarzburg was fast running out of male heirs, a feud would be played out between their grandsons.

The problems began with the death of the heir to the throne on 11 November 1845. Günther (1821-1845) was the last surviving son of reigning Prince Friedrich Günther (1793-1867), himself the son of the elder boy in the 1780 portrait. Friedrich Günther had three sons from his marriage to Auguste of Anhalt-Dessau, but the other two had already died as children. His heir was now his only brother Albrecht (1798-1869) and relationships between the two were not good[30].

The Kyffhäuser monument

The Kyffhäuser monument in northern Thuringia is a hugely popular attraction. We were there on German Unity Day when the whole of Thuringia seemed to be on the top of the Kyffhäuser mountain. 3 October is a public holiday in Germany to commemorate the anniversary of German reunification in 1990. There were fleets of coaches in the car park, hordes of bikers eating hot dogs from a stand, and flocks of families buying souvenirs. Everyone – from aged Grannie's to babies in prams – was toiling seven hundred yards up the hill to see the monument. At seven euros a head the organisers were doing very well.

The monument was funded by veterans of Bismarck's wars of German unification and built in the 1890s as a memorial to Kaiser Wilhelm I who became German emperor (kaiser) when the country was unified for the first time in 1871. The land on which it stands was part of the principality of Schwarzburg-Rudolstadt. Prince Günther Viktor (who usually avoided public appearances like the plague) made a speech at the inauguration on 18 June 1896.

Wilhelm I's memorial is massive, windswept, romantic, and great propaganda. It presents him as taking up the mantle of the famous Holy Roman Emperor Friedrich I Barbarossa (Redbeard). After Barbarossa died on crusade in 1190 the empire collapsed, and Germany fractured into small pieces of land. A legend took hold that Barbarossa was only asleep inside the Kyffhäuser mountain and one day would awake and emerge from his cave to herald in a new golden age.

It is well worth the climb to see Wilhelm I's memorial and experience the panoramic views. The monument is a nearly two-hundred-feet-high red sandstone tower sitting on an enormous platform and topped by a huge crown. At the base of the tower is a (twenty-feet-tall) statue of Barbarossa asleep on his throne. Above the sleeping emperor looms a copper statue (almost forty feet high) of Wilhelm I mounted on a horse. The symbolism and the message are clear. Here is Barbarossa's successor, who restored the glory of the German empire!

A further blow struck Friedrich Günther in 1854 when his wife Auguste died and then a few days later his mother. Karoline Luise (born Hesse-Homburg) had played a key role in his life, acting as regent while he was a minor and continuing to influence him. Friedrich Günther had come to the throne at thirteen and reigned for sixty years.

In the summer of 1855 Friedrich Günther disappeared from Rudolstadt for several weeks. During this time the sixty-one-year-old secretly married twenty-year-old Gräfin (countess) Helene von Reina as his second wife. The Schwarzburg-Rudolstadt family found out only after the event[31]. Helene was his first wife's niece, the daughter of Auguste's brother (Georg Bernhard of Anhalt-Dessau) by a morganatic marriage. In an attempt to make her of equal royal birth, Helene was adopted by her father's brother (Wilhelm Waldemar of Anhalt-Dessau) a few days before the wedding and declared to be a princess of Anhalt-Dessau[32]. The Schwarzburg-Rudolstadt family were appalled and insisted Friedrich Günther's second marriage was morganatic. It caused a family breach that never seems to have healed[33].

91. The internal courtyard with (right to left)
north wing, west wing (with tower) and south wing.

Helene died three days after giving birth to twins (a boy and a girl) in 1860[34]. Her little boy was named Sizzo, after a founder of the house of Schwarzburg, but he was not heir to the throne. It was determined that Sizzo (1860-1926) would only have succession rights in Schwarzburg-Rudolstadt after all other male dynasts in the family. When Friedrich Günther died in 1867 he was succeeded by his brother Albrecht and on his death two years later by Albrecht's only son Georg (1838-1890). When Georg died unexpectedly of the flu[35] the next heir was a second cousin (chart 21). Günther Viktor (1852-1925) was the grandson of the younger boy in the 1780 portrait. How upsetting this all must have been for Sizzo, who but for the decision taken on his mother's rank would already have been on the throne for over twenty years! It would not be surprising if Sizzo had grown up with a chip on his shoulder.

Günther Viktor was not born with the expectation of ruling. Neither his father nor grandfather were the reigning prince and there must have seemed every likelihood that his second cousin Georg, who was in the direct line of succession, would marry and have children. Georg did get engaged in 1871, to the young Marie of Mecklenburg-Schwerin, but this was quickly broken off when Marie's family discovered some unpalatable facts about her fiancé. Georg had a drinking problem[36] and was in a longstanding relationship with a local woman. After this ended, he began another relationship which lasted until his death and may have led to morganatic marriage[37]. His short-lived fiancé Marie of Mecklenburg-Schwerin went on to make a brilliant royal

92. Günther Viktor was the last prince of Schwarzburg-Rudolstadt.

match when in 1874 she married Grand Duke Vladimir Alexandrovich, a younger son of Tsar Alexander II. As Grand Duchess Marie Pavlovna senior, she is famous for her glamour, spectacular jewels, family ambition, and indomitable spirit. She survived the Revolution and escaped from Russia by ship across the Black Sea in March 1920.

Despite any shortcomings in his private life, Georg remained a popular ruler and was well-liked by his subjects. Günther Viktor in contrast lacked the common touch, and was far less popular in Schwarzburg-Rudolstadt than either his predecessor Georg or the semi-royal Sizzo. He suffered ill health from a child and some sources suggest he may have been epileptic[38]. He was a reserved and reclusive man who did not relish his royal responsibilities and shunned public appearances.

In 1891 Günther Viktor married Anna Luise of Schönburg-Waldenburg. Their only child was stillborn (see Schwarzburg) and the house of Schwarzburg faced a full-blown succession crisis. Günther Viktor was the last male dynast and after him there was only Sizzo. Chart 22 shows how the Schwarzburg-Rudolstadt family had run out of sons. Günther Viktor was also in line to inherit Schwarzburg-Sondershausen, where the ruling prince was childless and his younger brother unmarried (chart 20). There was only one solution. By a family law of 1 June 1896, Sizzo was recognised as heir after Günther Viktor to both Schwarzburg principalities with the title 'prince of Schwarzburg'. The following year, thirty-six-year-old Sizzo married Alexandra of Anhalt-Dessau, a cousin of his mother Helene[39]. Their only son Friedrich Günther was born in 1901.

Relationships between Günther Viktor and his heir were poor. Sizzo failed to live within his allowance and had financial problems. He accused Günther Viktor of being stingy and attacked him in the press. Günther Viktor retaliated by banning Sizzo from the family schlösser and downgrading his title. Sizzo had been created Prinz (prince) <u>von</u> Schwarzburg-Rudolstadt, but Günther Viktor reduced this to the lessor <u>zu</u> Schwarzburg-Rudolstadt. (It does not sound much but it mattered to them.) Things so deteriorated that in the 1920s Sizzo took his claims to court and the case was only settled with his death[40]. Günther Viktor died in 1925 and Sizzo in 1926, when Sizzo's only son Friedrich Günther (1901-1971) became the head of house Schwarzburg. He got married in 1938 (to Sophie of Saxe-Weimar-Eisenach), but it lasted only weeks and there were no children[41]. When Friedrich Günther died in 1971 the house of Schwarzburg became extinct in the male line.

I will always associate Heidecksburg with the glorious suite of rococo state rooms and with the gripping story of Günther Viktor and his cousin Sizzo (more fascinating by far than any modern soap opera). I look forward with great pleasure to returning to this schloss. I have yet to explore the schloss gardens, visit the *Rococo in Miniature* exhibition (a miniature kingdom that took fifty years to create, peopled by tiny figures), and more ...

Schwarzburg

In spring 2018, a special steam train arrived at the Fürstenbahnhof (Princes' railway station) carrying the final weapon to be returned to the famous armoury at Schloss Schwarzburg. Onlookers lined the route as a procession in historical costume solemnly carried the weapon from the small station to the schloss. There, in a ceremony charged with emotion, it was put back in place in the armoury rack[42]. Nearly eighty years earlier, the armoury had to be emptied in a hurry when the schloss was commandeered by the Nazis. Schwarzburg has a spectacularly scenic location among the wooded hills of the Thuringian Forest. This must have been a reason why Hitler coveted the schloss and planned to turn Schwarzburg into a Third Reich guest house (Reichgästeheim) for visiting dignitaries.

Schwarzburg is built on top of a steep mountain ridge in a deep u-bend of the River Schwarza. I gazed in wonder at the incomparable natural beauty of the site. For defensive purposes, the location is well-nigh perfect and there has been a schloss here for around a thousand years. The river flows past on three sides and the only way in is by a narrow causeway at the open (eastern) end. The top of the ridge is narrow and the schloss buildings are strung out in a line, rising above the wooded hillside like a frill. (From right to left in illustration 93 are the gatehouse and armoury, the schloss with grand portico, the schloss church and tower, and the Emperors' Hall.)

93. Schwarzburg has a spectacularly scenic location in the Thuringian Forest.

Schwarzburg came into the possession of the counts of Schwarzburg-Rudolstadt when the house of Schwarzburg divided in 1571. Their main residence became Heidecksburg in Rudolstadt (see above) and Schwarzburg was relegated to secondary status. Nevertheless, Schwarzburg always remained important to the family as a symbol of their illustrious history. Albrecht Anton of Schwarzburg-Rudolstadt (1641-1710) and his son Ludwig Friedrich I (1667-1718) built the Kaisersaal (Emperors' Hall) at Schwarzburg to honour the Schwarzburg Holy Roman emperor (Günther XXI (21)), and to mark their rise in rank from count to prince. Albrecht Anton declined the rank when it was first offered in 1697; he accepted it in 1710[43] but his son was the first to use it. Chart 21 shows a family tree for the princes of Schwarzburg-Rudolstadt. Friedrich Anton (1692-1744) rebuilt Schwarzburg in grand style after a disastrous fire in 1726. (He also rebuilt Heidecksburg after the big fire there in 1735.) Schwarzburg was used as a summer residence and for family birthdays, weddings, and other occasions. When Ludwig Friedrich I was buried here in 1718, the schloss church at Schwarzburg became the family burial place.

After the German monarchy fell, Schwarzburg became the property of the new Free State of Thuringia but the last prince and princess, Günther Viktor (1852-1925) and his wife Anna Luise (1871-1951), were granted the right to live there. Günther Viktor died in 1925 but Anna Luise continued to spend her summers in the schloss. All this changed suddenly in June 1940 when officials informed Anna Luise that her right of residence was summarily terminated by order of Hitler and she must vacate the schloss immediately[44].

Ownership of the schloss was being transferred from Thuringia to the central National Socialist (Nazi) government. After centuries of family occupation, Anna Luise had just one week to clear the schloss. Even the coffins of her husband and other family members had to be removed from the schloss church[45]. The collection of weapons in the Schwarzburg

94. Schwarzburg before World War II – the main wing (right) was gutted by the Nazis; the church wing (left) was demolished leaving only the tower.

armoury, prized by generations of princes, was packed up and sent into storage at Heidecksburg.

The Nazi government's original intention was to use Schwarzburg for the internment of King Leopold III of Belgium (he surrendered to Germany at the end of May 1940). This idea was quickly dropped, and King Leopold and his family spent the war years at Chateau Laeken in Belgium, before being moved to Germany when the allies invaded France in 1944. Work on the radical remodelling of Schwarzburg for a Reich guest house began almost before Anna Luise moved out. Forced foreign slave labour was used on the project. The principal wing of the schloss was gutted and the side wing housing the schloss church demolished, leaving only the church tower standing. The armoury building was spared only because it was earmarked as the guest house garage. Anna Luise fought the expulsion order and eventually received a one-off compensation payment under an agreement of October 1941[46]. By that time, the pace of work was slowing. With the war going badly for Germany the plans for Schwarzburg had to be abandoned; in 1942 work ceased altogether. The schloss was left an uninhabitable and structurally unsound ruin. On our first visit the building was fenced off and boarded up, but we could see enough to tell it was in a terrible state. A large hoarding announced that a restoration project was beginning.

By the time we visited Schwarzburg again, great progress had made on the restoration. The grand entrance portico with its eight Corinthian columns (illustration 94) was in plain sight and the church tower under scaffolding. Strips of paint on the cornice of the front suggested the restorers were trying out different colours. Although there was a long way to go, the structure was made safe to take the first groups of visitors inside during summer 2019 to view the ongoing work. This partial reopening was to celebrate the centenary of signing the Weimar constitution at Schwarzburg on 11 August 1919. Friedrich Ebert, president of the German republic (established at the end of World War I), was on holiday in Schwarzburg when he put his signature to the document. He stayed at the Weisser Hirsch (White Hart), near the entrance to the schloss. This famous hotel, which is still in business today, has seen royal visitors. Queen Wilhelmina of the Netherlands stayed here for a month in 1900 (8 May – 5 June) to meet potential marriage candidates. She chose Duke Heinrich of Mecklenburg-Schwerin and they were married in The Hague on 7 February 1901. Heinrich was closely related to the Schwarzburg-Rudolstadt family – his mother (Marie) was the sister of Günther Viktor. It is usually assumed that Friedrich Ebert stayed in the main hotel (as shown in illustration 95) but this was not the case. His room was in an annex a short distance away. A plaque on this building records the fact today.

95. The Weisser Hirsch at the entrance to Schloss Schwarzburg.

The highlight of my return visit to Schwarzburg was a tour of the newly refurbished armoury. It is a miracle that the weapons collection survived to return home to Schwarzburg decades later. In 1946 the collection was loaded onto railway wagons to be sent to Russia as part of war reparations. No one is completely sure why the wagons never left. It is thought that locals working in the railway yard took advantage of confusion to shunt the wagons into a siding. Here the collection remained hidden and undiscovered until 1949[47]. When the weapons were being restored for return to the armoury, an inventory commissioned by Günther Viktor in the 1890s proved invaluable. Many items still had their metal tag with unique identification number and were described in detail in the inventory list. A copy of this list was on display in the new gate house at Schwarzburg that houses the ticket office and shop. The old gate house was another building demolished by the Nazis.

Entry to the armoury at Schwarzburg is by guided tour in small groups. Our guide was first class and (joy of joys) spoke slowly and clearly so that my husband (who speaks some German) could follow most of her German commentary. The armoury building is small, but the tour was brilliantly stage-managed to maximise the visitor experience. Our guide led us slowly into the darkened space and around the edge to stand at the far end of the room. Then the lights went on and – What a display! The Schwarzburg armoury was first mentioned in the middle of the sixteenth century and began life as simply a place to store weapons. But when the counts of Schwarzburg-Rudolstadt were promoted to princes the armoury became more important as a statement of their new rank. Weapons were no longer just stored here; they were arranged in a dazzling display to impress noble visitors[48].

Exhibited around two lines of arches running down the centre of the room are symmetrical arrangements of body armour, helmets, canon, rifles, and other weapons. Above them hang colourful military banners. More items from this collection of over five thousand pieces are shown on a gallery that runs around the space. Anna Luise was an enthusiastic and accomplished photographer. Comparison with her photo of the armoury taken in 1892 shows it looks much the same today[49]. I liked the 'firing cup' (it fired shots after you drank from it) and the miniature weapons and uniforms of *the Children's Guard*, formed by Prince Georg (1838-1890) when a child, to protect the armoury during the revolutionary year of 1848[50]. The only minor irritant on a thoroughly enjoyable tour was an annoying alarm that sounded every time a visitor got too close to the exhibits. With the crowded group in a small space the alarm sounded frequently!

The other 'must see' at Schwarzburg is the Kaisersaal (Emperors' Hall) in the garden. This survived the ravages of the Nazis and was renovated in the time of the GDR. The building takes its name from a

gallery of portraits of the Holy Roman emperors on the first floor. The pictures are not hung on the walls in the usual way, but painted high up on wall panels in a tall lantern roof. There were originally forty-eight in number, covering all the Holy Roman emperors up to Karl VI, who held the

96. The Emperors' Hall takes its name from a portrait gallery of the Holy Roman emperors.

post when the Hall was built. Some have been lost, but those remaining include the Schwarzburg Holy Roman Emperor Günther XXI (21). The Emperor's Hall houses a small but fascinating museum about the history of Schwarzburg. I liked all the pictures, postcards, and family photos showing the schloss in its heyday before World War I.

The museum attendant in the Emperors' Hall first sparked my interest in Anna Luise of Schwarzburg-Rudolstadt, whom she called *Die Letzte Fürstin* (the last princess). This is because Anna Luise's husband, Günther Viktor, was the last of all the ruling German princes to abdicate when the monarchy fell. (He abdicated for Schwarzburg-Rudolstadt on 23 November 1918 and for Schwarzburg-Sondershausen on 25 November.) The life of Anna Luise spanned a tumultuous period in German history. She was born into privilege in 1871 when Germany was a monarchy; she died as a commoner in the GDR in 1951. Anna Luise lived through World War I, revolution, the end of the monarchy, the Third Reich, World War II, Soviet occupation, and the division of Germany. She kept a diary from adolescence and left behind hundreds of photographs, so her story is well documented.

The Schwarzburg Holy Roman emperor

Günther XXI (21) of Schwarzburg-Blankenburg (1304-1349), the future Holy Roman emperor, was born in Schloss Greifenstein in Bad Blankenburg (a town between Schwarzburg and Rudolstadt). His birthplace was first mentioned in 1208 and was known as Schloss Blankenburg until the name was changed to Greifenstein in the seventeenth century.

The reign of Günther (21) as emperor was contested and short. His name is sometimes left off the list of Holy Roman emperors, or he is shown as an 'anti-king' (pretender to the role). After the Emperor Ludwig the Bavarian died in 1347 there was no clear agreement on his successor. Günther (21) was elected on 30 January 1349 by a group of electors opposed to the rival candidate, Karl IV of Luxembourg. Günther was crowned in the cathedral at Frankfurt on 6 February. His support soon withered away and in May he was defeated by Karl IV at the Siege of Eltville. After negotiating a chunky severance payment and an amnesty for his followers, Günther (21) abdicated on 26 May 1349. His reign had lasted just 116 days; Karl IV went on to reign for thirty years. The new emperor was magnanimous in victory. When Günther (21) died from the plague only three weeks after his abdication, Karl IV arranged for him to be buried with royal honours in Frankfurt Cathedral. The Schwarzburg-Blankenburg line of the house of Schwarzburg died out with Günther (21)'s son.

Greifenstein is proud to be the birthplace of a Holy Roman emperor. The schloss is owned by the town of Bad Blankenburg and maintained by a Friends Association. It is open in the summer months when visitors can tour the museum and enjoy displays of birds of prey.

Anna Luise of Schönburg-Waldenburg married Günther Viktor of Schwarzburg-Rudolstadt in December 1891 when she was twenty years old. Anna Luise was not his first choice of bride. Günther Viktor had succeeded in Schwarzburg-Rudolstadt rather unexpectedly in January 1890 when his predecessor died suddenly of influenza (chart 21). Günther Viktor was the last male dynast in the Schwarzburg-Rudolstadt line and under huge pressure to get married, perhaps against his natural inclination[51]. In December 1890, to the great delight of his subjects, he became engaged to a princess of Saxe-Altenburg (the sister of Duke Ernst II, see chapter two). Three months later however, in March 1891, the engagement was broken off. The official reason given was that the couple had realised they were not compatible[52]. Günther Viktor now

97. Anna Luise of
Schwarzburg-Rudolstadt.

looked for a bride within his own family. He proposed to Anna Luise in November 1891 and they were married a month later. The couple were first cousins and had known each other since Anna Luise was born. Her father was the brother of Günther Viktor's mother and her grandmother (her father's mother) was also a Schwarzburg-Rudolstadt[53]. The arranged marriage of Günther Viktor and Anna Luise was not a love match, but their life together would show it was based on true affection[54]. They spent their honeymoon at Schwarzburg and the schloss became a favourite home.

The weight of expectation was on Anna Luise to produce an heir. She conceived quickly, but seven months into her pregnancy something went wrong and in September 1892 a baby boy was stillborn. Complications from the birth meant there could be no more babies. Anna Luise was gravely ill with puerperal fever and pleurisy and took a long time to recover. The lack of children was a dynastic disaster and a devastating personal blow. Günther Viktor retreated into private life and mostly left his public duties to his wife. Anna Luise became more unconventional in the way she dressed, eschewing fashion, and wearing her hair short. But Anna Luise had inner strength and showed fortitude and optimism through the ups and downs of her life. In January 1919, just weeks after her husband's abdication, she wrote to a friend that she would look for the best in her new role. This is the reason why her biographer suggests that 'To make life worth living at all times' could be Anna Luise's life motto[55].

Anna Luise left Schwarzburg for the last time on 13 June 1940. She was sixty-nine years old. The final years of her life were spent in Sondershausen (see above) in some privation. In January 1942 she adopted her grown-up nephew Wilhelm (the youngest son of her brother Ulrich) and his son, fifteen-month-old Ulrich. Wilhelm was killed on active service during the Normandy invasion in June 1944. As the war came to an end Sondershausen was filled with refugees and the homeless. Anna Luise's possessions were looted or given away to relieve the distress. The American army came and went and then the Russians. Still Anna Luise stayed on. Her stipend from the State of Thuringia was gone and she had to sell off art treasures or rely on charity to survive. In 1949 the new German Democratic Republic awarded her a small pension. Anna Luise of Schwarzburg-Rudolstadt died in Sondershausen on 7 November 1951. She made the last entry in her diary that same day[56]. We saw the rooms where she lived as part of the guided tour at Sondershausen. The curator said that for local people she was a symbol of what had been good in the old regime. Thousands turned out to mourn Anna Luise at her funeral.

8.

LAST WORDS

The covid-19 global pandemic disrupted the writing of this book. The weeks my husband and I had arranged to spend in Thuringia to complete on-site research had to be cancelled, as Europe went into lockdown. With a clinically vulnerable person in our household, we were still shielding many months later. I faced a dilemma. Abandon the book for the time being, or complete the research so far as possible from a distance? I decided to press on and not let the virus win. Looking back this was the right decision. As I complete the book, a year after the first peak of cases, the virus is still raging, Europe is again in lockdown, and the vaccine rollout beginning.

I so much look forward to returning to Thuringia as soon as it is safe to do so. This beautiful state is my favourite part of Germany. I long to experience the sensational ballroom at Heidecksburg once again, stroll in the Russian Garden at Belvedere, and toil up the hill to the Wartburg (it is so worth the effort)! For these and three other schlösser from previous books that I was unable to revisit for this one, I have of necessity focused more on their history and less on the visitor experience. High on my list of new schlösser to see when I can return to Thuringia are (amongst others) Wilhelmsthal near Eisenach, summer residence and hunting lodge of Ernst August I of Saxe-Weimar and Eisenach (see Dornburger Schlösser in chapter 5); Heldburg near Hildburghausen in south-west Thuringia, favourite home of Georg II of Saxe-Meiningen and his morganatic wife Baroness von Heldburg (see Elisabethenburg in chapter 4); and Löbichau near Gera, where fascinating Duchess Dorothea of Courland (what a colourful life story she has!) entertained the main protagonists in the Napoleonic Wars – Emperor Napoleon, Tsar Alexander I, and King Friedrich Wilhelm III of Prussia. Perhaps in the future there will be a second edition including these.

98. Heldburg is high on my list to visit next.

Schloss in Thuringia is my sixth book on *The Fascinating Royal History of German Castles*. My purpose in writing the series has been twofold – to add to the sparse literature in English about the German royal families and to encourage more English-speaking visitors to see their marvellous castles and palaces. Our view of German history is skewed by the unspeakable horrors of the twentieth-century Nazi years. Look on the shelves of any good bookshop and you should find numerous books in English on Hitler and the Third Reich, but relatively few about the one thousand years of German royal history (the Holy Roman Empire) that came before this.

Germany seen through the eyes of English-speaking tourists is also rather lopsided. Whilst Bavaria and Lake Constance in Baden-Württemberg are popular destinations, other states such as Thuringia and Mecklenburg-Western Pomerania on the Baltic coast (another area I love) are virtually unknown, perhaps because they once lay behind the Iron Curtain. Those schlösser in Thuringia that are part of the UNESCO World Heritage Sites (the Wartburg and Classical Weimar) enjoy visitors from around the world. But many other schlösser are little known outside Germany and some rarely see an English-speaking visitor. I hope the glimpses in this book will encourage you to visit Thuringia in the future.

My heartfelt thanks to the museum directors and curators, historians, fellow schloss enthusiasts and friends, who suggested sources and provided information for this book – including (in order of the book) Ulrich Schubert at Fröhliche Wiederkunft, Rainer Hohberg (Neues Schloss Hummelshain), Martin Modes (Saalfeld and Schwarzburg), Silke Opitz (Molsdorf), Mike Raimann (Tenneberg), Joachim Ortlepp and Andreas Paasche (Reinhardsbrunn), Michael Römhild (Hildburghausen), Jacqueline Bräunlich (Unteres Schloss Greiz), Ingrid Faber (Osterstein Gera) and Bearn Bilker (Ebersdorf). And a special thank you to Martin Modes and his team for our VIP day at Saalfeld and Schwarzburg.

A particular challenge I faced in writing this book was the lack of sources in English on the Thuringian royal families. (Notable exceptions include Arturo Beéche's wonderful book on the Saxe-Coburg and Gotha family and Charlotte Zeepvat's informative 'Family Album' series in Royalty Digest Quarterly – see the bibliography for both sources.) As a non-German speaker, translating the German sources was a slow and painstaking process for me, and I am most grateful for the help from my friends and translators Graham Billing and Gert Frisch.

Appendix D provides an index of all the schlösser featured in the *Schloss* series of books. As part of researching the six books, my husband and I have visited more than two hundred schlösser in many different parts of Germany; and revelled in the joys of what we call *schloss hunting.* Every visit is distinct and memorable in my mind. There is always the excitement of not knowing what we will find – a friendly museum director who wants to share his passion (Tenneberg), or a tour guide with a flair for the dramatic (Molsdorf); a sixteenth-century royal love story (Fröhliche Wiederkunft), or the birthplace of a nineteenth-century British queen (Elisabethenburg); a site of stunning natural beauty (Schwarzburg), or a work of art so magical it stops you in your tracks (*the Golden Carriage* of *the Diamond Prince* at Sondershausen)? I well remember the thrill of unexpectedly being filmed at Altenstein to appear on Thuringian TV (see *Schloss III*) – I still have the film clip.

From among the twenty-five schlösser in this book, of course I have some personal favourites and these are shown in the list below. I stress they are my personal choice and readers may well have their own favourites.

The author's favourite schlösser in this book

Fröhliche Wiederkunft – *fairy-tale confection of towers, steep roofs, and gables; this schloss has one of the most romantic stories in royal history.*
Molsdorf – *surprising schloss built by an eighteenth-century self-made celebrity: where the guide brought his story dramatically to life.*
Saalfeld – *kings or queens of fourteen European countries descended from this schloss known as 'The Cradle of European Dynasties'; the warm welcome makes it a favourite.*
Sondershausen – *ancestral schloss with a memorable portrait gallery covering six hundred years of family history: where curators went the extra mile to make our visit enjoyable.*
Wartburg – *iconic hilltop castle where the royal story of Thuringia began: a visit here is like walking through the pages of a history book.*

An ambition for the *Schloss* series of books has been to include schlösser from all thirty-one German royal states reinstated after the Napoleonic Wars to become members of the new German Confederation. At appendix E is a list of these states showing where in my books their schlösser are featured. As indicated in the appendix, only the duchy of Anhalt-Köthen is yet to be covered. My husband and I visited Schloss Köthen before the pandemic struck and it will be in the next book in the series to be called *Schloss in Saxony-Anhalt*. There are plenty more fascinating schlösser still out there to be explored. As a fellow royal author expressed it so vividly –

I am not 'schlossed-out' yet!

APPENDICES

APPENDIX A
MAP OF THURINGIA

Hand drawn map showing the approximate location of the twenty-five schlösser in this book.

1. Fröhliche Wiederkunft	10. Altenstein	18. Oberes Schloss Greiz
2. Altenburg	11. Hildburghausen	19. Sommerpalais Greiz
3. Neues Schloss Hummelshain	12. Residenzschloss Weimar	20. Osterstein Gera
4. Saalfeld	13. Wittumspalais	21. Ebersdorf
5. Friedenstein	14. Dornburger Schlösser	22. Sondershausen
6. Molsdorf	15. Belvedere	23. Neues Palais Arnstadt
7. Tenneberg	16. The Wartburg	24. Heidecksburg
8. Reinhardsbrunn	17. Unteres Schloss Greiz	25. Schwarzburg
9. Elisabethenburg		

APPENDIX B
THE ROYAL STATES IN THURINGIA

This list shows the eight royal duchies and principalities in Thuringia when Germany was a monarchy until World War I. It provides information on the royal house, the capital, and the size of each state measured by square miles and population in thousands (rounded).

Saxe-Altenburg
Wettin Ernestine Line: primogeniture 1685, extinct in male line 1991.
Capital: Altenburg.
Size: 510 square miles, 215k population[1].
Last monarch: Duke Ernst II (1871-1955), reigned from 1908.

Saxe-Coburg and Gotha
Wettin Ernestine Line: primogeniture 1747.
Capitals: Coburg and Gotha.
Size: Coburg 215 square miles, 55k population: Gotha 540 square miles 140k population[2].
Last monarch: Duke Karl Eduard (1884-1954), reigned from 1900.

Saxe-Meiningen
Wettin Ernestine Line: primogeniture 1800.
Capital: Meiningen
Size: 953 square miles, 280k population[3].
Last monarch: Duke Bernhard III (1851-1928), reigned from 1914.

Saxe-Weimar-Eisenach
Wettin Ernestine Line: primogeniture 1724.
Capital: Weimar.
Size: 1,393 square miles, 417k population[4].
Last monarch: Duke Wilhelm Ernst (1876-1923), reigned from 1901.

Reuss Elder Line (Reuss-Greiz)
Reuss: primogeniture 1690, extinct in the male line 1927.
Capital: Greiz.
Size: 120 square miles, 73k population[5].
Last monarch: Prince Heinrich XXIV (24) 1878-1927), reigned from 1902 (under a regency).

Reuss Younger Line (Reuss-Gera)
Reuss: primogeniture 1690, extinct in the male line 1945? (date not known, see Osterstein).
Capital: Gera.
Size: 320 square miles, 150k population[5].
Last monarch: Prince Heinrich XXVII (27) (1858-1928), reigned from 1908 (also regent of Reuss-Elder Line from 1908).

Schwarzburg-Sondershausen
Schwarzburg: primogeniture 1713, extinct in the male line 1909.
Capital: Sondershausen.
Size: 333 square miles, 90k population[6].
Last monarch: Günther Viktor (1852-1925), reigned from 1909 (also reigned in Schwarzburg-Rudolstadt from 1890).

Schwarzburg-Rudolstadt
Schwarzburg: primogeniture 1710, extinct in the male line 1971.
Capital: Rudolstadt.
Size: 360m square miles, 100k population[6].
Last monarch: Günther Viktor (1852-1925), reigned from 1890 (also reigned in Schwarzburg-Sondershausen from 1909).

APPENDIX C
CHARTS AND FAMILY TREES

1. The Ludowinger landgraves of Thuringia.
2. The house of Wettin and the Ernestine Line.
3. The Ernestine Line duchies in Thuringia.
4. The dukes of Saxe-Altenburg Elder Branch.
5. The seven sons of Duke Ernst the Pious.
6. The dukes of Saxe-Gotha-Altenburg.
7. The dukes of Saxe-Meiningen.
8. The three marriages of Duke Georg II of Saxe-Meiningen.
9. The dukes of Saxe-Hildburghausen.
10. The dukes of Saxe-Altenburg Younger Branch.
11. The daughters of Duke Joseph of Saxe-Altenburg.
12. The dukes of Saxe-Saalfeld and Saxe-Coburg-Saalfeld.
13. The succession to Saxe-Coburg and Gotha.
14. The dukes and grand dukes of Saxe-Weimar-Eisenach.
15. The princes of Reuss Elder Line (Reuss-Greiz).
16. The princes of Reuss Younger Line (Reuss-Gera).
17. The counts and princes of Reuss-Ebersdorf.
18. The thrones descended from Augusta of Reuss-Ebersdorf.
19. The princes of Schwarzburg-Sondershausen.
20. How the house of Schwarzburg ran out of sons: Schwarzburg-Sondershausen.
21. The princes of Schwarzburg-Rudolstadt.
22. How the house of Schwarzburg ran out of sons: Schwarzburg-Rudolstadt.

1. THE LUDOWINGER LANDGRAVES OF THURINGIA

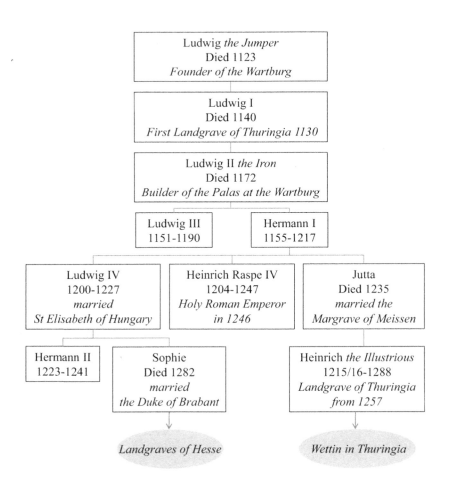

Family tree for the Ludowinger landgraves. After the death of Heinrich Raspe IV their lands in Thuringia were inherited by Heinrich *the Illustrious* of the house of Wettin.

2. THE HOUSE OF WETTIN AND THE ERNESTINE LINE

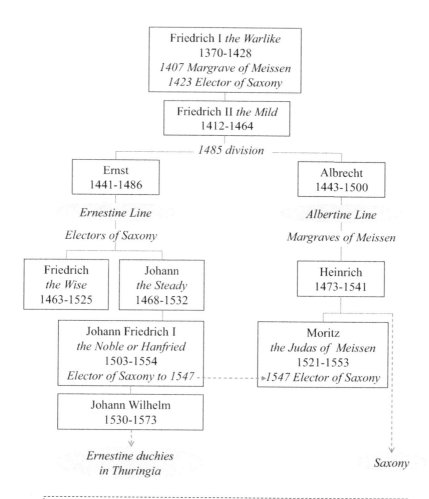

Chart shows the division of the House of Wettin in 1485. Chart also shows how the (senior) Ernestine line were electors of Saxony until, following the battle of Mühlberg in 1547, the title and lands were ceded to the (junior) Albertine line.

3. THE ERNESTINE LINE DUCHIES IN THURINGIA

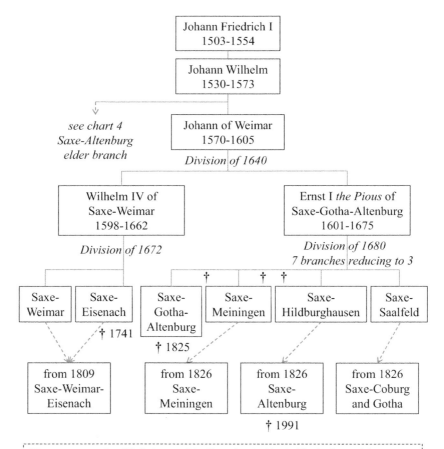

Johann Friedrich I
1503-1554

Johann Wilhelm
1530-1573

see chart 4
Saxe-Altenburg
elder branch

Johann of Weimar
1570-1605

Division of 1640

Wilhelm IV of
Saxe-Weimar
1598-1662

Ernst I *the Pious* of
Saxe-Gotha-Altenburg
1601-1675

Division of 1672

Division of 1680
7 branches reducing to 3

Saxe-Weimar

Saxe-Eisenach
† 1741

Saxe-Gotha-Altenburg
† 1825

Saxe-Meiningen

Saxe-Hildburghausen

Saxe-Saalfeld

from 1809
Saxe-Weimar-Eisenach

from 1826
Saxe-Meiningen

from 1826
Saxe-Altenburg

from 1826
Saxe-Coburg
and Gotha

† 1991

Chart presents a simplified picture of the Ernestine duchies in Thuringia surviving at
World War I. The four surviving duchies were Saxe-Weimar-Eisenach, Saxe-Meiningen,
Saxe-Altenburg, and Saxe-Coburg and Gotha. Chart also shows when branches became
extinct in the male line. Only selected territories are included.

4. THE DUKES OF SAXE-ALTENBURG ELDER BRANCH

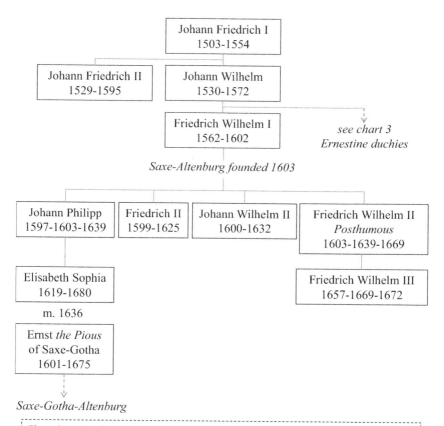

Johann Friedrich I
1503-1554

Johann Friedrich II
1529-1595

Johann Wilhelm
1530-1572

Friedrich Wilhelm I
1562-1602

see chart 3
Ernestine duchies

Saxe-Altenburg founded 1603

Johann Philipp
1597-1603-1639

Friedrich II
1599-1625

Johann Wilhelm II
1600-1632

Friedrich Wilhelm II
Posthumous
1603-1639-1669

Elisabeth Sophia
1619-1680

Friedrich Wilhelm III
1657-1669-1672

m. 1636

Ernst *the Pious*
of Saxe-Gotha
1601-1675

Saxe-Gotha-Altenburg

Chart shows the dukes of the Saxe-Altenburg Elder Branch from the creation of the duchy in 1603. When he came of age, Johann Philipp ruled on behalf of his younger brothers. On his death, the surviving brother, Friedrich Wilhelm II, became sole duke. The branch became extinct in the male line on the death of Friedrich Wilhelm III in 1672. Altenburg then passed to Duke Ernst *the Pious* of Saxe-Gotha by virtue of his wife Elisabeth Sophia, the only child of Johann Philipp.

5. THE SEVEN SONS OF DUKE ERNST THE PIOUS

Ernst *the Pious*	m.	Elizabeth Sophia
of Saxe-Gotha	1636	of Saxe-Altenburg
1601-1675		1619-1680

1. Friedrich I   ---▹*Saxe-Gotha-Altenburg*---------------▹*extinct 1825*
   1646-1691

2. Albrecht of
   Coburg
   1648-1699

3. Bernhard I   ---▹*Saxe-Meiningen*--------------------▹*Saxe-Meiningen*
   1649-1706   *including*
                                                               Hildburghausen
4. Heinrich of   *& Saalfeld*
   Römhild   *from 1826*
   1650-1710

5. Christian of
   Eisenberg
   1653-1707

6. Ernst   ---▹*Saxe-Hildburghausen*----------------▹*Saxe-Altenburg*
   1655-1715   *from 1826*

7. Johann Ernst ---▹*Saxe-Saalfeld*------▹*Saxe-Coburg*-----▹*Saxe-Coburg*
   1658-1729   *-Saalfeld*   *and Gotha*
                                          from 1735   *from 1826*

Chart shows the seven sons of Duke Ernst *the Pious* and the Ernestine Line duchies descending from them. The surviving duchies at World War I descended from the third son (Saxe-Meiningen), sixth son (Saxe Altenburg) and seventh son (Saxe-Coburg and Gotha). Chart also shows in simplified form how the duchies were reorganized in 1826.

6. THE DUKES OF SAXE-GOTHA-ALTENBURG

Ernst *the Pious* 1601-1640-1672-1675	Duke of Saxe-Gotha from 1640. Married Elisabeth Sophia of Saxe-Altenburg. Duke of Saxe-Gotha-Altenburg from 1672. Built Friedenstein.
Friedrich I 1646-1675-1691	Eldest son of Ernst *the Pious*. Remodelled the ducal apartments. Rebuilt the East Tower. Built the Ekhof theatre in the West Tower.
Friedrich II 1676-1691-1732	Succeeded as a minor. Father of Augusta (wife of Frederick Lewis, Prince of Wales). Built Friedrichsthal in the Friedenstein gardens. Remodelled Tenneberg as a widow's residence. Patron of Graf von Gotter.
Friedrich III 1699-1732-1772	Married Luise Dorothea of Saxe-Meiningen. Founded the Order of the Happy Hermits. Almanac de Gotha first published in his reign.
Ernst II 1745-1772-1804	Created one of the first English landscape parks in Europe at Friedenstein. Brought Konrad Ekhof to Gotha.
August 1772-1804-1822	Eldest son of Ernst II. Father of Luise (the mother of Prince Albert). Married twice but had no son.
Friedrich IV 1774-1822-1825	Younger son of Ernst II. Unmarried. Incapacitated and an invalid from war wounds.

Chart shows the seven dukes of Saxe-Gotha-Altenburg from 1672 (when Ernst *the Pious* acquired Altenburg by virtue of his wife's inheritance) to 1825 (when the branch died out on the death of Friedrich IV.)

7. THE DUKES OF SAXE-MEININGEN

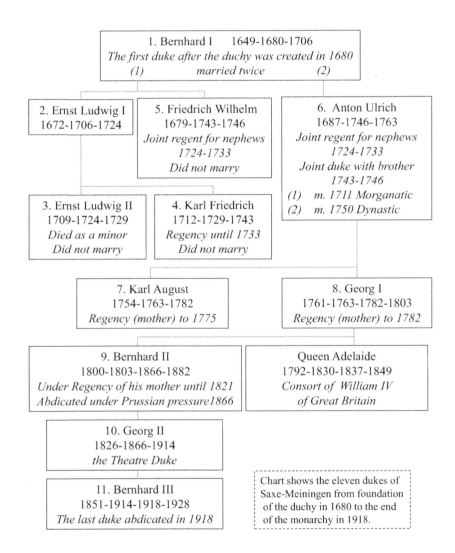

1. Bernhard I   1649-1680-1706
The first duke after the duchy was created in 1680
(1)   married twice   (2)

2. Ernst Ludwig I
1672-1706-1724

5. Friedrich Wilhelm
1679-1743-1746
Joint regent for nephews
1724-1733
Did not marry

6. Anton Ulrich
1687-1746-1763
Joint regent for nephews
1724-1733
Joint duke with brother
1743-1746
(1)   m. 1711 Morganatic
(2)   m. 1750 Dynastic

3. Ernst Ludwig II
1709-1724-1729
Died as a minor
Did not marry

4. Karl Friedrich
1712-1729-1743
Regency until 1733
Did not marry

7. Karl August
1754-1763-1782
Regency (mother) to 1775

8. Georg I
1761-1763-1782-1803
Regency (mother) to 1782

9. Bernhard II
1800-1803-1866-1882
Under Regency of his mother until 1821
Abdicated under Prussian pressure1866

Queen Adelaide
1792-1830-1837-1849
Consort of William IV
of Great Britain

10. Georg II
1826-1866-1914
the Theatre Duke

11. Bernhard III
1851-1914-1918-1928
The last duke abdicated in 1918

Chart shows the eleven dukes of
Saxe-Meiningen from foundation
of the duchy in 1680 to the end
of the monarchy in 1918.

8. THE THREE MARRIAGES OF
DUKE GEORG II OF SAXE-MEININGEN

Duke Georg II *the Theatre Duke*
1826-1866-1914

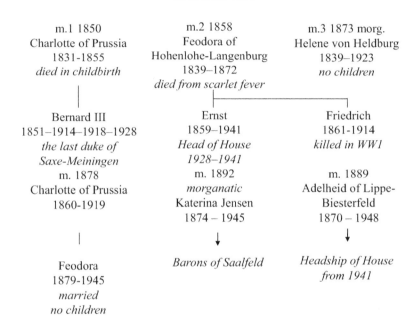

m.1 1850	m.2 1858	m.3 1873 morg.
Charlotte of Prussia	Feodora of	Helene von Heldburg
1831-1855	Hohenlohe-Langenburg	1839–1923
died in childbirth	1839–1872	*no children*
	died from scarlet fever	

Bernard III	Ernst	Friedrich
1851–1914–1918–1928	1859–1941	1861-1914
the last duke of	*Head of House*	*killed in WW1*
Saxe-Meiningen	*1928–1941*	
m. 1878	m. 1892	m. 1889
Charlotte of Prussia	*morganatic*	Adelheid of Lippe-
1860-1919	Katerina Jensen	Biesterfeld
	1874 – 1945	1870 – 1948
	↓	↓
Feodora	*Barons of Saalfeld*	*Headship of House*
1879-1945		*from 1941*
married		
no children		

Chart shows the three marriages of Duke Georg II of Saxe-Meiningen and his three surviving sons. The head of house today, Friedrich Konrad born in 1952, is a descendant (the grandson) of the youngest of the sons. Not all female descendants are included.

9. THE DUKES OF SAXE-HILDBURGHAUSEN

Ernst 1655-1680-1715	Sixth son of Ernst *the Pious* Founder of the duchy m. 1680 Sophia Henriette of Waldeck Built the schloss
Ernst Friedrich I 1681-1715-1724	Eldest son of Ernst m. 1704 Sophie Albertine of Erbach-Erbach Developed the baroque schloss garden
Ernst Friedrich II 1707-1724-1745	Third son of Ernst Friedrich I Succeeded as a minor and under his mother's regency to 1728 m. 1726 Caroline of Erbach-Fürstenau
Ernst Friedrich III 1727-1745-1780	Eldest son of Ernst Friedrich II Succeeded as a minor and under his mother's regency to 1748 m. (1) 1749 Luise of Denmark (2) 1757 Christiane of Brandenburg-Bayreuth (3) 1758 Ernestine of Saxe-Weimar Imperial debt commission formed 1769
Friedrich 1763-1780-1826-1834	Only son of Ernst Friedrich III Succeeded as a minor and under his great-great uncle's regency to 1784 m. 1785 Charlotte of Mecklenburg-Strelitz Ceded Hildburghausen to Meiningen in 1826 and became first duke of Saxe-Altenburg Younger Branch (see chart 10)

Chart shows the five dukes of Saxe-Hildburghausen from Ernst, who founded the state in 1680, to Friedrich, who ceded it to Meiningen in 1826 to become duke of Saxe-Altenburg.

10. THE DUKES OF SAXE-ALTENBURG YOUNGER BRANCH

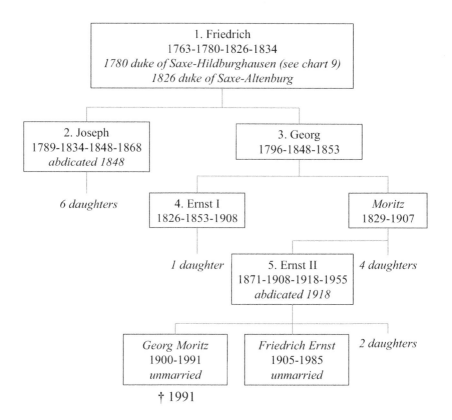

Chart shows the five dukes of the Saxe-Altenburg younger branch from 1826 (when the duchy of Saxe-Altenburg was re-created) to 1918 (when the monarchy came to an end). This branch of the Ernestine Line of the house of Wettin died out with the death of Georg Moritz in 1991.

11. THE DAUGHTERS OF DUKE JOSEPH OF SAXE-ALTENBURG

Joseph 1789-1868	m. 1817	Amalie of Württemberg 1799-1848

Marie 1818-1907	m. 1843	Georg V of Hannover 1819-1878	King & queen of Hannover from 1851 Deposed by Prussia 1866
Pauline 1819-1825	died as a child		
Therese 1823-1915	unmarried		
Elisabeth 1826-1896	m. 1852	Peter II of Oldenburg 1827-1900	Reigning grand duke and duchess of Oldenburg from 1853
Alexandra 1830-1911	m. 1848	Konstantin Grand duke of Russia 1827-1892	Founded the Konstantinovichi branch of the Russian royal family
Luise 1832-1833	died as a child		

Chart shows the daughters of Duke Joseph of Saxe-Altenburg Younger Branch with details of their marriages where appropriate. Through the marriage of the fifth daughter, Alexandra, Saxe-Altenburg became closely connected to the Russian royal family.

12. THE DUKES OF SAXE-SAALFELD AND SAXE-COBURG-SAALFELD

Johann Ernst
1658-1680-1729

m.1 1680
Sophie Hedwig of Saxe-Merseburg
1660-1686

m.2 1690
Charlotte Johanna of Waldeck
1664-1699

Christian Ernst
1683-1729-1745
m. 1724
Christiane Friederike von Koss
1686-1743

no children

Franz Josias
1697-1729-1764
m. 1723
Anna Sophia of
Schwarzburg-Rudolstadt
1700-1780

Ernst Friedrich
1724-1764-1800
m. 1749
Sophie Antonie of
Braunschweig-Wolfenbüttel
1724-1802

Chart shows the dukes of Saxe-Saalfeld
and Saxe-Coburg-Saalfeld. Johann Ernst
was the first duke of Saxe-Saalfeld from
1680. In 1735 when Coburg was added, the
duchy became Saxe-Coburg-Saalfeld. The
half-brothers Christian Ernst and Franz
Josias reigned jointly until the former's
death in 1745. Franz Josias then introduced
primogeniture. In 1826, following an
Ernestine Line re-organization, Ernst III
became Ernst I of Saxe-Coburg and Gotha
- *see chart 13.*

Franz Friedrich Anton
1750-1800-1806
m.2 1777
Augusta of Reuss-Ebersdorf
1757-1831

Ernst III
1784-1806-1844

see chart 13

13. THE SUCCESSION TO SAXE-COBURG AND GOTHA

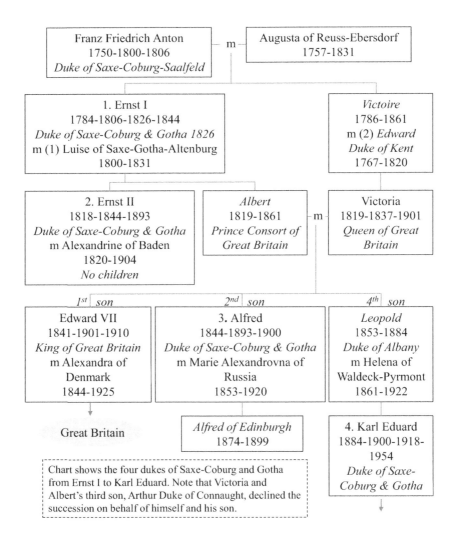

Franz Friedrich Anton
1750-1800-1806
Duke of Saxe-Coburg-Saalfeld

m

Augusta of Reuss-Ebersdorf
1757-1831

---

1. Ernst I
1784-1806-1826-1844
Duke of Saxe-Coburg & Gotha 1826
m (1) Luise of Saxe-Gotha-Altenburg
1800-1831

Victoire
1786-1861
m (2) *Edward*
Duke of Kent
1767-1820

---

2. Ernst II
1818-1844-1893
Duke of Saxe-Coburg & Gotha
m Alexandrine of Baden
1820-1904
No children

Albert
1819-1861
Prince Consort of
Great Britain

m

Victoria
1819-1837-1901
Queen of Great
Britain

1st son

Edward VII
1841-1901-1910
King of Great Britain
m Alexandra of
Denmark
1844-1925

2nd son

3. Alfred
1844-1893-1900
Duke of Saxe-Coburg & Gotha
m Marie Alexandrovna of
Russia
1853-1920

4th son

Leopold
1853-1884
Duke of Albany
m Helena of
Waldeck-Pyrmont
1861-1922

Great Britain

Alfred of Edinburgh
1874-1899

4. Karl Eduard
1884-1900-1918-
1954
Duke of Saxe-
Coburg & Gotha

Chart shows the four dukes of Saxe-Coburg and Gotha
from Ernst I to Karl Eduard. Note that Victoria and
Albert's third son, Arthur Duke of Connaught, declined the
succession on behalf of himself and his son.

14. THE DUKES AND GRAND DUKES OF
SAXE-WEIMAR-EISENACH

Ernst August I 1688-1707-1748	Duke of the twin duchies of Saxe-Weimar and Saxe-Eisenach from 1741. Built Belvedere and Dornburg Rococo Schloss
Ernst August II 1738-1748-1758	Under a regency to 1755. m. 1756 Anna Amalia of Brunswick-Wolfenbüttel 1739-1807
Carl August 1757-1758-1828	Under the regency of his mother to 1775. m. 1775 Luise of Hesse Darmstadt 1757-1830. Duke of the merged duchy from 1806. Grand duke from 1815. Patron of Goethe and Schiller. Built the Residenzschloss Weimar
Carl Friedrich 1783-1828-1853	m. 1804 Maria Pavlovna of Russia 1786-1859. Created the gardens at Belvedere.
Carl Alexander 1818-1853-1901	m. 1842 Sophie of the Netherlands 1824-1897. Restored the Wartburg
William Ernst 1876-1901-1918-1923	The last grand duke. Succeeded his grandfather (his father, Carl August, died in 1894). Abdicated in November 1918

Chart shows the dukes and grand dukes of Saxe-Weimar-Eisenach from Ernst August I of Saxe-Weimar. He also inherited Saxe-Eisenach in 1741 and ruled the twin duchies in a personal union. The two were merged to form Saxe-Weimar-Eisenach in 1806. Carl August was elevated from the rank of duke to grand duke in 1815.

15. THE PRINCES OF REUSS ELDER LINE (REUSS-GREIZ)

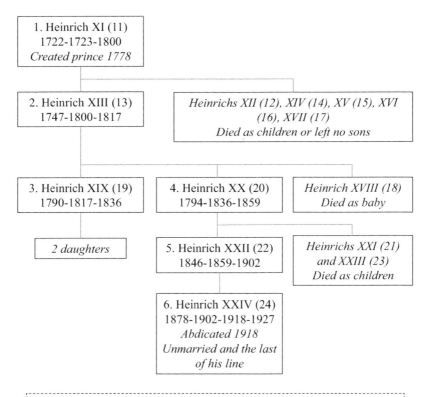

1. Heinrich XI (11)
1722-1723-1800
Created prince 1778

2. Heinrich XIII (13)
1747-1800-1817

Heinrichs XII (12), XIV (14), XV (15), XVI (16), XVII (17)
Died as children or left no sons

3. Heinrich XIX (19)
1790-1817-1836

4. Heinrich XX (20)
1794-1836-1859

Heinrich XVIII (18)
Died as baby

2 daughters

5. Heinrich XXII (22)
1846-1859-1902

Heinrichs XXI (21) and XXIII (23)
Died as children

6. Heinrich XXIV (24)
1878-1902-1918-1927
Abdicated 1918
Unmarried and the last of his line

Chart shows the six princes of Reuss Elder Line - from Heinrich XI (11) to Heinrich XXIV (24). Chart also shows the run of identification numbers in the Reuss Elder Line (from 11 to 24) and how it became extinct in the male line on the death of Heinrich XXIV (24).

16. THE PRINCES OF REUSS YOUNGER LINE (REUSS-GERA)

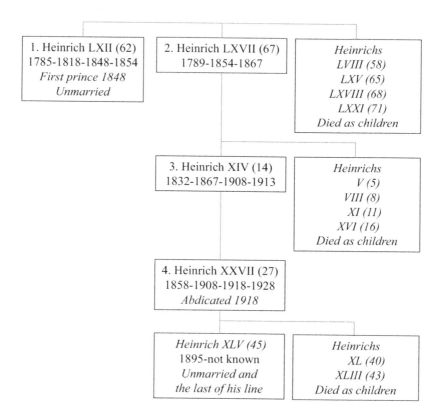

| 1. Heinrich LXII (62)
1785-1818-1848-1854
First prince 1848
Unmarried | 2. Heinrich LXVII (67)
1789-1854-1867 | *Heinrichs*
LVIII (58)
LXV (65)
LXVIII (68)
LXXI (71)
Died as children |

| 3. Heinrich XIV (14)
1832-1867-1908-1913 | *Heinrichs*
V (5)
VIII (8)
XI (11)
XVI (16)
Died as children |

| 4. Heinrich XXVII (27)
1858-1908-1918-1928
Abdicated 1918 |

| *Heinrich XLV (45)*
1895-not known
Unmarried and
the last of his line | *Heinrichs*
XL (40)
XLIII (43)
Died as children |

Chart shows the four princes of Reuss Younger Line from Heinrich LXII (62) to Heinrich XXVII (27). Chart also shows the run of identification numbers and how this branch of the house of Reuss became extinct in the male line on the death of Heinrich XLV (45). He died in captivity after arrest by the Soviets in 1945 and his date of death is not known. It is important to note that the numbering re-started with each new century and also included other branches on this side of the house. The numbers are therefore not consecutive.

17. THE COUNTS AND PRINCES OF REUSS-EBERSDORF

Heinrich X (10)
1662-1678-1711

Founder of the state
Succeeded as a minor
Built the schloss
Established Ebersdorf as
a religious centre of Pietism

Heinrich XXIX (29)
1699-1711-1747

Only son of Heinrich (10)
Succeeded as a minor

Heinrich XXIV (24)
1724-1747-1779

Eldest of 7 sons of Heinrich (29),
most of whom did not marry
Father of Augusta of
Saxe-Coburg-Saalfeld

Heinrich LI (51)
1761-1779-1822

Only surviving son of Heinrich (24)
Succeeded as a minor
Promoted to prince 1806

Heinrich LXXII (72)
1797-1822-1848-1853

Only son of Heinrich (51)
The "Principles Rider"
Abdicated 1848
Died unmarried

Chart shows the five rulers of Reuss-Ebersdorf from Heinrich X (10) who founded the state in 1678 to Heinrich LXXII (72) who abdicated in 1848.

18. THE THRONES DESCENDED FROM
AUGUSTA OF REUSS-EBERSDORF

Franz Friedrich Anton of - married - Augusta of
Saxe-Coburg-Saalfeld   1777   Reuss-Ebersdorf
1750-1806   1757-1831

Sophia - married - 1778-1835	Emmanuel of Mensdorf-Pouilly 1777-1852	
Antoinette - married - 1779-1824	Alexander of Württemberg Brother of King Friedrich 1771-1833	
Juliane - married - 1781-1860	Konstantin of Russia Brother of Tsar Alexander I 1779 -1831	
Ernst - married – 1784-1844 (1)	Luise of ⟶ Saxe-Gotha-Altenburg 1800-1831	(see entry for Victoire)
Ferdinand - married - 1785-1851	Antoinette of ⟶ Kohary 1797-1862	Portugal, Bulgaria. Brazil
Victoire - married – 1786-1861 (2)	Edward ⟶ Duke of Kent 1767-1820	Great Britain, Prussia/Germany Greece, Norway, Romania, Russia, Spain, Sweden, Yugoslavia
Leopold - married – 1790-1865 (2)*	Louise of ⟶ Orleans (France) 1812-1850	Belgium, Mexico, Italy, Luxembourg

Chart shows the seven children of Franz Friedrich Anton and Augusta who survived childhood and the thrones occupied by their descendants.
The name of the family changed to Saxe-Coburg and Gotha in 1826.
* Leopold's first wife was Charlotte of Wales (1796-1817), heiress to the British throne.

19. THE PRINCES OF SCHWARZBURG-SONDERSHAUSEN

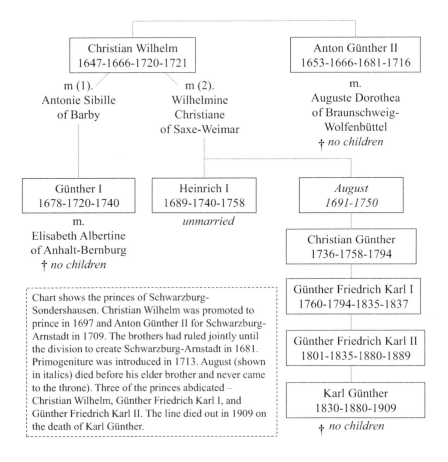

Christian Wilhelm
1647-1666-1720-1721

Anton Günther II
1653-1666-1681-1716

m (1).
Antonie Sibille
of Barby

m (2).
Wilhelmine
Christiane
of Saxe-Weimar

m.
Auguste Dorothea
of Braunschweig-
Wolfenbüttel
† *no children*

Günther I
1678-1720-1740

Heinrich I
1689-1740-1758

August
1691-1750

m.
Elisabeth Albertine
of Anhalt-Bernburg
† *no children*

unmarried

Christian Günther
1736-1758-1794

Günther Friedrich Karl I
1760-1794-1835-1837

Günther Friedrich Karl II
1801-1835-1880-1889

Karl Günther
1830-1880-1909
† *no children*

Chart shows the princes of Schwarzburg-Sondershausen. Christian Wilhelm was promoted to prince in 1697 and Anton Günther II for Schwarzburg-Arnstadt in 1709. The brothers had ruled jointly until the division to create Schwarzburg-Arnstadt in 1681. Primogeniture was introduced in 1713. August (shown in italics) died before his elder brother and never came to the throne). Three of the princes abdicated – Christian Wilhelm, Günther Friedrich Karl I, and Günther Friedrich Karl II. The line died out in 1909 on the death of Karl Günther.

20. HOW THE HOUSE OF SCHWARZBURG RAN OUT OF SONS
SCHWARZBURG-SONDERSHAUSEN

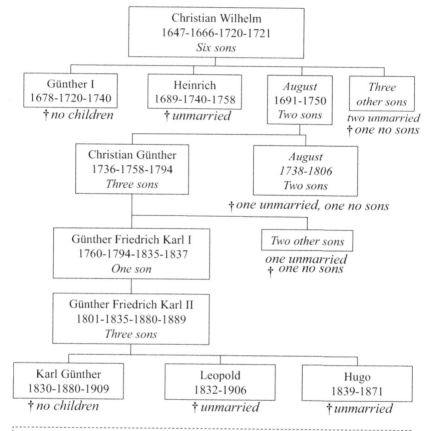

Christian Wilhelm
1647-1666-1720-1721
Six sons

Günther I
1678-1720-1740
† *no children*

Heinrich
1689-1740-1758
† *unmarried*

*August
1691-1750
Two sons*

*Three
other sons*
two unmarried
† *one no sons*

Christian Günther
1736-1758-1794
Three sons

*August
1738-1806
Two sons*

† *one unmarried, one no sons*

Günther Friedrich Karl I
1760-1794-1835-1837
One son

Two other sons
one unmarried
† *one no sons*

Günther Friedrich Karl II
1801-1835-1880-1889
Three sons

Karl Günther
1830-1880-1909
† *no children*

Leopold
1832-1906
† *unmarried*

Hugo
1839-1871
† *unmarried*

Chart includes the princes of Schwarzburg-Sondershausen from Christian Wilhelm (reigned 1666-1720). It shows how this branch of the house of Schwarzburg ran out of sons. The line became extinct on the death of Karl Günther (who was married but had no children) in 1909. His two younger brothers had already died unmarried. Chart only includes sons who survived childhood.

21. THE PRINCES OF SCHWARZBURG-RUDOLSTADT

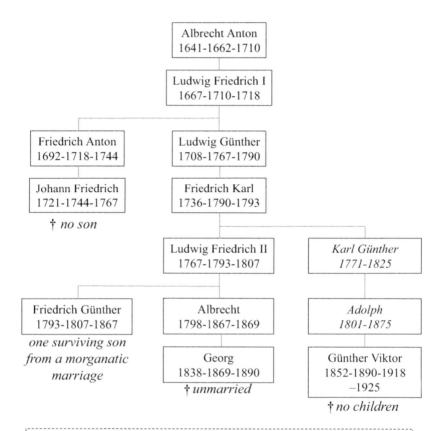

Chart shows the princes of Schwarzburg-Rudolstadt. Albrecht Anton accepted the rank of prince, but his son was the first actively to use it. Primogeniture was introduced in 1710. Karl Günther and Adolph (shown in italics) never came to the throne. When the marriage of the last prince, Günther Victor, proved childless the family law was changed in 1896. This declared the only surviving son of Friedrich Günther (from a morganatic marriage) to be an eligible dynast of the house.

22. HOW THE HOUSE OF SCHWARZBURG RAN OUT OF SONS
SCHWARZBURG-RUDOLSTADT

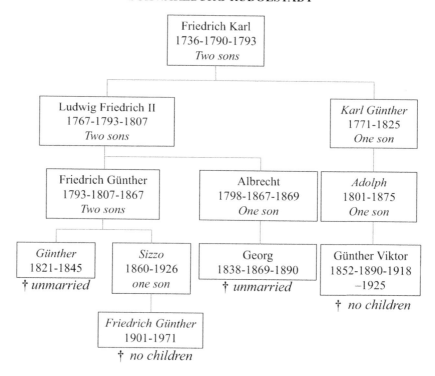

Chart includes the princes of Schwarzburg-Rudolstadt from Friedrich Karl (reigned 1790-1793). It shows how this line of the house of Schwarzburg ran out of sons. In 1896 Sizzo, the son of Friedrich Günther's second (morganatic) marriage, was declared as the next heir to both Schwarzburg principalities. The house of Schwarzburg became extinct on the death of his son, Friedrich Günther, in 1971. Chart only includes sons who survived childhood.

APPENDIX D
INDEX OF SCHLÖSSER IN THE *SCHLOSS* BOOKS

The schlösser are listed in alphabetical order by federal state, showing (1) the noble family with which the author most associates each schloss and (2) where it features in the books (book and page number). The book titles are shortened to *Schloss*, *Schloss II*, *Schloss III*, *Schloss IV* (*Schloss in Bavaria*), *Schloss V* (*Schloss in Baden-Württemberg*), and *Schloss VI* (*Schloss in Thuringia*).

Name (location if different)	Family	Book	Page no.
Baden-Württemberg			
Baden-Baden Neues Schloss	Baden	*Schloss V*	164
Bebenhausen (Tübingen)	Württemberg	*Schloss V*	88
Bruchsal	Prince-bishops Speyer	*Schloss V*	174
Ettlingen	Baden	*Schloss V*	173
Heidelberg	Palatinate	*Schloss V*	10
Heiligenberg	Fürstenberg	*Schloss V*	139
Hohenbaden (Baden-Baden)	Baden	*Schloss V*	155
Hohenheim (Stuttgart)	Württemberg	*Schloss V*	81
Hohenstaufen (Göppingen)	Staufer	*Schloss V*	100
Hohenzollern	Hohenzollern	*Schloss V*	106
Karlsruhe	Baden	*Schloss V*	152
Kirchheim (Kirchheim unter Teck)	Württemberg	*Schloss V*	86
Langenburg	Hohenlohe	*Schloss V*	36
Lichtenstein	Württemberg	*Schloss V*	93
Lorch	Staufer	*Schloss V*	100
Ludwigsburg	Württemberg	*Schloss V*	64
Ludwigsburg Favorite	Württemberg	*Schloss V*	65
Mannheim	Palatinate	*Schloss V*	17
Meersburg Altes Schloss	Prince-bishops Konstanz	*Schloss V*	134
Meersburg Neues Schloss	Prince-bishops Konstanz	*Schloss V*	134
Mergentheim (Bad Mergentheim)	Teutonic Knights	*Schloss V*	56
Monrepos (Ludwigsburg)	Württemberg	*Schloss V*	72
Montfort (Langenarden)	Montfort	*Schloss V*	133
Neckarbischofsheim	von Helmstatt	*Schloss V*	30
Neuenstein	Hohenlohe	*Schloss V*	50
Öhringen	Hohenlohe	*Schloss V*	55
Rastatt	Baden	*Schloss V*	160
Rastatt Favorite	Baden	*Schloss V*	166
Salem	Baden	*Schloss V*	144
Schwetzingen	Palatinate	*Schloss V*	24
Sigmaringen	Hohenzollern	*Schloss V*	112
Solitude (Stuttgart)	Württemberg	*Schloss V*	84
Stetten	Stetten	*Schloss V*	40

Teck (Owen)	Württemberg	*Schloss V*	96
Tettnang	Montfort	*Schloss V*	127
Villa Hohenlohe (Baden-Baden)	Hohenlohe	*Schloss V*	43
Weikersheim	Hohenlohe	*Schloss V*	44
Wurzach (Bad Wurzach)	Waldburg	*Schloss V*	120
Zeil (Leutkirch im Allgäu)	Waldburg	*Schloss V*	125
Zwingenberg	Palatinate	*Schloss V*	29

Bavaria

Ansbach	Brandenburg-Ansbach	*Schloss IV*	37
Bamberg New Residence	Prince-bishops Bamberg	*Schloss IV*	8
Berchtesgaden	Wittelsbach	*Schloss IV*	158
Berg	Wittelsbach	*Schloss IV*	125
Burghausen	Wittelsbach	*Schloss IV*	89
Burgraves Castle (Nuremberg)	Burgraves Nuremberg	*Schloss IV*	34
Callenberg (Coburg)	Saxe-Coburg and Gotha	*Schloss IV*	59
Dachau	Wittelsbach	*Schloss IV*	112
Donastauf	Thurn und Taxis	*Schloss IV*	75
Ehrenburg (Coburg)	Saxe-Coburg and Gotha	*Schloss IV*	46
Forchheim	Prince-bishops Bamberg	*Schloss IV*	30
Fürstenreid (Munich)	Wittelsbach	*Schloss IV*	147
Füssen	Prince-bishops Augsburg	*Schloss IV*	177
Greifenstein (Heiligenstadt)	Stauffenberg	*Schloss IV*	25
Herrenchiemsee	Wittelsbach	*Schloss IV*	140
Hohenschwangau	Wittelsbach	*Schloss IV*	168
Ketschendorf (Coburg)	Saxe-Coburg and Gotha	*Schloss IV*	65
Landshut Residence	Wittelsbach	*Schloss IV*	88
Laufen	Prince-bishops Salzburg	*Schloss IV*	99
Linderhof (Ettal)	Wittelsbach	*Schloss IV*	132
Neuburg	Wittelsbach	*Schloss IV*	101
Neuschwanstein (Hohenschwangau)	Wittelsbach	*Schloss IV*	173
Nuremberg	Holy Roman emperors	*Schloss IV*	32
Nymphenburg (Munich)	Wittelsbach	*Schloss IV*	113
Palais Edinburgh (Coburg)	Saxe-Coburg and Gotha	*Schloss IV*	53
Possenhofen	Wittelsbach	*Schloss IV*	124
Rosenau (Rödental)	Saxe-Coburg and Gotha	*Schloss IV*	51
Roseninsel Casino (Lake Starnberg)	Wittelsbach	*Schloss IV*	124
Royal Villa (Berchtesgaden)	Wittelsbach	*Schloss IV*	160
Schleissheim (Munich)	Wittelsbach	*Schloss IV*	106
Seehof (Memmelsdorf)	Prince-bishops Bamberg	*Schloss IV*	15
Seeon (Seeon-Seebruck)	Leuchtenberg	*Schloss IV*	152
St Emmeram (Regensburg)	Thurn und Taxis	*Schloss IV*	68
Tegernsee	Wittelsbach	*Schloss IV*	138
Tittmoning	Prince-bishops Salzburg	*Schloss IV*	95
Trausnitz (Landshut)	Wittelsbach	*Schloss IV*	82
Veste Coburg	Saxe-Coburg and Gotha	*Schloss IV*	54

Weissenstein (Pommersfelden)	Schönborn	*Schloss IV*	20
Wildenwart (Frasdorf)	Wittelsbach	*Schloss IV*	144
Berlin & Brandenburg			
Altes Palais (Berlin)	Hohenzollern	*Schloss*	56
Cecilienhof (Potsdam)	Hohenzollern	*Schloss*	78
Charlottenburg (Berlin)	Hohenzollern	*Schloss*	67
Kronprinzenpalais (Berlin)	Hohenzollern	*Schloss*	59
Neues Palais (Potsdam)	Hohenzollern	*Schloss*	63
New Pavilion (Berlin)	Hohenzollern	*Schloss*	75
Paretz (Ketzin)	Hohenzollern	*Schloss*	76
Rheinsberg	Hohenzollern	*Schloss II*	96
Sanssouci (Potsdam)	Hohenzollern	*Schloss*	60
Hesse			
Bad Homburg	Hesse-Homburg	*Schloss*	124
Darmstadt	Hesse-Darmstadt	*Schloss III*	114
Friedberg	Hesse-Darmstadt	*Schloss III*	134
Friedrichshof (Kronberg i/Taunus)	Hesse-Kassel	*Schloss*	112
Heiligenberg (Jugenheim)	Battenberg	*Schloss III*	126
Burgruine Königstein	Nassau	*Schloss*	120
Kranichstein (Darmstadt)	Hesse-Darmstadt	*Schloss III*	121
Kronberg	Lords of Kronberg	*Schloss*	118
Luxembourg (Königstein i/Taunus)	Nassau	*Schloss*	122
Rosenhöhe (Darmstadt)	Hesse-Darmstadt	*Schloss III*	119
Wilhelmshöhe (Kassel)	Hesse-Kassel	*Schloss III*	138
Wilhelmsthal (Calden)	Hesse-Kassel	*Schloss III*	144
Wolfsgarten (Langen)	Hesse-Darmstadt	*Schloss III*	125
Lower Saxony			
Ahlden	Hannover	*Schloss*	13
Bevern	Brunswick-Bevern	*Schloss III*	56
Braunschweig	Brunswick-Wolfenbüttel	*Schloss II*	151
Bückeburg	Schaumburg-Lippe	*Schloss II*	10
Celle	Hannover	*Schloss*	6
Fallersleben (Wolfsburg)	Brunswick-Lüneburg	*Schloss II*	178
Herrenhausen (Hannover)	Hannover	*Schloss*	16
Jever	Anhalt-Zerbst	*Schloss II*	33
Kaiserpfalz (Goslar)	Holy Roman emperors	*Schloss II*	169
Marienburg (Pattensen)	Hannover	*Schloss*	21
Oldenburg	Oldenburg	*Schloss II*	19
Pyrmont	Waldeck-Pyrmont	*Schloss III*	48
Rastede Palais	Oldenburg	*Schloss II*	24
Rastede Schloss	Oldenburg	*Schloss II*	24
Little Richmond (Braunschweig)	Brunswick-Wolfenbüttel	*Schloss II*	157
Salzdahlum	Brunswick-Wolfenbüttel	*Schloss II*	166

Stadthagen	Holstein-Schaumburg	*Schloss II*	13
Wolfenbüttel	Brunswick-Wolfenbüttel	*Schloss II*	162
Wolfsburg	Schulenburg-Wolfsburg	*Schloss II*	174
Mecklenburg-Pomerania			
Bad Doberan	Mecklenburg-Schwerin	*Schloss*	30
Blücher (Göhren-Lebbin)	Blücher	*Schloss II*	94
Gamehl	von Stralendorff	*Schloss*	52
Gelbensande	Mecklenburg-Schwerin	*Schloss*	46
Güstrow	Mecklenburg-Güstrow	*Schloss*	44
Hohenzieritz	Mecklenburg-Strelitz	*Schloss II*	76
Ludwigslust	Mecklenburg-Schwerin	*Schloss*	33
Mirow	Mecklenburg-Strelitz	*Schloss II*	68
Neustrelitz	Mecklenburg-Strelitz	*Schloss II*	82
Prinzenpalais (Bad Doberan)	Mecklenburg-Schwerin	*Schloss*	32
Schwerin	Mecklenburg-Schwerin	*Schloss*	41
Burg Stargard	Mecklenburg-Strelitz	*Schloss II*	90
Wiligrad (Löbstorf)	Mecklenburg-Schwerin	*Schloss*	50
North Rhine-Westphalia			
Altena	von Mark	*Schloss III*	33
Augustusburg (Brühl)	Wittelsbach	*Schloss III*	10
Bensberg (Bergisch-Gladbach)	Wittelsbach	*Schloss III*	24
Detmold	Lippe	*Schloss III*	38
Falkenlust (Brühl)	Wittelsbach	*Schloss III*	17
Nordkirchen	von Plettenberg	*Schloss III*	20
Türnich (Kerpen)	von Hoensbroech	*Schloss III*	19
Vischering (Lüdinghausen)	zu Vischering	*Schloss III*	30
Rhineland-Palatinate			
Bathhouse Palace (Bad Ems)	Nassau-Diez	*Schloss III*	150
Diez	Nassau-Diez	*Schloss III*	162
Marksburg (Braubach)	Hesse/Nassau	*Schloss*	135
Oranienstein (Diez)	Nassau-Diez	*Schloss III*	157
Phillipsburg (Braubach)	Hesse-Rheinfels	*Schloss*	136
Stolzenfels (Koblenz)	Hohenzollern	*Schloss III*	163
Vier Turme (Bad Ems)	von Thüngen	*Schloss III*	152
Saxony			
Colditz	Wettin	*Schloss*	102
Pillnitz (Dresden)	Wettin	*Schloss*	98
Residenzschloss (Dresden)	Wettin	*Schloss*	86
Rochlitz	Wettin	*Schloss*	107
Burg Stolpen	Wettin	*Schloss*	95
Taschenbergpalais (Dresden)	Wettin	*Schloss*	88

Saxony Anhalt

Bernburg	Anhalt-Bernburg	*Schloss III*	82
Luisium (Dessau)	Anhalt-Dessau	*Schloss III*	72
Johannbau (Dessau)	Anhalt-Dessau	*Schloss III*	62
Mosigkau	Anhalt-Dessau	*Schloss III*	67
Oranienbaum	Anhalt-Dessau	*Schloss III*	72
Quedlinburg	Abbesses of Quedlinburg	*Schloss III*	77
Wörlitz Country House	Anhalt-Dessau	*Schloss III*	71

Schleswig-Holstein

Blomenburg (Selent)	von Blome	*Schloss II*	66
Eutin	Holstein-Gottorf	*Schloss II*	42
Glücksburg	Holstein-Glücksburg	*Schloss II*	54
Gottorf	Holstein-Gottorf	*Schloss II*	53
Hemmelmark	Hohenzollern	*Schloss II*	54
Husum	Holstein-Gottorf	*Schloss II*	62
Kiel	Hohenzollern	*Schloss II*	47
Salzau (Fargau-Pratjau)	von Blome	*Schloss II*	66

Thuringia

Altenburg	Saxe-Altenburg	*Schloss VI*	20
Altenstein (Bad Liebenstein)	Saxe-Meiningen	*Schloss III, VI*	100,87
Arnstadt Neues Palais	Schwarzburg-Sondershausen	*Schloss VI*	186
Belvedere (Weimar)	Saxe-Weimar-Eisenach	*Schloss II, VI*	133,123
Burg Gleichen (Drei Gleichen)	Hohenzollern	*Schloss VI*	58
Dornburg Altes Schloss	Saxe-Weimar-Eisenach	*Schloss VI*	117
Dornburg Renaissance Schloss	Saxe-Weimar-Eisenach	*Schloss VI*	121
Dornburg Rococo Schloss	Saxe-Weimar-Eisenach	*Schloss VI*	117
Ebersdorf	Reuss Younger Line	*Schloss VI*	170
Elisabethenburg (Meiningen)	Saxe-Meiningen	*Schloss III, VI*	94, 78
Friedenstein (Gotha)	Saxe-Gotha-Altenburg	*Schloss II, VI*	113,42
Friedrichsthal (Gotha)	Saxe-Gotha-Altenburg	*Schloss VI*	50
Fröhliche Wiederkunft (Wolfersdorf)	Saxe-Altenburg	*Schloss VI*	10
Greifenstein (Bad Blankenburg)	Schwarzburg	*Schloss VI*	207
Greiz Oberes Schloss	Reuss Elder Line	*Schloss VI*	151
Greiz Unteres Schloss	Reuss Elder Line	*Schloss VI*	142
Greiz Sommerpalais	Reuss Elder Line	*Schloss VI*	157
Heidecksburg (Rudolstadt)	Schwarzburg-Rudolstadt	*Schloss II, VI*	138,192
Hildburghausen	Saxe-Hildburghausen	*Schloss VI*	94
Hummelshain Neues Schloss	Saxe-Altenburg	*Schloss VI*	29
Kromsdorf	Saxe-Weimar-Eisenach	*Schloss VI*	115
Molsdorf (Erfurt)	Von Gotter	*Schloss VI*	53
Mühlburg (Drei Gleichen)	Hohenzollern	*Schloss VI*	58
Osterburg (Weida)	Saxe-Weimar-Eisenach	*Schloss VI*	168
Osterstein (Gera)	Reuss Younger Line	*Schloss VI*	162

Palais Weimar (Bad Liebenstein)	Saxe-Meiningen	*Schloss III, VI*	106,92
Reinhardsbrunn (Friedrichroda)	Saxe-Coburg and Gotha	*Schloss II, VI*	120,67
Residenzschloss Weimar	Saxe-Weimar-Eisenach	*Schloss II, VI*	128,102
Saalfeld	Saxe-Coburg-Saalfeld	*Schloss II, VI*	106,36
Schwarzburg	Schwarzburg-Rudolstadt	*Schloss II, VI*	145,200
Sondershausen	Schwarzburg-Sondershausen	*Schloss VI*	178
Tenneberg (Waltershausen)	Saxe-Gotha-Altenburg	*Schloss VI*	61
Tiefurt (Weimar)	Saxe-Weimar-Eisenach	*Schloss VI*	114
Tinz (Gera)	Reuss Younger Line	*Schloss VI*	164
Veste Wachsenburg (Drei Gleichen)	Saxe-Coburg and Gotha	*Schloss VI*	59
Wartburg (Eisenach)	Saxe-Weimar-Eisenach	*Schloss III, VI*	86, 130
Wilhelmsburg (Schmalkalden)	Hesse-Kassel	*Schloss III*	106
Wittumspalais (Weimar)	Saxe-Weimar-Eisenach	*Schloss VI*	110

APPENDIX E
THE GERMAN ROYAL HOUSES

Listed in alphabetical order are the thirty-one sovereign states ruled by a German royal family that were reinstated at the Congress of Vienna in 1815 after the Napoleonic Wars. The list shows where schlösser of each royal house are featured in the *Schloss* books (book and chapter number). The book titles are shortened to *Schloss, Schloss II, Schloss III, Schloss IV (Schloss in Bavaria), Schloss V (Schloss in Baden-Württemberg)*, and *Schloss VI (Schloss in Thuringia)*.

	Schloss	Schloss II	Schloss III	Schloss IV	Schloss V	Schloss VI
Anhalt-Dessau			4			
Anhalt-Bernburg			4			
Anhalt-Köthen*						
Baden					7	
Bavaria			2	5, 6, 7		
Brunswick		7	3			
Hannover	2					
Hesse-Darmstadt			6			
Hesse-Homburg	6					
Hesse-Kassel			6			
Hohenzollern-Hechingen					5	
Hohenzollern-Sigmaringen					5	
Lippe-Detmold			2			
Mecklenburg-Schwerin	3					
Mecklenburg-Strelitz		4				
Nassau	6					
Oldenburg		2				
Prussia	4, 6	5	7		5	
Reuss Elder Line						6
Reuss Younger Line						6
Saxe-Coburg-Saalfeld		6		3		3
Saxe-Gotha-Altenburg		6				3
Saxe-Hildburghausen						4
Saxe-Meiningen			5			4
Saxe-Weimar-Eisenach		6	5			5
Schaumberg-Lippe		2				
Saxony	5					
Schwarzburg-Rudolstadt		6				7
Schwarzburg-Sondershausen						7
Waldeck-Pyrmont			3			
Württemberg					4	

* To be included in Schloss in Saxony-Anhalt (*Schloss VII*).

ILLUSTRATIONS

The illustrations listed below (by illustration number or page number), are reproduced by courtesy of the individuals or organisations shown. All other illustrations are from the author's collection.

1. 2. 4. Schloss Fröhliche Wiederkunft
3. Wikimedia Commons, Aschroet, CC0
9. 12. Förderverein Schloss Hummelshain/Jürgen Friedel
11. Förderverein Schloss Hummelshain/Anita Volkamer
13. Förderverein Schloss Hummelshain/Steffen Sptizner
18. Votimedia/Shutterstock
26. 27. 29. Schloss Tenneberg/Manfred Windus
28. Schloss Tenneberg/Stadtverwaltung Waltershausen
30. Joachim Ortlepp, guided tours of Reinhardsbrunn
34. Wikimedia Commons, Kramer96
41. 42. 43. 44. Stadtmuseum Hildburghausen
57. Mike Fuchslocher/Shutterstock
58. Marzolino/Shutterstock
59. Harald Lueder/Shutterstock
64. 65. 67. 70. Tourist-Information Greiz
74. 76. 77. Stadtarchiv Gera
Page 164. Stadtarchiv Gera
Page 168. Fotoarchiv der Stadt Weida
78. 80. Stadtarchiv Gera
81. Wikimedia Commons, HieRo GlyPhe
85. Kulturbetrieb Arnstadt, Clemens Bauerfeind
86. Kulturbetrieb Arnstadt
87. 88. Kulturbetrieb Arnstadt, Thomas Wolf

NOTES

Chapter 1

1. Franz Haarman, *Das Haus Sachsen-Coburg und Gotha.* Werl: Borde-Verlag, 2013, 11.
2. Shephard Thomas Taylor, *An Historical Tour: or, the early ancestors of the Prince of Wales, of the House of Wettin.* London: Williams and Norgate, 1884, iii. Reprinted by British Library for The History of Britain and Ireland collection.

Chapter 2

1. Sylvia Weigelt, *Das Wasserschloss 'Zur Fröhlichen Wiederkunft' in Wolfersdorf: 'Fürwahr ein heiteres Haus'.* Wolfersdorf: Schloss Wolfersdorf Verwaltungsgemeinschaft mbH, 2014, 12.
2. Elke Anna Werner, 'Vier Gemälde mit Szenen aus dem Leben Johann Friedrich des Grossmütigen von Sachsen.' *Deutsches Historisches Museum Magazin.* Heft16, 6. Jahrgang. Berlin Winter 1995/96, 2.
3. Ibid, 3.
4. After the town of Schmalkalden in Thuringia where it was founded in 1531 (see Wilhelmsburg in *Schloss III*).
5. Werner, 'Vier Gemälde mit Szenen aus dem Leben Johann Friedrich des Grossmütigen von Sachsen.', 6.
6. The grandfathers of the two men were brothers. Johann Friedrich's grandfather (Ernst) founded the Ernestine line of the house of Wettin; and Moritz's grandfather (Albrecht) the Albertine line (see chart 2).
7. Guided tour at Fröhliche Wiederkunft.
8. Weigelt, *Das Wasserschloss 'Zur Fröhlichen Wiederkunft' in Wolfersdorf*, 20.
9. Ibid, 10.
10. Guided tour at Fröhliche Wiederkunft.
11. Weigelt, *Das Wasserschloss 'Zur Fröhlichen Wiederkunft' in Wolfersdorf*, 77.
12. Guided tour at Fröhliche Wiederkunft.
13. Weigelt, *Das Wasserschloss 'Zur Fröhlichen Wiederkunft' in Wolfersdorf*, 104.
14. Ibid, 110.
15. Shephard Thomas Taylor, *An Historical Tour: or, the early ancestors of the Prince of Wales, of the House of Wettin.* London: Williams and Norgate, 1884. Reprinted by British Library for The History of Britain and Ireland collection, 97.
16. Thomas Gehrlein, *Das Haus Sachsen-Altenburg vormals Sachsen-Hildburghausen.* Werl: Borde-Verlag, 2018, 30.
17. Ibid, 14.

18. Uta Künzl and Toralf Keil, *Das Altenburger Schloss in Wort, Bild und Ton*. Altenburg: Residenz Schloss Altenburg, 2011, 26.

19. Ibid.

20. At that time Russia was still using the old-style Julian calendar which was behind the more modern Gregorian calendar. The date of the marriage in Russia was 30 August 1848.

21. Greg King and Penny Wilson, *Gilded Prism: The Konstantinovichi Grand Dukes & the Last Years of the Romanov Dynasty*. East Richmond Heights: Eurohistory.com, 2006, 12.

22. Olga Barkovets, Feodor Federov, and Alexander Krylov. *Peterhof ist ein Traum: Deutsche Prinzessin in Russland*. Berlin: Quintessenz Verlag, 2001, 78. Quoted in King & Wilson, *Gilded Prism*, 12.

23. Olga's first child was born the year after her marriage. She would become the mother of eight and the grandmother of Prince Philip, Duke of Edinburgh.

24. Coryne Hall, 'Aunt Sanny: Grand Duchess Alexandra Iosifovna of Russia.' *The European Royal History Journal*. June 2011, 5.

25. Susan Symons, *Schloss in Baden-Württemberg: The Fascinating Royal History of German Castles*. St Just-in-Roseland: 2019, 78. Queen Olga was unhappily married to King Karl of Württemberg who was homosexual.

26. David Chavchavadze, *The Grand Dukes*. New York: Atlanta International, 1990, 62. Quoted in King & Wilson, *Gilded Prism*, 41.

27. Vera Konstantinovna and Irene W. Galaktionova, 'Fragments of Memoirs: Part I – My Father'. *Royal Russia Annual No 7: A Celebration of the Romanov Dynasty and Imperial Russia in Words & Photographs*. Ontario: Gilbert's Books for Royal Russia, Winter 2015, 96.

28. Arturo E. Beéche (edited), *The Other Grand Dukes: Sons and Grandsons of Russia's Grand Dukes*. East Richmond Heights: Eurohistory.com, 2012, 83.

29. King & Wilson, *Gilded Prism*, chapter 15, 134-142.

30. A shilling is ten pence in present-day currency. This is a small amount now but was worth a lot more in 1884.

31. Taylor, *An Historical Tour*, 99.

32. Weigelt, *Das Wasserschloss 'Zur Fröhlichen Wiederkunft' in Wolfersdorf*, 87.

33. Gehrlein, *Das Haus Sachsen-Altenburg*, 32.

34. Künzl and Keil, *Das Altenburger Schloss in Wort, Bild und Ton*, 30.

35. Claudia and Rainer Hohberg, *Jagd-und Residenzschloss Neues Schloss Hummelshain*. Regensburg: Schnell & Steiner, 2016. 2.

36. Ibid, 20.

37. Ibid, 15.

38. Künzl and Keil, *Das Altenburger Schloss in Wort, Bild und Ton*, 28.

Chapter 3
1. Bearn Bilker, 'The November 1918 Abdications, Part V.' *Royalty Digest Quarterly.* 4 2019, 51.
2. The fourteen European countries are Belgium, Bulgaria, Germany, Great Britain, Greece, Italy, Luxembourg, Norway, Portugal, Romania, Russia, Spain, Sweden, Yugoslavia. Excluded from this list are numerous sovereign houses within Germany. For a comprehensive family tree including all lines of descent see *The Coburg Dynasty* family tree in Arturo E. Beéche, *The Coburgs of Europe: The Rise and Fall of Queen Victoria and Prince Albert's European Family.* East Richmond Heights: Eurohistory.com, 2014, 354-355.
3. Banner outside the chapel at Schloss Saalfeld.
4. Information from Schloss Saalfeld.
5. Ingrid Bachmeier, 'Das Schloss in Saalfeld' in Roswitha Jacobsen and Hendrik Bärnighausen (edited), *Residenz-Schlösser in Thüringen: Kulturhistorische Porträts.* Jena: quartus-Verlag, 1998. 130.
6. Niels Fleck, *Fürstliche Repräsentation in Sakralraum: Die Schlosskirchen der Thüringisch-ernestinischen Residenz in 17. Und Beginnenden 18. Jahhundert.* Berlin München: Deutscher Kunstverlag, 2015.
7. Fleck, *Fürstliche Repräsentation in Sakralraum*, 248.
8. Information from Schloss Saalfeld.
9. Franz Haarmann, *Das Haus Sachsen-Coburg und Gotha.* Werl: Borde-Verlag, 2013, 11.
10. Ibid, 13.
11. Ernst and two older brothers agreed to split their territory after a fourth (eldest) brother died. In their inheritance agreement, Wilhelm got Saxe-Weimar; Albrecht, Saxe-Eisenach; and Ernst, Saxe-Gotha. When Albrecht died childless in 1644, his share was split between the two remaining brothers.
12. Roswitha Jacobsen, 'Schloss Friedenstein in Gotha.' in Roswitha Jacobsen and Hendrik Bärnighausen (edited), *Residenz-Schlösser in Thüringen: Kulturhistorische Porträts.* Jena: quartus-Verlag, 1998, 78.
13. Kamen Pawlow, *Gotha, A City Worth Visiting: Travel Guide Including Useful Information about Art, Nature and Sport.* Kamen Pawlow (self-published), 2008, 27.
14. Schloss Friedenstein audio guide.
15. Ibid.
16. Thomas Gehrlein, *Das Haus Sachsen-Altenburg vormals Sachsen-Hildburghausen.* Werl: Borde-Verlag, 2018, 18.
17. Jacobsen, 'Schloss Friedenstein in Gotha', 88.

18. Stella Tillyard, *A Royal Affair: George III and his Troublesome Siblings*. London: Chatto and Windus, 2006, 7.

19. Lucy Worsley, *Courtiers: The Secret History of Kensington Palace*. London: Faber and Faber, 2010, 196.

20. Janice Hadlow, *The Strangest Family: The Private Lives of George III, Queen Charlotte and the Hanoverians*. London: William Collins, 2014, 59. The comment was made by George II to his prime minster Sir Robert Walpole.

21. William Duke of Cumberland (1721-1765).

22. Tillyard, *A Royal Affair*, 15.

23. Hadlow, *The Strangest Family*, 70.

24. Worsley, *Courtiers*, 306.

25. Quoted in William Makepeace Thackeray, *The Four Georges*. London: Smith, Elder and Co, 1866, 133.

26. Hadlow, *The Strangest Family*, 110.

27. RA VIC/MAIN/QVJ(W) Thursday 28 August 1845 (Queen Victoria's draft) retrieved 16 May 2020. Written at Gotha (Friedrichsthal).

28. Haarmann, *Das Haus Sachsen-Coburg und Gotha*, 13.

29. English handout for the guided tour at Schloss Molsdorf.

30. Translated in the English handout for the guided tour as 'Enjoy all pleasures to the full'.

31. Stiftung Thüringer Schlösser und Gärten.

32. Helmut-Eberhard Paulus, *Schloss und Garten Molsdorf: Graf Gotters Residenz der Aufklärung*. Regensburg: Schnell & Steiner, 2012, 89.

33. Silke Opitz, *Les Belles Dames de Molsdorf – Das Damenkabinett im Schloss des Grafen Gotter*.

34. Gotter's collection of portraits in the Silver Cabinet was removed prior to the sale of Molsdorf in 1909 to the writer Gräfin (countess) Maria von Gneisenau. The pictures shown now are not original. The original portrait of Duchess Luise Dorothea of Saxe-Gotha-Altenburg is at Schloss Callenberg in Coburg (email correspondence with curator at Schloss Molsdorf). Molsdorf had many owners after Gotter, but the only one to leave a lasting mark was Countess Maria. Visitors can still see her marble bathroom in art noveau style.

35. Silke Opitz (edited), *At Molsdorf Palace*. Berlin: Revolver Publishing, 2015, 119.

36. Paulus, *Schloss und Garten Molsdorf*, 89 translated by Graham Billing.

37. Opitz (edited), *At Molsdorf Palace*, 112-3. Includes a translated extract (pages 111-122) of the biography of Gotter by August Emil Alfred Beck (1812-1874), archivist at the Gotha court. *Graf Gustav Adolph von Gotter. Ein Lebensbild aus der Zeit Friedrich's des Grossen und Maria Theresia's*. Gotha, 1867.

38. Ibid, 113.
39. Ibid, 129.
40. Ibid, 116.
41. RA VIC/MAIN/QVJ(W) Sunday 31 August 1845 (Queen Victoria's draft) retrieved 27 May 2020. Written at Gotha (Friedrichsthal).
42. Opitz (edited), *At Molsdorf Palace*, 121.
43. Email correspondence with the curator at Schloss Molsdorf.
44. Guided tour at Schloss Molsdorf.
45. www.waltershausen.de
46. Museum Director Schloss Tenneberg.
47. Ibid.
48. Günter Schuchardt, *The Wartburg – World's Heritage*. Regensburg: Schnell & Steiner, 2006, 59.
49. Shephard Thomas Taylor. *An Historical Tour, or, The Early Ancestors of the Prince of Wales, of the House of Wettin*. London: Williams and Norgate, 1884. Reprinted by British Library for The History of Britain and Ireland collection, 159.
50. Story from Ludwig Bechstein. *Der Sagenschatz und die Sagankreise des Thüringer Landes*. Hildburghausen, 1835, volume 1, 104-106.
51. www.waltershausen.de
52. Ibid.
53. RA VIC/MAIN/QVJ(W) Thursday 28 August 1845 (Queen Victoria's drafts) retrieved 12 June 2020. Written at Gotha (Friedrichsthal).
54. *Reinhardsbrunn Castle in Thuringia and the Siberian Money* [in German]. Deutsche Welle, 16 July 2018. Referenced in Wikipedia, *Reinhardsbrunn*.
55. www.schloss-reinhardsbrunn.de
56. Fleck, *Fürstliche Repräsentation in Sakralraum*, 52.
57. RA VIC/MAIN/QVJ(W) Thursday 28 August 1845 (Queen Victoria's drafts) retrieved 12 June 2020. Written at Gotha (Friedrichsthal).
58. There were originally thirty-two portraits but one is missing.
59. RA VIC/MAIN/QVJ(W) Thursday 28 August 1845 (Queen Victoria's drafts) retrieved 12 June 2020. Written at Gotha (Friedrichsthal).
60. RA VIC/MAIN/QVJ(W) Tuesday 19 August 1845 (Queen Victoria's draft) retrieved 27 May 2020. Written at Coburg (Rosenau).
61. Delia Millar, *Views of Germany from the Royal Collection at Windsor Castle: Queen Victoria and Prince Albert on Their Journeys to Coburg and Gotha*. London: The Royal Collection, 1998, 19.
62. Illustrated London News of 6 September 1845. Quoted in Millar, *Views of Germany from the Royal Collection at Windsor Castle*, 162.

63. David Duff, *Victoria Travels: Journeys of Queen Victoria between 1830 and 1900 with Extracts from her Journal.* London: Frederick Muller, 1970, 92.
64. Ibid, 93.
65. RA VIC/MAIN/QVJ(W) Saturday 30 August 1845 (Queen Victoria's drafts) retrieved 13 June 2020. Written at Gotha (Friedrichsthal).
66. www.schloss-reinhardsbrunn.de
67. Friends of Schloss Reinhardsbrunn.

Chapter 4
1. Storyboard at Schloss Elisabethenburg, Meiningen.
2. Ibid.
3. Audio-guide at Schloss Elisabethenburg, Meiningen.
4. Marlene Eilers-Koenig, 'Queen Adelaide.' *Royalty Digest Quarterly.* 2. 2006, 58.
5. Alfred Erck and Hannelore Schneider, 'Schloss Elisabethenburg in Meiningen'. Roswitha Jacobsen and Hendrik Bärnighausen (edited), *Residenz-Schlösser in Thüringen: Kulturhistorische Porträts.* Jena: quartus-Verlag, 1998. 93.
6. *Theatre Town Meiningen* (tourist information brochure). Erfurt: Verein Städtourismus in Thüringen E.V., 6.
7. Ricardo Mateos Sáinz de Medrano, 'The Theatre Duke.' *Royalty Digest: A Journal of Record*, August 1995, 35, 37.
8. Harold A Albert, *Queen Victoria's Sister.* London: Robert Hale, 1967, 175.
9. John van der Kiste, *Charlotte and Feodora: A Troubled Mother-Daughter Relationship in Imperial Germany.* South Brent: A&F Publications, 2015, 14.
10. Ibid.
11. Storyboard at Schloss Elisabethenburg, Meiningen.
12. Maren Goltz, *Meiningen – Muse's Court Between Weimar and Bayreuth: Bach, Bülow, Brahms, Wagner and Reger in Meiningen.* Meiningen: Meininger Museen, 2011. 7.
13. Ibid.
14. Thomas Gehrlein, *Das Haus Sachsen-Meiningen: Über 1000 Jahre Gesamtgeschichte mit Stammfolgen.* Werl: Börde-Verlag, 2013, 46.
15. Roger Fulford (edited), *Darling Child: Private Correspondence of Queen Victoria and the German Crown Princess 1871-1878.* London: Evans Brothers Ltd, 1976, 82.
16. Günther Thim and Bertram Lucke (edited), *Schloss und Park Altenstein.* Rudolstadt: Stiftung Thüringer Schlösser und Gärten with München Berlin: Deutscher Kunstverlag, 1997, 12.

17. Edith Raddatz. 'Georg I and der Altenstein.' *Altensteiner Blätter.* Schweina 2003/2004, 14-33. Referenced in the Wikipedia German entry for *Schloss Altenstein.* The arson that destroyed the schloss was an act of revenge against the tenants. After the fire they moved into the stables to set up a farm there and it took decades to force them out.
18. Gehrlein, *Das Haus Sachsen-Meiningen,* 37.
19. He named Friedrich II of Saxe-Gotha-Altenburg who was the son of the elder brother of Bernhard I of Saxe-Meiningen.
20. Gehrlein, *Das Haus Sachsen-Meiningen,* 36.
21. Ibid, 37.
22. Elisabeth Christine of Brunswick-Wolfenbüttel was the daughter of the brother of Anton Ulrich of Saxe-Meiningen's mother.
23. Gehrlein, *Das Haus Sachsen-Meiningen,* 39.
24. Charlotte Zeepvat, 'Saxe-Meiningen: A Family Album.' *Royalty Digest Quarterly.* 4, 2011, 14.
25. Gehrlein, *Das Haus Sachsen-Meiningen,* 41.
26. Ibid.
27. Mary Hopkirk, *Queen Adelaide.* London: John Murray, 1946, 44.
28. Thim and Lucke (edited), *Schloss und Park Altenstein,* 21.
29. Saxe-Hildburghausen was a principality until 1806 when it joined Napoleon's Confederation of the Rhine as the Holy Roman Empire was breaking up. The principality was then upgraded to a duchy. Correspondence with Stadtmuseum Hildburghausen.
30. Niels Fleck, *Fürstliche Repräsentation in Sakralraum: Die Schlosskirchen der Thüringisch-ernestinischen Residenz in 17. Und Beginnenden 18. Jahhundert.* Berlin München: Deutscher Kunstverlag, 2015, 225.
31. Thomas Gehrlein, *Das Haus Sachsen-Altenburg vormals Sachsen-Hildburghausen.* Werl: Borde-Verlag, 2018, 26.
32. Ibid.
33. Peter H. Wilson, *The Holy Roman Empire: A Thousand Years of Europe's History.* Allen Lane, 2016, 541.
34. Olaf Jaenicke, 'Prinz Joseph von Sachsen-Hildburghausen – Eine biographische Skizze.' *Hildburghäuser Stadtgeschichte: Kleines Universum 2.* Stadtmuseum Hildburghausen, 12/2002, 13. Gives the debt as four million guilders, annual interest as two hundred thousand guilders, and the annual tax revenues as seventy-one thousand eight hundred guilders.
35. Ibid, 6.
36. *The Imperial Festival Palace Hof: An Illustrated Guide through Austria's Largest Countryside Palace Estate.* Marchfeldschlösser Revitalisierungs-Betriebsges, 2005, 11.

37. Franz Sattlecker and Birgit Lindner (edited), *Baroque Lust for Life: Schloss Hof & Schloss Niederweiden*. Wien: Amalthea Signum Verlag, 2017, 23.
38. Jaenicke, 'Prinz Joseph von Sachsen-Hildburghausen', 15-16.
39. Heinrich Ferdinand Schöppl, *Die Herzoge von Sachsen-Altenburg.* Bolzano 1917, reprint Altenburg, 1992, 158. Quoted in Wikipedia, *Duchess Charlotte Georgine of Mecklenburg-Strelitz.*
40. Constance Wright, *Louise, Queen of Prussia: A Biography.* London: Frederick Muller, 1970, 12.
41. Letter of 25 May 1799 to a friend. From Dr Rudolf Armin Human, *Chronik der Stadt Hildburghausen.* Hildburghausen, 1886, 204. Quoted in Wikipedia, *Duchess Charlotte Georgine of Mecklenburg-Strelitz.*
42. Correspondence with Stadtmuseum Hildburghausen regarding the visits of Queen Luise.
43. Friederike had a somewhat scandalous marital career. Widowed at eighteen in 1796 she went on to marry twice more. Her third husband was Duke Ernst August of Cumberland (fifth son of George III) and they became king and queen of Hannover on the death of William IV (Queen Adelaide's husband) in 1837. The fourth sister, Therese, married into the hugely wealthy Thurn und Taxis family who ran the postal system in the Holy Roman Empire (see St Emmeram in *Schloss in Bavaria*).
44. The novel was *Titan* published in four volumes between 1800 and 1803.
45. H.P. Wulf-Woesten, *Hilburghäuser Hoheiten – Dem Volk verbunden.* Hildburghausen, 1992, 24. Quoted in Wikipedia, *Duchess Charlotte Georgine of Mecklenburg-Strelitz.*
46. Correspondence with Stadtmuseum Hildburghausen.

Chapter 5

1. Detlef Ignasiak, 'Das Stadtschloss in Weimar'. Roswitha Jacobsen and Hendrik Bärnighausen (edited), *Residenz-Schlösser in Thüringen: Kulturhistorische Porträts.* Jena: quartus-Verlag, 1998, 16.
2. Ibid, 20.
3. Frances Gerard, *A Grand Duchess: The Life of Anna Amalia Grand Duchess of Saxe-Weimar-Eisenach and The Classical Circle of Weimar.* London: Hutchinson & CO, 1902, 100.
4. Ibid, 92-94.
5. Ibid, 403.
6. Sven Michael Klein, *Das Haus Sachsen-Weimar-Eisenach.* Werl: Borde Verlag, 2013, 27.
7. Ibid, 29 and Ignasiak, 'Das Stadtschloss in Weimar', 24.

8. Bearn Bilker, 'The November 1918 Abdications, Part II.' *Royalty Digest Quarterly.* 1 2019, 55.
9. Gerard, *A Grand Duchess*, 211.
10. Ignasiak, 'Das Stadtschloss in Weimar', 14.
11. Ibid, 23.
12. Klein, *Das Haus Sachsen-Weimar-Eisenach*, 34.
13. Bilker, 'The November 1918 Abdications, Part II.', 55.
14. Ignasiak, 'Das Stadtschloss in Weimar', 27.
15. UNESCO is part of the United Nations and stands for United Nations Educational, Scientific, and Cultural Organisation. A World Heritage Site is recognised as being of outstanding international importance and therefore deserving of special protection.
16. Klein, *Das Haus Sachsen-Weimar-Eisenach*, 24.
17. Gerard, *A Grand Duchess*, 39. Gerard quotes from Anna Amalia's *Gedanken* (Recollections).
18. Klein, *Das Haus Sachsen-Weimar-Eisenach*, 25.
19. Letter of February 1759 from Anna Amalia to Frederick the Great quoted in Gerard, *A Grand Duchess*, 57.
20. Gerard, *A Grand Duchess*, 55.
21. Klein, *Das Haus Sachsen-Weimar-Eisenach*, 25-26.
22. Gerard, *A Grand Duchess*, 368-9.
23. Wikipedia. *Ernest Augustus I, Duke of Saxe-Weimar-Eisenach.* The entry references Karl von Beaulieu-Marconnay, *Ernst August, Herzog von Sachsen-Weimar-Eisenach.* Allgemeine Deutsche biographie ADB0. Band 6, Duncker & Humblot, Leipzig 1877, 317.
24. Klein, *Das Haus Sachsen-Weimar-Eisenach*, 22.
25. Dietger Hagner, Helmut-Eberhard Paulus and Achim Todenhöfer (edited), *Dornburger Schlösser und Gärten.* Berlin München: Deutscher Kunstverlag, 2011, 15. Called the Zeithainer Lustlager (Zeithain Pleasure Camp) this grandiose military show took place at Zeithain near Meissen and was attended by dukes and princes from around Europe.
26. Wilhelmsthal near Eisenach – high on my list for a future visit.
27. Klein, *Das Haus Sachsen-Weimar-Eisenach*, 17.
28. Ibid, 20.
29. Ibid, 21.
30. Ibid, 22.
31. Ibid, 23.
32. Hagner and others, *Dornburger Schlösser und Gärten*, 32.
33. Translation www.melodicverses.com

34. Erich Taubert, *Grand Princess Maria Pavlovna in Weimar*. Weimar: Eric Taubert, 2002, 3. Quoted in Marion Wynn, 'Maria Pavlovna: Memories of a Russian Grand Duchess in Weimar.' *Royalty Digest Quarterly* 1. 2014, 51.

35. Ignasiak, 'Das Stadtschloss in Weimar', 20.

36. Storyboard at Schloss Belvedere.

37. Wynn, 'Maria Pavlovna, 51.

38. William Mead Lalor, 'The Daughters of Tsar Paul I'. Arturo E. Beéche (edited), *The Grand Duchesses: Daughters and Granddaughters of Russia's Tsars*. Oakland: Eurohistory.com, 2004. 3.

39. Ibid.

40. Storyboard at the Residenzschloss, Weimar.

41. Klein, *Das Haus Sachsen-Weimar-Eisenach*, 30.

42. Ibid, 31.

43. Rita Seifert, *Weimar: European Cultural Centre, Cradle of German Classicism*. Lübeck: Schoning Verlag, 3rd edition, 2-3.

44. Elise's mother was the daughter of Prince Ferdinand of Prussia, a younger brother of Frederick the Great.

45. Mead Lalor, 'The Daughters of Tsar Paul I', 5.

46. Theo Aaronson, *The Kaisers*. Indianapolis/New York: The Bobbs-Merrill Company, 1971, 13.

47. Gert-Dieter Ulferts, *Belvedere Palace*. Weimar: Klassik Stiftung Weimar, 2009.

48. Taylor, Shephard Thomas. *An Historical Tour: or, the early ancestors of the Prince of Wales, of the House of Wettin*. London: Williams and Norgate, 1884. Reprinted by British Library for The History of Britain and Ireland collection, 150.

49. Count Ludwig *der Springer* (the *Jumper* or *Leaper*) acquired his epithet by allegedly jumping out of a castle window into the river to escape his pursuers.

50. Joachim Zeune, *Castles and Palaces: Germany*. Regensburg: Schmidt Verlag, 2004, 106.

51. Günter Schuchardt, *The Wartburg – World's Heritage* (Regensburg: Schnell & Steiner, 2006), 5.

52. Ibid, 7.

53. English handout for the German guided tour at the Wartburg.

54. Ibid.

55. Schuchardt, *The Wartburg*, 12-13.

56. Klein, *Das Haus Sachsen-Weimar-Eisenach*, 32.

57. Schuchardt, *The Wartburg*, 18.

58. Taylor, *An Historical Tour*, 168.

59. Zeune, *Castles and Palaces*, 109.
60. Carl Alexander was also closely related to the Dutch and Russian royal families. He was the brother-in-law of King Willem II of the Netherlands (his wife Sophie was Willem's sister) and a first cousin of Tsar Alexander II of Russia (his mother Maria Pavlovna was the sister of Alexander's father, Tsar Nikolai I).
61. Schuchardt, *The Wartburg*, 50.
62. English handout for the German guided tour at the Wartburg.
63. Schuchardt, *The Wartburg*, 16.
64. Martyn Rady, *The Hapsburgs: The Rise and Fall of a World Power*. Allen Lane 2020, 67.
65. Schuchardt, *The Wartburg*, 14.

Chapter 6
1. Thomas Gehrlein, *Das Haus Reuss: Aelterer und Jüngerer Linie*. Werl: Borde-Verlag, 2012, 21.
2. Sven Michael Klein, *Fürst Heinrich XXII, Reuss Aelterer Linie:Sein Leben, sein Wirken und seine Zeit*. Greiz: Thüringischen Staatsarchiv Greiz, 2002, 20.
3. Ibid, 25.
4. Moniek Bloks, *Hermine: An Empress in Exile. The Untold Story of the Kaiser's Second Wife*. Winchester, Washington: Chronos Books, 2020, 3-4, quoting Empress Hermine, *Days in Doorn*, London: Hutchinson, 1928, 38 and 44.
5. Klein, *Fürst Heinrich XXII*, 27.
6. Ibid, 30.
7. Ibid, 31.
8. The regent was initially Heinrich XIV (14) of Reuss-Gera (1832-1913) and from 1908 his son, Heinrich XXVII (27) of Reuss-Gera (1858-1928).
9. Storyboard at Unteres Schloss Greiz.
10. Charlotte Zeepvat, 'The House of Reuss zu Greiz (Elder line): A Family Album.' *Royalty Digest Quarterly*. 3. 2018, 26.
11. Ibid.
12. Bloks, *Hermine*, 10.
13. Storyboard at Unteres Schloss Greiz.
14. Bloks, *Hermine*, 12.
15. Letters of October 1922 from Wilhelm to his friend Max Fürstenberg. Quoted in John C. G. Röhl, *Wilhelm II: Into the Abyss of War and Exile, 1900-1941*. Cambridge: Cambridge University Press, 2014, 1209. From Donaueschingen archives.
16. Bloks, *Hermine*, 112.
17. Ibid, 118-120.

18. Tourist-Information Greiz (edited), *Greiz 800 Jahre, 1209-2009: Greiz's Upper Palace*. Greiz: Tourist-Information, 2009, 8.

19. Thomas Gehrlein, *Das Haus Reuss: Teil I und II*. Werl: Börde-Verlag, 2015, 93.

20. Ibid, 91.

21. Ibid, 92.

22. Gotthard Brandler and others, *Sommerpalais und Fürstlich Greizer Park*. Berlin München: Deutscher Kunstverlag, 2014, 14.

23. Ibid.

24. Ibid, 25.

25. Gehrlein, *Das Haus Reuss:Teil I und II*, 92.

26. The last prince of Reuss Elder Line, Heinrich XXIV (24) (1878-1927), was mentally incapable of ruling and his reign was subject to a regency (see Unteres Schloss Greiz). When the monarchy came to an end in November 1918 the regent abdicated on his behalf.

27. Brandler and others, *Sommerpalais und Fürstlich Greizer Park*, 36.

28. Ibid, 35.

29. Siegfried Mues, 'Schloss Osterstein in Gera'. Roswitha Jacobsen and Hendrik Bärnighausen (edited), *Residenz-Schlösser in Thüringen: Kulturhistorische Porträts*. Jena: quartus-Verlag, 1998, 206.

30. Thomas Gehrlein, *Das Haus Reuss:Teil III und IV*, Werl: Borde-Verlag, 2015, 39.

31. Ibid, 42.

32. Information on the history of Tinz from Anja Löffler and others, *Monument Topography of the Federal Republic of Germany. Cultural Monuments in Thuringia Volume 3: City of Gera*. Thuringian State Office for the Preservation of Monuments and Archaeology of Thuringia, Sandstein Verlag, 2007.

33. Information on the history of Osterstein from Siegfried Mues and Klaus Brodale, *City Guide Gera*, Gondrom Verlag, Bindach, 1st edition 1995.

34. Gehrlein, *Das Haus Reuss:Teil III und IV*, 47.

35. Gehrlein, *Das Haus Reuss: Aelterer und Jüngerer Linie*, 23.

36. Gehrlein, *Das Haus Reuss:Teil III und IV*, 48.

37. Bürgerinformation Der Stadt Weida, *Weida: Die Wiege des Vogtlandes*. Stadt Weida – Stadtverwaltung, 2018, 5.

38. Curator at Osterburg.

39. Ibid.

40. Gehrlein, *Das Haus Reuss: Teil III und IV*, 27.

41. Ibid, 28.

42. Franz Friedrich Anton of Saxe-Coburg-Saalfeld's first wife was Sophie of Saxe-Hildburghausen, a daughter of Duke Ernst Friedrich III of

Saxe-Hildburghausen (see chart 9). They were married in Schloss Hildburghausen on 6 March 1776 and Sophie died in October the same year.

43. Augusta, Duchess of Saxe-Coburg-Saalfeld, *In Napoleonic Days: Extracts from the Private Diary of Augusta, Duchess of Saxe-Coburg-Saalfeld, Queen Victoria's maternal grandmother, 1806-1821: Selected and Translated by H.R.H. The Princess Beatrice.* London: John Murray, 1941, vi. From Princess Beatrice's introduction, quoting Frederic Schoberl.

44. Arturo E. Beéche, *The Coburgs of Europe: The Rise and Fall of Queen Victoria and Queen Albert's European Family.* East Richmond Heights: Eurohistory. com, 2013, 7.

45. Augusta, Duchess of Saxe-Coburg-Saalfeld, *In Napoleonic Days*, 66-67.

46. Gehrlein, *Das Haus Reuss:Teil III und IV*, 30.

47. Ibid.

48. James Morton, *Lola Montz: Her Life & Conquests.* London: Portrait, 2007, 40.

49. Ibid, 42. Also Gehrlein, *Das Haus Reuss: Teil III und IV*, 32.

50. Gehrlein, *Das Haus Reuss: Teil III und IV*, 31.

51. Bearn Bilker, 'Woizlawa-Feodora: Royal Centenarian' *Royalty Digest Quarterly*, 2, 2019, 57-63. The mother of Princess Woizlawa-Feodora, who died the day after she was born, was Viktoria-Feodora of Reuss-Gera, the sister of Heinrich (45). Mr Bilker's wife was a close friend of Princess Woizlawa-Feodora.

52. Bearn Bilker, 'You Always Have to Give a Ray of Hope: A Visit to Princess Woizlawa-Feodora Reuss, Duchess of Mecklenburg' *Royalty Digest Quarterly*, 2, 2007, 31.

53. Correspondence with Bearn Bilker. The father of Heinrich XIX was the younger brother of the father of Heinrich XIV.

54. www.burgerbe.de/2017/12/25prinz-reuss

Chapter 7

1. Hendrik Bärnighausen and others (edited), *Schloss Sondershausen mit Park.* Rudolstadt: Thüringer Schlösser und Gärten with München Berlin: Deutscher Kunstverlag, 1997, 40.

2. Ulrich Hahnemann, *Das Haus Schwarzburg: 1249 Jahre Familiengeschichte eines thüringischen Adelsgeschlechtes.* Werl: Borde-Verlag, 2013, 8.

3. Bearn Bilker, 'The November 1918 Abdications, Part V.' *Royalty Digest Quarterly*. 4 2019, 54.

4. Hahnemann, *Das Haus Schwarzburg*, 25.

5. Hendrik Bärnighausen 'Das Schloss In Sondershausen' in Roswitha Jacobsen and Hendrik Bärnighausen (edited), *Residenz-Schlösser in*

Thüringen: Kulturhistorische Porträts. Jena: quartus-Verlag, 1998, 161.

6. Hahnemann, *Das Haus Schwarzburg*, 37.
7. To Duke Ernst Friedrich who reigned in Saxe-Coburg-Saalfeld from 1764-1800 (chart 12).
8. Bärnighausen and others (edited), *Schloss Sondershausen mit Park*, 11.
9. Bärnighausen 'Das Schloss In Sondershausen', 161.
10. Bärnighausen and others (edited), *Schloss Sondershausen mit Park*, 11.
11. Information at Schloss Sondershausen.
12. Ibid.
13. Curator at Schloss Sondershausen.
14. Bärnighausen and others (edited), *Schloss Sondershausen mit Park*, 11.
15. Bärnighausen, 'Das Schloss In Sondershausen', 164.
16. Ted Rosvall, 'Schwarzburg-Sondershausen: A Family Album'. *Royalty Digest Quarterly*. 4, 2020.
17. 'A Princely Slugging Match', The Omaha Excelsior, 3 May 1890, 1. Referenced in Wikipedia, *Charles Gonthier, Prince of Schwarzburg-Sondershausen*.
18. When Günther XL (40) died in 1552, Günther XLI (41) and his three brothers ruled Schwarzburg-Sondershausen jointly until they divided it in 1571. Günther (41) took Neideck as his residence and rebuilt it in the 1550s. On the division of 1571 he became count of Schwarzburg-Arnstadt.
19. Hendrik Bärnighausen 'Die Schlösser in Arnstadt' in Roswitha Jacobsen and Hendrik Bärnighausen (edited), *Residenz-Schlösser in Thüringen: Kulturhistorische Porträts*. Jena: quartus-Verlag, 1998, 168.
20. Ibid, 170.
21. Hahnemann, *Das Haus Schwarzburg*, 33.
22. Empress Elisabeth Christine, the wife of Emperor Karl VI was a princess of Braunschweig-Wolfenbüttel.
23. Story board in the doll museum at the Neues Palais, Arnstadt.
24. Hahnemann, *Das Haus Schwarzburg*, 37.
25. Bärnighausen 'Die Schlösser in Arnstadt', 171.
26. Story board in the *Bach in Arnstadt* exhibition at the Neues Palais, Arnstadt.
27. Their grandfather Albrecht Anton (1641-1710) introduced the primogeniture rule in 1710.
28. Frank Esche, 'Friedrich Anton' in *Die Fürsten von Schwarzburg-Rudolstadt: 1710-1918*. Thüringer Landesmuseum Heidecksburg Rudolstadt, 2001, 39.
29. Painted by Friedrich Wilhelm Morgenstern.
30. Jens Henkel, 'Friedrich Günther' in *Die Fürsten von Schwarzburg-Rudolstadt*, 123.
31. Ibid, 124.
32. House Laws of Schwarzburg. www.heraldica.org.

33. Charlotte Zeepvat, 'Schwarzburg-Rudolstadt: A Family Album.' *Royalty Digest Quarterly*. 2. 2014, 24.

34. A year later Friedrich Günther married for a third time (morganatically) to twenty-year-old Marie Schulze, the daughter of a doctor.

35. Jens Henkel, 'Georg Albert' in *Die Fürsten von Schwarzburg-Rudolstadt*, 158.

36. Galina Korneva and Tatiana Cheboksarova, *Grand Duchess Marie Pavlovna*. Richmond Heights: Eurohistory, 13.

37. Henkel, 'Georg Albert' in *Die Fürsten von Schwarzburg-Rudolstadt*, 155-6.

38. Gerlinde Gräfin von Westphalen, *Anna Luise von Schwarzburg: Die Letzte Fürstin*. Jena: Jenzig-Verlag Gabriele Köhler, 2011, 22. Bearn Bilker, Eurohistory Royal Gatherings Conference, November 2016.

39. Alexandra's grandfather, Leopold IV of Anhalt-Dessau, was the eldest brother of Helene's natural father Georg Bernhard, her adopted father Wilhelm Waldemar, and her aunt Auguste (Friedrich Günther's first wife).

40. Doreen Winker, 'Günther Viktor' in *Die Fürsten von Schwarzburg-Rudolstadt*, 169.

41. Hahnemann, *Das Haus Schwarzburg*, 62.

42. Thüringer Staatsanzeiger Nr.25/2018 Montag 18 Juni 2018.

43. Lutz Unbehaun, 'Schloss Heidecksburg in Rudolstadt.' Jacobsen and Bärnighausen (edited). *Residenz-Schlösser in Thüringen*, 147.

44. Gräfin von Westphalen, *Anna Luise von Schwarzburg*, 128.

45. Unbehaun, 'Schloss Heidecksburg in Rudolstadt' in *Residenz-Schlösser in Thüringen*, 194.

46. Gräfin von Westphalen, *Anna Luise von Schwarzburg*, 131.

47. Jens Henkel, *Fürstliches Zeughaus Schwarzburg*. Rudolstadt: Thüringer Landesmuseum Heidecksburg Rudolstadt, 2017, 82.

48. English handout for the guided tour at the Schwarzburg Zeughaus, 1.

49. Henkel, *Fürstliches Zeughaus Schwarzburg*, 45.

50. English handout for the guided tour at the Schwarzburg Zeughaus, 4.

51. Bearn Bilker, expert on the German royal families, suggested in a talk at the Eurohistory Royal Gatherings Conference, November 2016, that Günther Viktor could have been homosexual.

52. Winker, 'Günther Viktor' in *Die Fürsten von Schwarzburg-Rudolstadt*, 166.

53. Thekla of Schwarzburg-Rudolstadt, the daughter of Ludwig Friedrich II (1767-1807) – see chart 21.

54. Gräfin von Westphalen, *Anna Luise von Schwarzburg*, 23.

55. Ibid, 11.

56. Bearn Bilker, Eurohistory Royal Gatherings Conference, November 2016.

Appendix B

1. Thomas Gehrlein. *Das Haus Sachsen-Altenburg vormals Sachsen-Hildburghausen.* Werl: Borde-Verlag, 2018, 7.
2. Franz Haarmann. *Das Haus Sachsen-Coburg und Gotha.* Werl: Borde-Verlag, 2013, 13.
3. Thomas Gehrlein. *Das Haus Sachsen-Meiningen*: Über 1000 Jahre Gesamtgeschichte mit Stammfolgen.* Werl: Börde-Verlag, 2013, 6.
4. Sven Michael Klein, *Das Haus Sachsen-Weimar-Eisenach.* Werl: Borde Verlag, 2013, 4.
5. Thomas Gehrlein. *Das Haus Reuss: Aelterer und Jüngerer Linie.* Werl: Borde-Verlag, 2012, 4.
6. Ulrich Hahnemann, *Das Haus Schwarzburg: 1249 Jahre Familiengeschichte eines Thüringischen Adelsgeschlechtes.* Werl: Borde-Verlag, 2013, 8.

BIBLIOGRAPHY

Anonymous. *A Diary of Royal Movements and of Personal Events and Incidents in the Life and Reign of Her Most Gracious Majesty Queen Victoria: Compiled from Official Documents and Public Records, Volume the First.* London: Elliot Stock, 1883. Reprinted by Franklin Classics.

Ahrendt, Dorothee. *Belvedere Palace Park.* Weimar: Klassik Stiftung Weimar, 2009.

Apfelstadt, F. *Haus Kevernburg-Schwarzburg von seinem Ursprunge bis auf unsere Zeit: Dargestellt in den Stammtafeln seiner Haupt-und Nebenlinien.* Thüringer Chronik-Verlag, H.E. Müllerott, Sondershausen 1890, Arnstadt 1996.

Augusta, Duchess of Saxe-Coburg-Saalfeld. *In Napoleonic Days: Extracts from the Private Diary of Augusta, Duchess of Saxe-Coburg-Saalfeld, Queen Victoria's maternal grandmother, 1806-1821: Selected and Translated by H.R.H. The Princess Beatrice.* London: John Murray, 1941.

Bärnighausen, Hendrik and others (edited). *Schloss Sondershausen mit Park.* Rudolstadt: Thüringer Schlösser und Gärten with München Berlin: Deutscher Kunstverlag, 1997.

Beéche, Arturo E. *The Coburgs of Europe: The Rise and Fall of Queen Victoria and Prince Albert's European Family.* East Richmond Heights: Eurohistory.com, 2014.

Beéche, Arturo E (edited). *The Grand Duchesses: Daughters and Granddaughters of Russia's Tsars.* Oakland: Eurohistory.Com, 2004.

Beeck, Clemens. *Weimar Highlights: The Practical Guide to discovering the City.* Berlin: Jaron Verlag, 2012.

Bilker, Bearn. 'The November 1918 Abdications, Part II.' *Royalty Digest Quarterly.* 1, 2019; and Part V.' *Royalty Digest Quarterly.* 4, 2019.

Bloks, Moniek. *Hermine: An Empress in Exile. The Untold Story of the Kaiser's Second Wife.* Winchester, Washington: Chronos Books, 2020.

Brandler, Gotthard and others. *Sommerpalais und Fürstlich Greizer Park.* Berlin München: Deutscher Kunstverlag, 2014.

Bürgerinformation Der Stadt Weida. *Weida: Die Wiege des Vogtlandes.* Stadt Weida – Stadtverwaltung, 2018.

Doran, Dr. John. *Memoir of Queen Adelaide: Consort of William IV (first published 1861).* Fairford: The Echo Library, 2011.

Duff, David. *Victoria Travels: Journeys of Queen Victoria between 1830 and 1900 with Extracts from her Journal.* London: Frederick Muller, 1970.

Eilers-Koenig, Marlene. 'Queen Adelaide.' *Royalty Digest Quarterly.* 2, 2006.

Fleck, Niels. *Fürstliche Repräsentation in Sakralraum: Die Schlosskirchen der Thüringisch-ernestinischen Residenz in 17. Und Beginnenden 18. Jahrhundert.* Berlin München: Deutscher Kunstverlag, 2015.

Fleischer, Horst and others. *Die Fürsten von Schwarzburg-Rudolstadt: 1710-1918.* Thüringer Landesmuseum Heidecksburg Rudolstadt, 2001.

Gehrlein, Thomas. *Das Haus Reuss: Aelterer und Jüngerer Linie.* Werl: Borde-Verlag, 2012.

Gehrlein, Thomas. *Das Haus Reuss: Teil I und II.* Werl: Borde-Verlag, 2015.

Gehrlein, Thomas. *Das Haus Reuss: Teil III und IV.* Werl: Borde-Verlag, 2015.

Gehrlein, Thomas. *Das Haus Sachsen-Altenburg vormals Sachsen-Hildburghausen.* Werl: Borde-Verlag, 2018.

Gehrlein, Thomas. *Das Haus Sachsen-Meiningen: Über 1000 Jahre Gesamtgeschichte mit Stammfolgen.* Werl: Börde-Verlag, 2013.

Gerard, Frances. *A Grand Duchess: The Life of Anna Amalia Grand Duchess of Saxe-Weimar-Eisenach and The Classical Circle of Weimar.* London: Hutchinson & Co, 1902.

Goltz, Maren. *Meiningen – Muse's Court Between Weimar and Bayreuth: Bach, Bülow, Brahms, Wagner and Reger in Meiningen.* Meiningen: Meininger Museen, 2011.

Gräfin von Westphalen, Gerlinde. *Anna Luise von Schwarzburg: Die Letzte Fürstin.* Jena: Jenzig-Verlag Gabriele Köhler, 2011.

Haarmann, Franz. *Das Haus Sachsen-Coburg und Gotha.* Werl: Borde-Verlag, 2013.

Hadlow, Janice. *The Strangest Family: The Private Lives of George III, Queen Charlotte and the Hanoverians.* London: William Collins, 2014.

Hagner, Dietger, Helmut-Eberhard Paulus and Achim Todenhöfer (edited). *Dornburger Schlösser und Gärten.* Berlin München: Deutscher Kunstverlag, 2011.

Hahnemann, Ulrich. *Das Haus Schwarzburg: 1249 Jahre Familiengeschichte eines thüringischen Adelsgeschlechtes.* Werl: Borde-Verlag, 2013.

Hall, Coryne. 'Aunt Sanny: Grand Duchess Alexandra Iosifovna of Russia.' *The European Royal History Journal,* June 2011.

Henkel, Jens. *Fürstliches Zeughaus Schwarzburg.* Rudolstadt: Thüringer Landesmuseum Heidecksburg Rudolstadt, 2017.

Hohberg, Claudia and Rainer. *Jagd-und Residenzschloss Neues Schloss Hummelshain.* Regensburg: Schnell & Steiner, 2016.

Hopkirk, Mary. *Queen Adelaide.* London: John Murray, 1946.

Jacobsen, Roswitha and Hendrik Bärnighausen (edited). *Residenz-Schlösser in Thüringen:Kulturhistorische Porträts.* Jena: quartus-Verlag, 1998.

Jaenicke, Olaf. 'Prinz Joseph von Sachsen-Hildburghausen – Eine biographische Skizze.' *Hildburghäuser Stadtgeschichte: Kleines Universum 2.* Stadtmuseum Hildburghausen, 12/2002.

Jaenicke, Olaf. 'Der Schlosspark Hildburghausen.' *Hildburghäuser Stadtgeschichte: Kleines Universum 2.* Stadtmuseum Hildburghausen, 12/2002.

King, Greg and Penny Wilson. *Gilded Prism: The Konstantinovichi Grand Dukes & the Last Years of the Romanov Dynasty*. East Richmond Heights: Eurohistory. com, 2006.

Klein, Sven Michael. *Fürst Heinrich XXII, Reuss Aelterer Linie:Sein Leben, sein Wirken und seine Zeit*. Greiz: Thüringischen Staatsarchiv Greiz, 2002.

Klein, Sven Michael. *Das Haus Sachsen-Weimar-Eisenach*. Werl: Borde Verlag, 2013.

Konstantinovna, Vera and Irene W. Galaktionova. 'Fragments of Memoirs: Part I – My Father' and 'Fragments of Memoirs: Part II – My Family.' *Royal Russia Annual No 7: A Celebration of the Romanov Dynasty and Imperial Russia in Words & Photographs*, Winter 2015.

Krüger, Kurt. *Gustav Adolph Graf von Gotter: Leben in Galanter Zeit*. Erfurt: Verlag Kleine Arche, 1993.

Künzl, Uta and Toralf Keil. *Das Altenburger Schloss in Wort, Bild und Ton*. Altenburg: Residenz Schloss Altenburg, 2011.

Künzl, Uta and Margaret Marks. *Schloss Altenburg*. Regensburg: Schnell & Steiner Verlag, 2001.

Lass, Heiko and others. *Schloss Heidecksburg Rudolstadt*. Berlin München: Deutscher Kunstverlag, 2013.

Louda, Jiří and Michael Maclagan. *Lines of Succession: Heraldry of the Royal Families of Europe*. London: Orbis Publishing, 1981.

Merten, Klaus. *German Castles and Palaces*. London: Thames and Hudson, 1999.

Millar, Delia. *Views of Germany from the Royal Collection at Windsor Castle: Queen Victoria and Prince Albert on Their Journeys to Coburg and Gotha*. London: The Royal Collection, 1998.

Müller, E-J (edited). *Die Reformation in Weida: Eine Erinnerung An Der Den 500 Jahrestag Der Erneuerung*. Stadt Weida – Stadtverwaltung, 2017.

Nagel, Franz (edited). *Residenz Gotha: Schloss Friedenstein und Herzoglicher Park Gotha*. Petersberg: Stiftung Thüringer Schlösser und Gärten, Rudolstadt und Michael Imhof Verlag, 2014.

Opitz, Silke (edited). *At Molsdorf Palace*. Berlin: Revolver Publishing, 2015. Published in conjunction with the exhibition FULL HOUSE at Schloss Molsdorf.

Paulus, Helmut-Eberhard. *Schloss und Garten Molsdorf: Graf Gotters Residenz der Aufklärung*. Regensburg: Schnell & Steiner, 2012.

Pawlow, Kamen. *Gotha, a City Worth Visiting: Travel Guide Including Useful Information about Art, Nature and Sport*. Kamen Pawlow (self-published), 2008.

Pörnbacher, Hans. *St. Elizabeth of Hungary*. Regensburg: Schnell & Steiner, 2003.

Rausch, Wilhelm. *Auf Den Spuren Thüringer Fürsten: Die Ahnengalerie im Schloss Reinhardsbrunn*. Gotha: Justus Perthes Verlag Gotha, 1995.

Rosvall, Ted. Schwarzburg-Sondershausen: A Family Album. *Royalty Digest Quarterly*. 4, 2020.

Sáinz de Medrano, Ricardo Mateos. 'The Theatre Duke.' *Royalty Digest: A Journal of Record*. August 1995.

Sandars, Mary F. *The Life and Times of Queen Adelaide*. London: Stanley Paul & Co, 1915.

Schuchardt, Günter. *The Wartburg – World's Heritage*. Regensburg: Schnell & Steiner, 2006.

Schuchardt, Günter. *Martin Luther (1483-1546): Monk – Preacher – Reformer*. Regensburg: Schnell & Steiner, 2006.

Seifert, Rita. *Weimar: European Cultural Centre, Cradle of German Classicism*. Lübeck: Schoning Verlag, 3rd edition.

Sotnick, Richard. *The Coburg Conspiracy: Victoria and Albert – Royal Plots and Manoeuvres*. Great Britain: Ephesus Publishing, 2010.

Taylor, Shephard Thomas. *An Historical Tour: or, the early ancestors of the Prince of Wales, of the House of Wettin*. London: Williams and Norgate, 1884. Reprinted by British Library for The History of Britain and Ireland collection.

Thim, Günther and Bertram Lucke (edited). *Schloss und Park Altenstein*. Rudolstadt: Stiftung Thüringer Schlösser und Gärten with München Berlin: Deutscher Kunstverlag, 1997.

Thornton, Richard. 'Prince Albert's Stepfather: His Life and Descendants.' *Royalty Digest Quarterly*. 3. 2010.

Tillyard, Stella. *A Royal Affair: George III and his Troublesome Siblings*. London: Chatto and Windus, 2006.

Ulferts, Gert-Dieter. *Belvedere Palace*. Weimar: Klassik Stiftung Weimar, 2009.

Van der Kiste, John. *Charlotte and Feodora: A Troubled Mother-Daughter Relationship in Imperial Germany*. South Brent: A&F Publications, 2015.

Victoria, Queen of Great Britain and Ireland. *Queen Victoria's Journals*. www.queenvictoriasjournals.org

Weigelt, Sylvia. *Das Wasserschloss 'Zur Fröhlichen Wiederkunft' in Wolfersdorf: 'Fürwahr ein heiteres Haus'*. Wolfersdorf: Schloss Wolfersdorf Verwaltungsgemeinschaft mbH, 2014.

Werner, Elke Anna. 'Vier Gemälde mit Szenen aus dem Leben Johann Friedrich des Grossmütigen von Sachsen.' *Deutsches Historisches Museum Magazin*. Heft16, 6. Jahrgang. Berlin Winter 1995/96.

Worsley, Lucy. *Courtiers: The Secret History of Kensington Palace*. London: Faber and Faber, 2010.

Wyn, Marion. 'Memories of a Russian Grand Duchess in Weimar.' *Royalty Digest Quarterly.* 1, 2014.

York, The Duchess of and Benita Stoney. *Travels with Queen Victoria.* London: Weidenfeld and Nicolson, 1993.

Zeepvat, Charlotte. 'The Dukes of Saxe-Altenburg: A Family Album.' *Royalty Digest Quarterly.* 3, 2009.

Zeepvat, Charlotte. 'Saxe-Meiningen: A Family Album.' *Royalty Digest Quarterly.* 4, 2011.

Zeepvat, Charlotte. 'Saxe-Weimar-Eisenach: A Family Album.' *Royalty Digest Quarterly.* 2, 2008.

Zeepvat, Charlotte. 'Schwarzburg-Rudolstadt: A Family Album.' *Royalty Digest Quarterly.* 2, 2014.

Zeepvat, Charlotte. 'The House of Reuss zu Greiz (Elder line): A Family Album.' *Royalty Digest Quarterly.* 3, 2018.

Zeune, Joachim. *Castles and Palaces: Germany.* Regensburg: Schmidt Verlag, 2004.

Schloss is the German word for castle or palace, and you are never far from one of these in Germany. For most of its history Germany was not a single country but a patchwork of royal states, held together under the banner of the Holy Roman Empire. The dukes and princes who ruled these states were passionate builders. Their beautiful castles and palaces, and their compelling personal stories, provide the material for the *Schloss* series of books.

This book can be seen as an inspiration ... to get out there and find the lesser known palaces and learn more about their history. Royalty Digest Quarterly Journal.

Each of the *Schloss* books includes twenty-five beautiful castles and palaces in Germany and looks at these from two perspectives. The first is the author's experience as an overseas visitor to each schloss; the second, colourful stories of the historical royal families connected with them. Royalty have always been the celebrities of their day, and these stories from history can rival anything in modern-day television soap operas.

The second volume is as good as the first, maybe even better – a must... Amazon review.

The stories in the *Schloss* books include the mistress of the king who tried to blackmail him and was imprisoned for forty-nine years; the princess from a tiny German state who used her body and her brains to become the ruler of the vast Russian empire; the prince who defied his family to marry a pharmacist's daughter and then bought her the rank of royal princess; and the duke whose personal story is so colourful he has been called the Bavarian Henry VIII!

Susan Symons has done another fantastic job, proving the point that history can also be fun...
The European Royal History Journal.

The German princes abdicated in 1918, at the end of World War I, and Germany became a republic. As they lost their royal families, many castles and palaces went into decline and became prisons, workhouses, and other institutions. Some were damaged or destroyed in World War II; others lay behind the Iron Curtain for fifty years. The books chart these difficult years and their resurgence and use today as public buildings, museums, and hotels.

The latest addition visits Bavaria – and what a treat it is. Fascinating reading!
The European Royal History Journal

The castles and palaces in the books range in time from fortified castles of the middle-ages; to grand palaces built in imitation of Louis XIV's Versailles; to stately homes from the turn of the early twentieth century. Many are not well known outside Germany and some rarely see an English-speaking visitor. The *Schloss* books might encourage you to go and see these wonderful places for yourself.

The books are sympathetic to our fascinating German royal history and make linkages and connections in a clear and interesting way.
European Castles Institute, Schloss Philippsburg, Germany.

The *Schloss* books are intended to be light-hearted and easy to read. Illustrated throughout and supplemented with charts and family trees, they should appeal to anyone who likes history or sightseeing or is interested in people's personal stories. With dozens of royal families in Germany before the monarchy fell, there are still many more castles and palaces to go, and Susan is already at work on the next book.

This is a well-written, entertaining display of the castles ... I am definitely off to Thuringia, Symons' book in hand.
Royalty Digest Quarterly Journal

SCHLOSS WURZACH
A JERSEY CHILD INTERNED BY HITLER
– GLORIA'S STORY

In the early hours of 16 September 1942 there was a knock on the door of ten-year-old Gloria Webber's home in Jersey. Gloria, her parents and four younger children were all on a list of Jersey civilians to be

deported to Germany on the direct orders of Hitler. Gloria and her siblings, with hundreds of other Jersey children, spent the next years of their childhood interned in an old castle in the south of Germany, called Schloss Wurzach.

Schloss Wurzach was a grand baroque palace built in the eighteenth century by one of Germany's noble families. But by World War II it had fallen on hard times and was used as a prison camp. The schloss was cold, damp, in poor condition, and very dirty. The internees were horrified by what they found. Twelve of the islanders died in Wurzach during their detention and are buried in the town; others suffered fractured lives.

This short book recalls Gloria's childhood experience and is illustrated with vivid pictures of camp life painted by her father during their confinement. It also describes how she and other internees returned to Germany in later life to celebrate their liberation with the people of Wurzach, showing there can be reconciliation and friendship between former enemies.

Queen Victoria is the monarch from history that everyone knows. These three books focus on the Queen as a woman – her personal life, events that formed her resolute character, and relationships that were important to her. They use some of her own words from her journal, to help tell the story; and are illustrated with portraits and memorabilia from the author's own collection.

Victoria has a life story full of drama, intrigue and surprises. *Young Victoria* covers the bizarre events of her birth, with a scramble to produce the heir to the throne; her lonely childhood under a tough regime; and how she came to the throne at 18.

Victoria & Albert is the story of her marriage to Albert and how she balanced the roles of monarch and Victorian wife and mother. *The Widowed Queen* covers the long years of her life alone after Albert's early death, when she became an icon of the age; the longest serving European sovereign; and matriarch of a huge clan.